MASH

M A S H

An Army Surgeon in Korea

Otto F. Apel Jr., M.D.
and Pat Apel

THE UNIVERSITY PRESS OF KENTUCKY

Publication of this volume was made possible in part
by a grant from the National Endowment for the Humanities.

Editorial and Sales Offices: The University Press of Kentucky
663 South Limestone Street, Lexington, Kentucky 40508-4008

02 01 00 99 98   5 4 3 2

Library of Congress Cataloging-in-Publication Data

Apel, Otto F., 1923-
    Mash: an army surgeon in Korea / Otto F. Apel and Pat Apel.
      p.   cm.
    Includes bibliographical references and index.
    ISBN 0-8131-2070-5 (hard cover : alk. paper)
    1. Apel, Otto F., 1923-   . 2. Korean War, 1950-1953—Personal
narratives, American. 3. Korean War, 1950-1953—Medical care—
United States. 4. Mobile hospitals—Korea (South). 5. United
States. Army—Surgeons—Biography. I. Apel, Pat, 1948-
II. Title.
DS921.6.A58 1998
951.904'2'092—dc21   98-15170

For Jeep, the young patron of the playing field,
and Matt, the Airborne Ranger,
our beloved of the next generation.

May they never have to do this.

CONTENTS

Preface   ix

Maps   xvi

1. From the Gridiron to the Iron Triangle   1

2. "The Spirit of '76"   18

3. The MASH in Action   43

4. The Mechanized Angels   66

5. Where We Lived   91

6. In the OR   126

7. "We're Going to Be Court-Martialed"   149

8. The Friends We Left Behind   178

9. Rotating Out   203

Bibliography   217

Index   220

PREFACE

One great irony of warfare is that the more humanity increases its proficiency to inflict injury upon human beings—through technology, tactics, and psychological manipulation—the more humanity must advance its capability to deliver emergency medical care to the swelling number of casualties.

The Korean War, 1950-53, was a significant point in that great tension between the destruction of armies and the preservation of individual lives. The designation "police action," given facetiously by President Harry S. Truman in response to a reporter's question, does not begin to describe the commitment and heroism and ferocity and sacrifice of all who participated in the rugged war on the Korean Peninsula nearly fifty years ago. Young Americans grappled with Chinese and North Koreans in the toe-to-toe, slug-it-out grind of the jagged Korean mountains. The climate for this donnybrook vacillated from a dusty, stifling, sticky heat to penetrating subzero temperatures that froze everything from automotive fluids to the stubble on the soldier's chin.

The first of the three years of the war showcased the high mobility characteristic of later American involvement in Vietnam and the Persian Gulf. On June 25, 1950, the North Koreans blitzed across the thirty-eighth parallel into South Korea and pushed through the South Korean capital of Seoul. American troops, withdrawn from Korea by 1948 and stationed in Japan, came to the aid of the soldiers of the Republic of Korea (ROKs). The North Korean armor and infantry columns steamrollered south until the Americans and the ROKs dug in their heels for a last-ditch defense in a large semicircle around the port city of Pusan on the southern tip of the Korean peninsula. Backs to the sea, the Americans and the ROKs held their ground. That defensive position came to be known as the Pusan Perimeter.

General Douglas MacArthur, commander of U.S. forces in the Far East, responded with a controversial plan to flank the North Koreans. On September 15, 1950, not quite three months after the initial invasion, U.S.

and ROK air, naval, and land forces executed MacArthur's gamble with an amphibious invasion at the coastal city of Inchon, near Seoul, just below the thirty-eighth parallel, the dividing line between North and South Korea. The invasion forces thrust inland behind the North Koreans and threatened the supply lines and the North Korean troops advancing through South Korea toward Pusan. The North Koreans retreated northward with the Americans and the South Koreans in hot pursuit.

The war, now a United Nations action, was carried into North Korea. With the United Nations forces approaching the Yalu River, which marks the border between China and North Korea, the Chinese moved into North Korea at the end of October 1950 and made preparations in their staging areas without being noticed by the United Nations troops. Then, surprising nearly everyone, the Chinese attacked the United Nations forces with unexpected savagery. The war once again scrambled south. With the influx of American and United Nations troops, the Chinese invasion was stifled and the Chinese were expelled from South Korea. A deadlock developed near the thirty-eighth parallel, the boundary established between North and South Korea at the end of World War II. After the first year to eighteen months, the war settled into a stalemate of infantry struggles and massive artillery duels over the rugged ridgelines of central Korea.

The battles of the Korean War have been etched into American military history. The Pusan Perimeter, the Chosin Reservoir, the Punch Bowl, Bloody Ridge, Heartbreak Ridge, Old Baldy, Pork Chop Hill, and the names of countless other ridges and valleys stained with the blood of our young soldiers are now among the bywords of American bravery.

American casualties in Korea were very heavy: 33,629 killed in action and 103,284 wounded in action. Overall, the American death toll from all causes has been placed as high as 55,000.

This memoir is about war, but it addresses a different aspect of war: the struggle of men and women in the U.S. Army who were called upon to expend their efforts and their lives preserving human life during this vicious combat. Most Americans are familiar with the term *M*A*S*H* from the popular film and television series, which began in the 1970s. The Mobile Army Surgical Hospital (MASH), designed to provide immediate emergency surgical care to the wounded, was first used in Korea and persisted in its original form approximately two years before its mission was changed to reflect the changing tactical situation.

How did the U.S. medical personnel perform in providing this immediate surgical care to the soldiers? Through the movie and the television series, most Americans are also familiar with the portrayal of the irreverent attitudes of the doctors and nurses of the MASH units in Korea. My personal experience confirms that many of the attitudes of the doctors and nurses in the MASH were indeed irreverent. In fact, several of the episodes of the television series were based upon events that occurred in the 8076th MASH during my stay there in 1951-52.

A distinct series of occurrences after World War II created an environment that gave rise to those attitudes. By the very nature of the MASH, its doctors and nurses were separated physically from the military medical community. Beyond that, the military unpreparedness of the army, the lack of training and regimentation of the doctors and nurses drafted for the Korean War, the mobility of the units, and the intensity of the combat separated the doctors and nurses in the MASH units physically and philosophically from the established military medical community. The doctors and nurses of the MASH units were not acculturated into the military medical community and therefore did not share the traditions, customs, and attitudes of the army. Consequently, their attitudes were sometimes considered irreverent.

That should not surprise anyone. The army made little effort to acculturate its drafted doctors and nurses into the ways and customs of the military medical community. For the purpose of acculturating people into any military community, three tools are generally available: first, a pool of experienced soldiers to share accumulated knowledge of military customs and ways; second, training programs to teach the new soldiers the military and professional knowledge required to perform the mission; and third, the mutual support of the present community, which can encourage the accomplishment of the mission. The latter is often manifested as unit cohesion or esprit de corps. None of those methods of acculturation were available to the doctors and nurses in the MASH units in the first half of the Korean War.

First, it is axiomatic that a battle-tested unit is a better unit. Any army tries to keep a pool of experienced personnel to provide a cadre of soldiers who know the customs and mores of the military community. The series of events that created a special culture in the MASH began with the rapid loss of personnel after World War II, which stripped the army of its pool of experienced doctors and nurses. In 1950, with its Medical

Corps at approximately one-third strength, the army drafted civilian doctors, many of whom were residents or interns, and assigned them to the newly organized MASH units. Upon arrival in the combat zone, many of these draftees began their careers in military medicine unfamiliar with—and unhindered by—the customs, traditions, and procedures of the military medical community. Had experienced doctors been assigned to the units in Korea, perhaps they could have passed on their collected knowledge of the military. In the absence of the "old salts," the MASH doctors and nurses were left to improvise with the equipment and knowledge available to them.

Second, most armies try to provide the best training possible for their soldiers. Training, designed to instill within the soldier the discipline and the ability to perform the tasks necessary to accomplish the military mission, can in some instances overcome the lack of a pool of experienced personnel in the combat units. The army failed to provide adequate training for its medical personnel in the Korean War. Even during the war, inadequate medical training was a vexing and volatile issue in the Department of Defense. Few of the doctors assigned to Korea had any training in the treatment of the wounds and diseases common to warfare, in military operations in a field combat environment, or in the customs and traditions of military organizations. On the one hand, without the guidelines of military medical procedures or the physical proximity to the pooled military experience in the rear echelon hospitals, the doctors and nurses had to learn military field operations and military medicine on the job in order to provide the medical care required in the combat zone. On the other hand, the lack of training meant that the MASH doctors and nurses began with a clean slate in providing military medical care. The unintended consequence of that clean slate was an irreverent environment that promoted improvisation and innovation in medical care delivery.

Third, the tactical mobility and the intensity of combat in the first half of the war has rarely been matched in the annals of military history. The mobility of the MASH units separated the doctors and nurses physically from their medical peers. The intensity of the combat separated them experientially and attitudinally from the medical community. The doctors and nurses in the MASH units saw and heard and felt and smelled and tasted on a daily basis what the infantry soldiers lived and what was seen only at second hand by the rest of the military medical community. The stark reality of the war provided the lens through which these doctors and nurses interpreted life and purpose and the experience of Korea. Although this was not the first time in history that doctors and nurses have been in the midst of the fighting at the front lines, it was the first time that a hospital was designed and assigned to operate so close to the combat.

These factors led to a different working environment for the MASH doctors and nurses, one that produced young men and women who were not checked by the customs and traditions of the rest of the military medical community and who were not impeded by military medical training but who were willing to step out and try new procedures and new ideas. In attitudes toward the rank structure and the discipline of the military, MASH personnel exhibited the irreverence commonly found not in undisciplined or untrained troops but in the hardened combat soldier who has lived in the face of battle.

War has been the crucible for medical innovation throughout the centuries, perhaps because war provides a perverse opportunity for innovation. In Korea the environment of the MASH in the larger general context of war led to several significant medical innovations in emergency medical care delivery, the most notable of which were the advances in arterial repair and the transport of the wounded to the hospitals by helicopter. Both saved the lives and limbs of many Americans. During the life of the MASH, important advances were made also in the use of antibiotics, in the distribution and use of blood plasma and type O blood for the treatment of blood-loss shock, and in the early ambulation of the wounded in the hospitals.

This memoir is the tribute of one doctor to those doctors and nurses and enlisted personnel who had that "irreverent attitude" and who worked so hard under those conditions to pioneer the army into the modern era of medical care on the battlefield. This is also the story of one doctor who, at age twenty-eight, found himself assigned as the chief surgeon of the 8076th MASH, Korea. But more than one doctor's story, it is the story of the MASH in its unique experiences and contributions. I rely on my own experiences, but I also rely on the work of others, most notably the official records of the Medical Corps in Korea as published by the Army Center of Military History in Dr. Albert E. Cowdrey's excellent work, *The Medics' War.* From that work I have taken excerpts of official documents, statistics of persons wounded and treated, and certain anecdotes of the MASH. I have also drawn on accounts of other doctors and friends with whom I have discussed this matter or from whom I have received correspondence concerning our shared experiences in Korea. For the sake of readability, I have not footnoted those references. Since this is a memoir not of a single doctor, but of the MASH, I do not contend that the account belongs to me but rather to the men and women who shared the honor of Korea.

I try to remain faithful to the facts, experiences, emotions, and perceptions involved in the MASH and in the war and in the unexpected and undesired confrontation with the Korean culture. The conversations throughout the manuscript are for the most part reconstructed from specific recollection, from individual attitudes of doctors and nurses in the Medical Corps, and from general attitudes in the medical community in the United States. Many who shared this experience and who are as sincere about it as I am may remember events differently than they are recorded here. Others may ascribe different motives or interpretations to words and deeds. We are all, of course, limited by our own resources, experiences, and interests. My recollections of events and conversations, although often clouded by the vagueness that the passage of fifty years visits upon us, have been greatly assisted by the several hundred photographs (color slides) that I took during my tour in Korea. These photographs are a treasure of memories that I have used to relive again and again my experiences and upon which I have based the several public presentations I have been privileged to give on the MASH. They have been invaluable in writing this memoir. As I review the photographs, some names and faces and places I will never forget. Others I have long since forgotten, but that is a comment on my limitations, not upon the individuals involved.

This is of necessity a transient observation, an observation made through the lenses of the American culture of the twentieth century, an observation that began with little or no understanding of—and, if the truth were known, little desire to understand—the vast reaches of Asia, its cultures, its peoples, or its problems. In following an obligatory sense of American calling to a war fought thousands of miles from the cities and towns and playing fields of the United States, I discovered the land of Korea—its culture, its people, and its problems—to be very real and vaguely understandable. This account is undertaken with a longing to grasp more firmly our part in the sad and often forgotten and unappreciated era that has arisen from the universal human experience that was—and is—Korea.

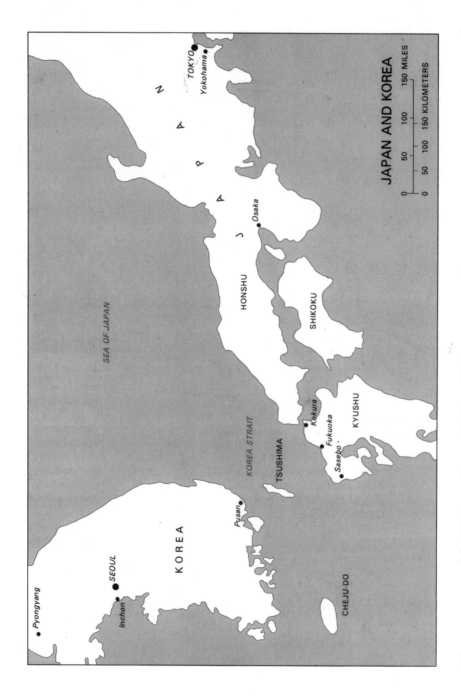

JAPAN AND KOREA

All maps courtesy of the U.S. Army Center of Military History.

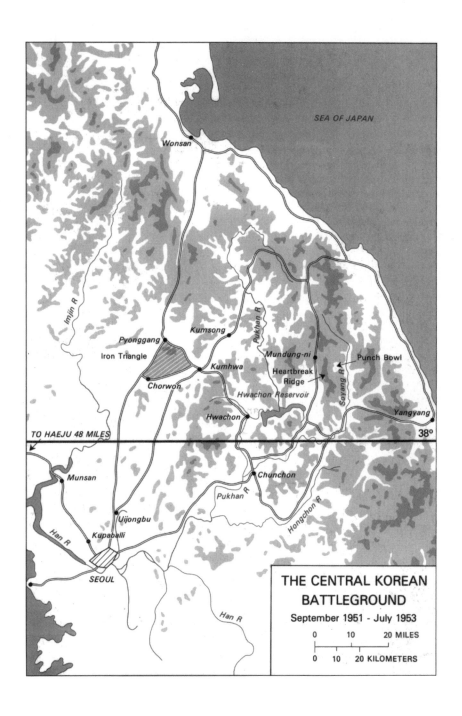

SEA OF JAPAN

Wonsan

Imjin R

Kumsong

Pukhan R

Pyonggang
Iron Triangle
Kumhwa
Mundung-ni
Punch Bowl
Heartbreak
Ridge
Chorwon
Soyang R
Hwachon Reservoir
Hwachon
Yangyang

TO HAEJU 48 MILES
38°

Munsan
Chunchon
Pukhan R
Uijongbu
Hongchon R
Kupaballi
Han R

SEOUL

**THE CENTRAL KOREAN
BATTLEGROUND**

September 1951 - July 1953

Han R

0   10   20 MILES

0   10   20 KILOMETERS

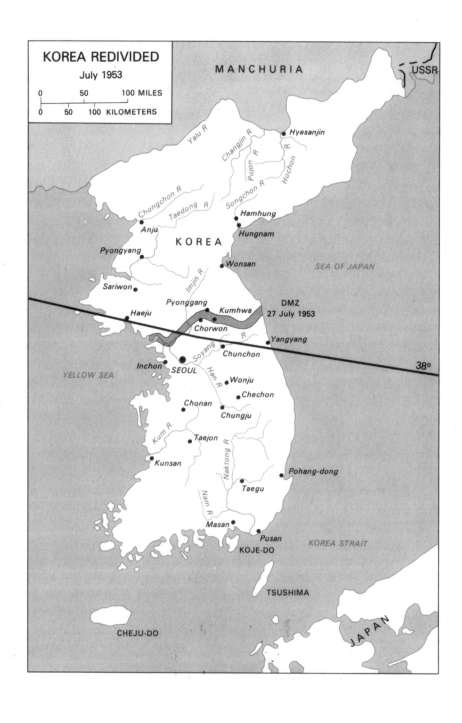

KOREA REDIVIDED
July 1953

0   50   100 MILES
0   50   100 KILOMETERS

MANCHURIA

USSR

Hyesanjin

Yalu R
Changjin R
Pujon R
Hochon R
Chongchon R
Taedong R
Songchon R

Hamhung

Anju

KOREA

Hungnam

Pyongyang

Wonsan

SEA OF JAPAN

Sariwon

Imjin R

Haeju

Pyonggang

Kumhwa

DMZ
27 July 1953

Chorwon

R

Yangyang

Soyang

Chunchon

38°

Inchon

SEOUL

Han R

Wonju

YELLOW SEA

Chechon

Chonan

Kum R

Chungju

Taejon

Naktong R

Kunsan

Pohang-dong

Nam R

Taegu

Masan

Pusan

KOREA STRAIT

KOJE-DO

TSUSHIMA

JAPAN

CHEJU-DO

1 FROM THE GRIDIRON TO THE IRON TRIANGLE

Korea was a long time ago. Korea was a mountainous country far away and the war there happened a long time ago. Even now, time and distance separate us. Korea was far from my mind on a recent autumn evening as I drove from my office in the Ohio River town of Portsmouth, out the rural roads into the hills and farms and communities, to my home back up the county road away from everything. In the Appalachian foothills of southern Ohio in the fall, when the leaves turn colors and the weather cools and the geese flock south, the mushrooms are out in the fields. As I turned up the county road toward home, I was followed by a man and a woman in a pickup truck. My wife, Joan, saw them too. Neither of us said anything.

We left the gravel county road and eased into our own lane, and the truck followed us. The lane, nearly half a mile of new gravel, rolled over the hills and up to the house. We stopped and the truck stopped about fifty yards behind us. I watched cautiously in the rear view mirror. The man got out, grasped a strand of barbed wire fence, pushed it down, and stepped through into the field. He was a tall, slender, clean-cut man with thin threads of graying hair slicked straight back, and he wore a faded old army field jacket. He sauntered into the field. He stopped and searched the ground, strolled on, stopped and searched some more. He looked up at us. We looked at him. He dropped his gaze to the ground and continued his slow, deliberate walk about the field.

"Who is that?" Joan asked.

"I don't know," I said.

I put the car in reverse and eased back toward him. Several yards away, I stopped and stepped out. The man glanced up, unsurprised. He was a handsome man who appeared to be in his late fifties or early sixties. I looked back at the truck and saw the woman staring at us. The man's clear eyes searched the ground as he ambled on over to the fence. He clutched something in his clean, lean-fingered hand.

"Can I help you?" I said. I stood cautiously on the other side of the fence.

"Naw, I don't need no help. I'm just out here looking for mushrooms."

"I don't know whether there are any mushrooms out there," I said. I glanced involuntarily to the fading green pasture.

"This your property?" he asked.

I said it was. Joan watched from the car.

He came a little closer until he stood several yards from me. Beneath the old, torn army field jacket he wore a plaid shirt and overalls.

"You Dr. Apel?" he asked.

I said I was.

"You the surgeon?"

I nodded. "Can I help you with anything?"

"You the one I read about in the paper a couple months ago? The one who was in the MASH unit in Korea?"

I nodded.

He looked over his shoulder quickly and back to me. He smiled. "You remember me?"

I searched his face. "I don't think I do."

He said his name and it did not ring a bell.

"I lived on Fourth Street all my life. Grew up there, went to the high school four or five years behind you. I lived there all my life."

I could see that he held a mushroom in his hand; he pulled it up close to his face and studied it. He turned it, then pinched it open as if he were dissecting it. Without looking up from his mushroom, he told me where he worked.

"I worked there ever since I got back from Korea," he said proudly.

In the silence of the evening, a tractor engine roared slowly over the field. A distant car with its lights on pushed down the county road.

"You still don't remember me?"

For the life of me, I could not place him.

"I was in your MASH back in 1951. I was with the 17th Infantry, 7th Division. Was hit in the shoulder near the Hwachon Reservoir. They brought me in and I seen you working there and asked one of them nurses if it was you. I said to the nurse, I said, 'Is that man from Ohio?' And the nurse, she looked and she said you was."

He lobbed the mushroom underhand out into the field.

"I was there in 1951 and '52," I said.

"I know you was," he said quickly. "You worked on me and next thing I knew I was back in Japan in one of them hospitals. I never got to say thanks to you. Hadn't been for you, they tell me I woulda been dead."

I had to smile.

He scrunched his face. "Yeah, ever since I got back, I been meaning to come out here and say 'thanks' to you."

"That was nearly fifty years ago," I said.

"Yeah," he said with a sheepish grin. "I guess time just gets away from you, don't it? I been meaning to come out here and just never got around to it. Kept meaning to come out sooner or later. I thought today's as good a time as any."

I laughed warmly. "I appreciate it."

"Anyway," he said, "thanks for all you done."

I stood for a moment in silence. The locusts screeched in the trees.

"Well," he said, "can't keep the wife waiting."

And with that, he turned and sauntered back toward the truck. I watched as he walked slowly, grasped the barbed wire, opened a place, and crawled through. He hopped across the gully to the pickup and stepped in. The engine started with the roar of the rusted-out muffler, and he went on down the roadway. In a moment he was out of sight.

"You're welcome," I said.

Korea and the MASH were a long time ago. I have not been back since 1952—except frequently when I have involuntarily jerked at a loud noise that sounded like artillery or when I have cried out in the darkness from a deep and vivid dream. Now even the thoughts and the dreams are less frequent. But all this time I have intended to go back. I have wondered what that war was about and what we were doing there. I know it is a part of us and a part of me, and all these years I have intended to go back.

I never would have dreamed of a place like Korea. In all my youth, I never even knew it existed. In fact, I'm not sure how I became acquainted with the name Korea. My ancestors came to these southern Ohio hills from Germany. Maybe they stopped here because these hills, I am told, look like the southern part of Germany. Maybe it's a twist of irony that they look like some parts of Korea. I have never seen the southern part of

Germany, but I know that many of our distant relatives live in the small towns there and many of them fought on the German side in World War I and World War II. My first ancestor on this side of the Atlantic, George Apel, is listed as an immigrant at the port of Baltimore, Maryland, in 1839. He set out on what came to be the German Trail—east from the port of New York or Boston or Baltimore, across the mountains north of Philadelphia into the coal and iron country of western Pennsylvania, passing his predecessors, the Pennsylvania Dutch, and on down the juncture of the Monongahela and the Allegheny and into the Ohio River Valley. All the Ohio River Valley from Pittsburgh to Louisville is heavily German. Cincinnati, about a hundred miles downriver from us, is a city with a hefty German flavor. George Apel did not make it all the way to Cincinnati. He settled in Lawrence County, Ohio, and took up farming.

George Apel's nephew, whose name was also George, came to the port of Baltimore in 1844. He followed his uncle's footsteps on the German Trail and came to Lawrence County and found a job in a small industry. The work must have been tough because both George and his uncle moved west into Scioto County and farmed the rolling green hills. There they multiplied and there they stayed. Both are buried in a small cemetery surrounding a small Lutheran church in Scioto County. The lettering on their grave markers is in the gothic German. My father (George's grandson) and his seven brothers and sisters were required to speak German in their household until they were sixteen.

When my turn came, I reversed the journey on the German Trail. At the South Shore, Kentucky, railway station that served Portsmouth, Ohio, I boarded the *George Washington,* a passenger train of the Chesapeake and Ohio Railroad, and headed through the Appalachian foothills up the Ohio River valley, back through West Virginia and the Pennsylvania Dutch country and into New York City. I was fresh out of high school back before World War II. New York City, in this awestruck midwesterner's eyes, was the center of the world and the home of Columbia University. I was just one of a procession of young, wide-eyed kids from the rest of the nation who came to New York for an education and found homesickness, big-city ways, and a longing to get it over with and get out.

At Grand Central Station the *George Washington* was renamed the *Fast Flying Virginian* for the return trip. Every afternoon at four, the *Vir-*

ginian chugged across the northern tip of Manhattan Island, past Harlem, past Morningside Heights, out past Baker Field, Columbia's football stadium, and into the heartland of America. At football practice every fall afternoon, my heart yearned to be on board. The *Virginian* wound through the Appalachians and stopped at every gray, wooden depot across Pennsylvania and West Virginia and Kentucky. I wanted to sprint off that football field and hop that train back to some sense of permanence and warmth. But Coach Little, the legendary Lou Little, never would have allowed that. He was Woody Hayes, Bear Bryant, and Tom Osborne all rolled into one. He would have run right after me, grabbed me firmly under the shoulder pads, and jerked me back to Baker Field, where I would have been standing out in the cold rain and sleet watching the *Fast Flying Virginian* chug by and wishing once more that I were at home.

Then came Pearl Harbor, and all the plans that were permanent in life were now up for grabs. Europe and Asia were on fire, and it seemed that every young man in America was headed that way. I was on the scholarship program with the navy and stayed behind at Columbia; when I finished undergraduate school, I entered Columbia College of Physicians and Surgeons. The war was an omnipresent threat, but we went on. I was voted to the All-American football team at Columbia and was offered NFL contracts, but all that was secondary in my thoughts.

I was graduated from Columbia as a V-12, an apprentice seaman in the navy's tuition program, and I got my first taste of medicine in the summer before my first year in medical school. I was assigned to Sampson Naval Base Hospital in Geneva, New York. Without the first minute of medical training, I was given a set of green scrubs, pointed in the direction of one of those long, antiseptic, tile-floored government hallways, and assigned to assist the nursing staff in patient care. The days were long, and we shifted from one nurses' station to another, one ward to another, one floor to another. We learned the basic things such as taking temperature and pulse rate and blood pressure. The most exciting thing we did was to give shots.

Penicillin was just beginning to be used in civilian and naval hospitals as the number one antibiotic. It was highly regarded as a new drug and was given only under close observation and in the most sterile of conditions. I was directed to prepare an injectable solution by removing the powder from a sterile vial, placing it in a sterile solution, and injecting the solution into the patient. Left to my own devices, I laid the vial on the lab table and searched for the solution. When I turned back to the table, the vial of penicillin powder scooted on its side and the contents made a nice white trail across the black tabletop.

I glanced outside the lab door quickly to see who was there. I expected to receive a good lecture for dropping the vial. Seeing no one around, I took a sheet of paper from my notebook, scraped the powder across the tabletop and back into the vial. I searched it diligently for foreign substances. None. I quickly put the powder into the solution and the solution into the syringe and the syringe into the patient's arm. The patient made a rapid recovery, and all was well with the navy.

The rest of my time at Sampson—which was the sum total of my military medical training—was uneventful; the summer was saved by periodic ventures into Ovid, New York, with the Waves and the nurses. And then on to medical school.

The only stabilizing thing in the lives of us medical students during those first years of medical school was the pursuit of education. Classes came regularly and we had to be there on schedule. I was probably the only guy in the country who played football during his first year in medical school and had to attend class on Saturday mornings before ball games. In 1943 we played Yale in New Haven. The team left Baker Field by bus early Saturday morning before the traffic was bad. But I was not willing to miss my Saturday morning class.

The last thing Coach Little said to me was, "Apel, you better be there by two o'clock."

"Yes, sir," I said quickly. "I have a train ticket."

"I don't care about the ticket. You be there."

One of the New York newspapers carried the description of my arrival at the Yale Bowl in a brief article the following day. I finished class on Saturday, caught the subway to the train station, and caught the train to New Haven. Throughout the entire trip I could see mental images of Coach Little pacing the sidelines during the warmups and muttering my name in vain.

I took a cab from the New Haven train station to the Yale Bowl, and the cab got caught in the game traffic.

"Goin' to the game?" the cabbie asked as we waited for the cars to move. I said I was.

"Who you like?" he said without much real interest.

"I wouldn't give much for Columbia's chances right now," I said.

He shrugged his heavy shoulders. "I don't know. Yale's not much this year."

The manager was at the locker room door with my equipment. "Hurry. They're tossin' the coin right now."

I returned kickoffs in addition to playing on offense and defense. I hoped we lost the toss so we would have to kick to them and I would have a few extra minutes to dress and warm up.

At two o'clock straight up, I trotted out of the locker room and along the sideline toward Coach Little. His face relaxed when he saw me; then when he realized they were lining up for the kickoff, he growled, "Get out there. Right now."

I did not break stride. I went right out on the field as the referee blew the whistle to signal Yale's kickoff to Columbia.

Medical School was far removed from the European and Pacific theaters of operations, but the presence of the war hung like the smell of disinfectant over the classrooms and wards and operating rooms. Like millions of other Americans, we thought about the war all the time. It was always there. Soldiers and sailors returned to school and brought with them the ghosts of all those who had gone to war and had not returned. Movie reels, newspapers, local bond drives, calls to support the war effort constantly reminded us of the frail course of our present lives.

When Victory in Europe Day came, we sighed, we celebrated, and we thought it was all over. We were happy for ourselves that we did not have to go, and we were happy for those who were coming home. Personnel officers in the military scurried about to construct an equitable way to demobilize the military and the Medical Corps. Everyone wanted to go home, but the war in the Pacific still raged on. The War Department devised plans to release units and individuals over an extended period of time and in a manner that was "fair" to those who actually fought the war. The result was the Adjusted Service Rating, an elaborate point system based on time in service, days in combat, number of dependents, and decorations. The application of the Adjusted Service Rating to the Medical Corps meant a drastic reduction of overall strength through the summer of 1945. It was devised with good intentions, but like many government projects started with good intentions, it only added to the turmoil. This cumbersome system created not an orderly process for demobilization but a lot of hard feelings toward the army.

In September 1945 the war in the Pacific came to a sudden end. With a collective sigh of relief, the soldiers of the U.S. Army, including those in the Medical Corps, looked back to the States and to families and businesses and getting on with life. Doctors and medical students joined the rest of the population in the age-old game of getting out of the service. We at home could not blame them. Our generation was probably as adept as any other in exerting congressional pressure, in writing letters, in calling friends in government and business, in pressuring relatives in the higher offices of the military—our generation did it all to get out of military service. And no one blamed anybody for it. The war was over and our generation had fought it. Now we deserved to get out.

In our view, bad fortune rested upon one class of people in the entire world. No less enviable position could be found in the years after World War II than to be a doctor on active duty in the military. Within a year after V-E Day, the number of army doctors dropped from approximately forty-five thousand to eighty-five hundred. For the thousands of doctors escaping the military, the world of medicine and plenty beckoned. It was time to get on with the business of practicing medicine.

The plans for those of us in school were no different. The burden of the war lifted, we could finish medical training and go on to practice. I had married Marjorie Griffin, my high school sweetheart, who had gone to Swarthmore in Philadelphia. We lived in a minuscule apartment in New York City as I finished my last years in medical school. Our first son, Barney, came soon. We wanted to go home to southern Ohio for keeps—first internship, then residency, then home.

You have to give it to the army. They tried to maintain the strength of the Medical Department in the years after the war; but no one wanted to serve. The demobilization after World War II had created a vacuum in the medical service that had to be filled from the civilian sector. In December 1947 the Army Medical Corps was authorized a total of 3,000 officers but had assigned only 1,926. The Army Nurse Corps was authorized 2,258 and had an actual strength of 1,148.

In order to rebuild the Medical Department, the army had to overcome several problems, not the least of which was the perception of army service held by those the army hoped to recruit. Army pay was not the only issue. Military doctors were seen in the medical community as second-class citizens. Civilian doctors and medical students perceived the army as unduly regimented, inequitable in its treatment of active duty and reserve officers, and archaic in its medical doctrine. The military was simply not a place where a doctor could progress in the field of medicine. And after spending that much time and effort in training, getting ahead in the chosen field was of major importance.

Those perceptions of the army arose out of the low morale in the Medical Corps at the end of World War II. The doctors on active duty—those who would take their view of the army into the civilian sector when they were discharged—had negative attitudes toward the freedom to practice medicine within the army. Surveys among doctors and nurses taken by the army in 1946 indicated that two-thirds of the doctors and over 90 percent of the nurses would leave the army immediately if given the opportunity. Of 210 nurses polled in June 1946, only 15 said they wanted to stay on active duty. The same attitudes were common among technicians and enlisted personnel.

Military medical doctrine, in the eyes of the young doctors and interns in America, was unmoving and antiquated. It simply could not compete with the exciting innovations in the teaching institutions and hospitals in the United States. The new things being tried and developed were in the civilian sector. Maj. Gen. Norman T. Kirk, army surgeon general, wrote in 1946 to the army chief of staff, "Much of the unwillingness of the young physician to enter the military service is due to his belief that the Army denies to him . . . opportunities for professional advancement, for postgraduate education for specialization, for certification by professional specialty boards and for clinical research and self expression."

Nobody was going to serve in the army. But the army tried. During this period three thousand reserve officers were asked to take voluntary tours of active duty in the army. Forty-one applied for active duty. No one was going to volunteer. Later, in 1950, immediately after the passage of the Doctors Draft Act, applications for active and reserve commissions swamped the air force and the navy, and those branches met their needs for the war effort. But the army's applications for active duty lagged far behind its requirements. The general sentiment was that doctors would have done just about anything to avoid service in the military, and particularly in the army.

The army came up with an idea to counter all this bad press: follow the lead of the civilian sector and turn to professional specialization. Specialization was the order of the day in the medical field, and the military needed to compete for the young doctors graduating from the nation's medical schools. Military doctors had always been considered general practitioners. In particular, army combat doctors were not specialists: they were hard-driven surgeons whose sole job was to save the lives of the young soldiers wounded in combat. In following the civilian lead, the army, so the debate went, gave up that primary role for the sake of numbers in the Medical Corps. Specialization would later become a greater issue in the Korean War.

The army's major effort to convince people to serve in the Medical Corps was training programs such as the newly enlarged Army Specialized Training Program (ASTP), which paid a volunteer student's tuition to medical school. The navy's program was called the Navy Specialized Training Program or the V-12 program. I attended medical school at Columbia as a V-12. That meant that the navy paid my undergraduate and medical school tuition. In return I was to serve in the navy if needed. During World War II nearly 80 percent of the students in American medical schools were involved with the specialized training programs (55 percent in the army and 25 percent in the navy).

The ASTP and V-12 programs instituted in World War II yielded their harvest in the postwar years. People like me who went to school during the war were now graduating into a military that was downsizing. Although we had willingly accepted the tuition support during wartime, we, like everyone else, were unhappy with the prospect of serving in the peacetime army. The surgeon general concluded, "The ASTP's were the most disgruntled lot of doctors ever encountered by the Army."

During the postwar years, the Democratic party smiled upon us. President Truman and his secretary of defense, Louis Johnson, slashed the defense budget. They parted with defense money as if it was their own. The military, only a few years earlier the favorite son of the federal treasury, now languished at the end of the fiscal soup line. Uncle Sam's checking account for training was about to bounce some checks. In December 1947 the cutbacks in military strength overall and the political climate of the time reduced the number of ASTPs beginning active duty. Although ASTPs made up the majority of officers, the number of doctors on active duty was still below the number required for the Medical Corps.

But the army was undaunted: in February 1949 the Medical Corps unveiled the Moral Suasion Campaign, another attempt to persuade doctors and nurses to volunteer for service in the armed forces. The American Medical Association agreed to publish an appeal in its journal and did so with little success. The Department of Defense followed with a campaign to persuade young doctors to enter the military. On March 7, 1949, the secretary of defense mailed 10,863 letters to ASTP- and V-12-trained doctors and dentists, inviting them to apply for a commission in one of the three services. Almost 9,000 replies were received. But although this was a good response, in the period from February 1949 until mid-1950, only 522 of those 9,000 responses resulted in applications for active duty in any of the branches of the service. Only 180 applications came to the army. Everyone else said emphatically *no*.

By 1950 the army was truly in sad shape. Budgetary cutbacks, popular disenchantment with the military, postwar euphoria, focus on the good life, all things pointed away from the military. Assigned strength in army units in general had fallen perilously below the authorized strength. Combat units in the Far East Command were at approximately 50 percent strength, and combat service support units (which included medical units) were at 25 percent strength. The Far East Command surgeon, Maj. Gen. James A. Bethea, sounded the alarm: "The outlook for medical service within the FEC [Far East Command] during the year ... presents a grim picture from a personnel standpoint. Commencing in January 1950 and increasing each month through June 1950 the losses in the Medical Corps in the Far East Command will be extremely heavy ... so much so that no suitable solution can be foreseen."

At the outbreak of the Korean War, only two hundred doctors were assigned to the Far East Command, which included Japan, Okinawa, Guam, the Philippines, and Korea. In the early months of the Korean War, the medical battalions of the 1st Cavalry Division and the 24th and 25th Infantry Divisions averaged only fourteen of the authorized forty-two medical officers. At no time in the first six months of the Korean War did the number of doctors in any of the medical battalions of these divisions reach over twenty-four of the authorized forty-two.

That was the condition of the Army Medical Corps when Korea visited us in Cleveland, Ohio. I was out of medical school and, I thought, out of the navy. When I was graduated, they were not taking doctors. The navy told me to go my merry way and I did. I did not know that the navy V-12 program still existed; the navy, indeed the military in general, was the farthest thing from my mind.

No one outside the army or the government expected a military crisis in those days. We now know of the development of American foreign policy in Korea and Asia through a variety of historical studies on the Cold War. We can read the accounts of the Roosevelt and Truman administrations and their varying attitudes toward containment of the Soviet Union, the support of European colonialism to stifle the expansion of communist movements in Europe and Asia, and the nationalist fervor to secure foreign markets for American business. But in the aftermath of World War II, all that was lost on those of us in the general public who were trying to make a living.

Then came the big surprise: June 25, 1950, and the North Korean blitz into South Korea. I was in a surgical residency at Saint Luke's Hospital on the east end of Cleveland. We had had another son and then a daughter, three children in all. The comfort and security of all our plans to settle down in our hometown and begin an idyllic life in the practice of medicine were also blitzed by the North Korean Army.

The news began to spread by word of mouth. The army was taking doctors wherever they could find them. The morale in the civilian medical community plummeted in those first days. It was absolutely unthinkable for most of us that we might have to go to a war.

The house staff had a softball team that played on the fields beneath the windows of the huge Saint Luke's Hospital complex. We were known by our uniforms: surgical scrub pants and white T-shirts. We played City Hospital, Western Reserve Hospital, and college and pickup teams from around the city. We were pretty good.

One bright Saturday afternoon in the late summer of 1950, I trotted off the field after infield warmups. Several teammates huddled outside the dugout. It was hot and dry.

"What are you going to do about Korea?" one said. It was the topic of frequent conversation.

"Where is Korea, anyway?" said another. "I never heard of it."

"It's a nightmare," said a third. There was a conspiratorial air about this conversation. "And we're getting into another war and we're getting our fancy fannies whupped right now."

Another intern listened. He pulled his hat down to shade his eyes. All faces had frowns when it came to Korea.

"They need everybody," the first intern said. "They're going to pass a Doctors Draft Act."

"They won't draft any doctors," the second intern answered. "They'll draft interns and put them out there while the doctors stay in private practice and make all the money."

"That's true," said another intern. He thumbed his chest. "They're getting ready to take guys like us to the cleaners. Mark my words. We're going to get screwed."

One intern leaned into the conversation. "A friend of mine at Walter Reed told me that right now they have thousands of wounded who don't see doctors. They have sergeants operating on them and the sergeant calls a doctor on the field radio and the doctor tells him what to do."

"I heard that," said the first intern. "All the surgeon does is talk to sergeants over the radio and tell them how to do the operation."

I looked at him. He held a bat with a hand at each end and lifted it over his head to stretch. He looked back at me.

"It's the truth," he said. "I'm not making it up. All those government so-called doctors have really messed this thing up and we have to pay for their mistakes. They need doctors and nurses anywhere they can get them."

"I'll tell you this," one said. "I'm not going. I guarantee you I'm not going. I'm going to be in private practice and I'm not going. Let those politicians fix their own mistakes. They got themselves into this. Let's see them get out of it."

"I was up in the pathology department last week," the second intern said. "I heard some guys talking up there and they know how to stay out of it. And they said they can get all of us out of it. None of us will have to go."

"You don't have to go," another pitched in. "All the smart people are going to get out of it."

"What about you?" the first intern said to me. "I'll get you this guy's name and he can get you out of it."

The umpire swept his hand across the plate and shouted, "Batter up!"

"Call me tomorrow," the intern said. "You can get out of this. Nobody in his right mind is going to Korea."

It was hot and the sweat had popped out on my forehead. I glanced over at my wife in the stands. Our kids were beneath the bleachers playing in the sand. The sun was bright, and Marge shaded her eyes as she looked over my way. I knew I was going. I did not know how I was going. To my knowledge, I was no longer a part of the military. Part of it could probably be called patriotism. I did not know anything about the Korean War, but I knew they would need some doctors. Part of it could probably be called obligation since the navy had paid for my education. Like it or not, I owed this to them. And part of it could probably be called stubbornness. Like Shakespeare's Falstaff, I believe that discretion is the better part of valor. And part of discretion is knowing when to step into a fight and when to avoid it. That depends not upon your circumstances but upon the circumstances of those in the fight. For better or for worse, our nation, to the layman's utter astonishment, had jumped right into the middle of a melee. Whether we were prepared for that fight rests on the shoulders of President Truman and Secretary Johnson and the military command. Their job is the national defense and all the responsibilities included in the national defense, particularly the preservation of as many American lives as possible. But the accomplishment of those responsibilities did not determine whether I should help those who had answered their country's call to fight the Korean War. I knew I was going because, in the back of my mind, I knew that's what doctors were for. The ancient duty of doctors called, and for better or for worse, I intended to answer.

"You're up, Ottie," someone said. I took a bat and went to the plate.

On September 1, 1950, nine weeks after the North Korean invasion, Public Law 779 passed both houses of Congress. Called the Doctors Draft Act, this legislation had the support of the military and the American Medical Association, the American Dental Association, and the Association of American Veterinary Medicine. The bill itself provided for the registration of all doctors fifty years old and under with induction eligibility to age fifty-one.

Priority of induction was set out in the statute. First were those doctors who had been students in the specialized training programs administered by the army, the navy, and the air force but who had served for less than ninety days. That was the ASTPs and the V-12s. That was me. Second were those in the same category but who had served for more than ninety days. There were a few of those. Most of the ASTPs and V-12s had used a great deal of ingenuity to get out of serving even ninety days. Third were those doctors who had no military service and fourth, those who had served since September 16, 1940, in inverse ratio to the length of their active service after that date.

What happened with the Doctors Draft Act should not have surprised anyone. The Doctors Draft Act did exactly what we all knew it would do. First, from the rather narrow perspective of the intern or resident trying to complete his or her education, it would take care of the concerns of the politicians who were trying to find bodies for the Medical Corps. Second, it immunized established doctors, veteran or nonveteran, from service. Third, the draftees would salve the concerns of career military doctors by providing a corps of young doctors who would serve their time and leave the service, eliminating future competition. Fourth, and last, the Doctors Draft Act was attentive to the needs of the young men and women going to Korea who would be injured and require medical support.

By drafting residents and interns first, the Congress of the United States made a determination not to call on the wealth of experienced doctors in private practice, many of whom had been combat doctors only five years before. Instead, the government drafted the inexperienced into the service. That is not to say that the younger doctors should not have been drafted. They should have. The ASTPs and the V-12s, like the National Guard today, knew that the time for service could come in the future.

The consequence of the Doctors Draft Act was that it did not provide a substitute for the pool of experienced officers lost after World War II. When the draftees entered the service, no "old salts" were there to take the new officers under their wings to ease the transition from a peacetime to a wartime army. The army had lost more than numbers. It had lost the experienced members of the military community who would have guided the Medical Corps in the early months of the war. The Doctors Draft Act did not remedy that loss.

I did not know it at the time, but I was a part of what the Defense Department called Operation NavMed. The secretary of defense instructed the secretary of the navy to make available to the army 570 reserve doctors. The notice came by mail. I had expected something. Two weeks earlier two notices had come, one to a doctor on the staff and another to an intern. We called them "death notices" or "obituaries." They were terse directions to report to the Armed Forces Induction Center for transport to service in the U.S. Army.

I stood in the lounge of the operating rooms at Saint Luke's Hospital in Cleveland. "I heard you got your obituary," an intern said. He sat in the lounge in a green scrub suit. I showed him the letter.

"There's still time, Ottie," he said. "A classmate of mine at Johns Hopkins got out of it after he had gotten his obituary and even after his reporting date had passed."

We talked a moment. I told him I thought I would go.

"Don't go flag-waving on us," he said. "This is a dirty war that nobody wants to have anything to do with. We got better things to do. In fact, I heard a whole dental section in a National Guard unit threatened to walk out if they got called."

"My father-in-law knows the governor," I said.

"There you go," he said. "That'll get you in the National Guard as a mechanic or something. Then they won't send you."

"A mechanic?" I said.

"Yeah, if you go in as a doctor, you're gone. You're dead meat, MacArthur's cannon fodder. Go directly to the Pusan Perimeter, do not pass go, do not collect two hundred dollars."

I laughed. "I'll probably go."

He shook the letter in the air. "Don't do anything rash. Think about this. Someone can take care of this for you. All you got to do is ask."

That night, my wife sat at the dinner table with the letter in front of her. I told her what little I knew about it.

"You mean there's some way that you can get out of it?" she asked. She had her own ideas about Korea and the army and President Truman and Secretary Johnson and General MacArthur.

"That's what they say."

"What do you think about it?"

"I owe the navy," I said.

"This Korea thing is crazy," she said. "I don't want you involved. World War II was one thing. This Korea thing is something else." She was approaching exasperation. "Most people don't even know where Korea is."

"Even fewer care," I said.

"Ottie," she said. She was very serious. "If you have to go, I want you to go. I want you to do the right thing."

"I've been thinking about you and the kids."

"We'll go back to Portsmouth. We can live with my folks or we'll get an apartment or a house. Don't you worry about that. We'll be well taken care of there."

"I don't want to leave you behind."

She understood.

2 "THE SPIRIT OF '76"

In the late spring and early summer of 1951, the 8076th Mobile Army Surgical Hospital (MASH) was a dreary formation of tents in the linebacker position behind the 2d, 7th, and 24th Infantry Divisions and the 2d and 6th Republic of Korea (ROK) Divisions. It also supported elements of the 1st Cavalry Division, the 25th Infantry Division, and a smattering of United Nations troops near Chunchon, Korea. I boarded a rickety old C-23 at Osaka, Japan, for the short lift to the airstrip at Pusan on the southern tip of Korea. Several other officers and noncommissioned officers (NCOs) made the hop that day over the glistening Sea of Japan. All would be picked up and routed to the front lines north of the 38th parallel. We placed our duffel bags beneath the sling seats in the C-23 and closed our eyes for the ride.

We had not been in the air long before we saw Korea on the horizon. As I looked out the small window, the first thing I saw was the bright blue sky, so bright I had to squint, and then immediately the rugged mountain ranges. I was surprised at the beauty and the majesty of the mountains. I do not know what I expected, but I was surprised at the beauty of the country as we viewed it from the air. I had been told that the first thing you notice about Korea when you step through the door of the aircraft is the smell. I had been told that it comes from the agricultural use of certain fertilizers. Whatever the source, the smell, according to my information, hung over the entire country. It was not so when we arrived. I had expected it and looked for it. Only a trace of the smell was apparent, and it was covered by the pungent odor of petroleum products and engine exhaust from the aircraft and the vehicles scurrying around the airstrip. There was no smell of agriculture. I was later told that fertilizer was not available in large quantities during the war.

As the major port of Korea, Pusan was bustling with the resupply of United Nations troops. An endless circle of airplanes came in to the huge airport, and a constant flotilla of cargo ships entered the advanced commercial port. The airport looked like so many other busy commercial airports around the world: stacks of crates and boxes, soldiers loading and unloading aircraft, front-end loaders hoisting the stacks onto the backs of two-and-a-half-ton trucks (commonly called deuce-and-a-halfs), and the constant buzz and bustle of the major lifeline to the soldiers in combat. We looked with wide eyes as we passed through.

At the replacement station in the airport, we were directed to another C-23, which carried us several thousand feet above the Main Supply Route (MSR) to Wonju. We looked down on the convoys moving like dark brown caterpillars over the hot, dusty roads. The MSR wound along the riverbeds and curved around the mountains. In the brightness and the heat, I could feel the sensation of asthma, anxiety, and seasickness, none of which I normally had but all of which presently afflicted each of us.

At Wonju a driver, a private first class, searched our faces as we exited the aircraft.

"Any doctors here?" he said. I told him I was a doctor.

"Got orders for the 8076th?" he asked. I nodded.

"Throw your duffel in the back of that jeep over there. We're moving out in about five minutes."

I got in the jeep and waited. The driver stood among several NCOs and swapped war stories. As I looked over my shoulder, I saw him hand a rumpled piece of cloth to a sergeant. The sergeant quickly secreted the cloth in a small bag. The pfc jumped in the driver's seat, cranked the jeep, and off we went.

When we were out on the road away from the airport, I asked him, "Was that a flag you gave that man back there?"

I did not know whether I should ask, but I figured that since he was driving me I had better have some idea of what was going on.

"North Korean flag," he said, matter-of-factly.

After a short moment I asked, "Where'd you get it?"

He glanced over at me with a twinge of suspicion in his squint. "We made it."

"You made it?" I said.

"Yeah," he shrugged. "These rear echelon tractor jockeys go crazy over souvenirs. They'll give anything for a North Korean flag. We make them and find a chicken or something and kill it and sprinkle blood on it. Tell them it was captured. They love it. They think it's the real thing. That one got us ten cases of whiskey that was supposed to go to some officers' club."

I have to admit I smiled. "What do you do that for?"

"Everything good that comes in from the States headed to the front gets stolen by these jerks back here and it ends up in some colonel's quarters. Probably some doctor who has a clean hotel room and doesn't want to get out in the heat. At the front we get all the stuff that nobody else wants to steal."

"You get back at 'em, huh?"

"Yeah, we're averaging about three or four flags a week. We get some good stuff with them."

The road from Pusan to Wonju looked like an interstate compared to the road to Chunchon. Wide enough for two vehicles to pass if they rubbed fenders, the road wound up and down and around and through. The roadbed was not much more than a tank trail the engineers had cut out on the move north. The heat from the jeep engine as well as the yellowish-red dust clogged our lungs. We stopped frequently for oxcarts filled with household goods or hay or manure. In the stifling heat, the smells and the brightness of the sun and the persistence of the civilian refugees scurrying about like ants on the roads baffled even those with the patience of Job. The driver honked and shouted even though he knew it would do no good. This was an awful trip.

I saw the dust trail first. Around the mountain a huge, yellowish-red pillar rose to the sky. As the pillar approached us, I was convinced that it was a tank column—probably the whole North Korean army. They were close to us when they came around a bend in the road into our sight. It was a column of trucks led by a jeep.

The men in the jeep, all Americans, smiled and waved as if we were long lost brothers. The driver seemed to know them for he waved back with the same enthusiasm. The passenger in the other jeep was a captain, and he smiled at me, waved, and shouted something I could not understand over the engine noise.

When we cleared the column and the racket died down, I asked the driver who was in the lead jeep.

"That's the guy you're replacing," he shouted. "For the last three months, he's been counting the days until you'd get here."

The strange thought that popped into my mind was that I was glad to see him upright in a jeep and not horizontal in an ambulance.

The 8076th in 1951. In the early part of the war the entire hospital was tentage. Mobility required quick disassembly of the MASH.

The city of Chunchon, a small industrial center near the 38th parallel, had suffered severe damage during the early part of the war. Several small factories had been gutted, and only shells of twisted steel remained. Bomb and artillery craters pocked the roads and streets and fields in and around the city. But the once proud city of Chunchon had licked its serious wounds and was continuing with life until the armies came back to destroy it again.

I had never seen a MASH before. I thought I had an idea of what to expect, but even in the glaring midday sun I never would have recognized as a medical facility the conglomeration of dark brown tents, the sides down and tied, that appeared quickly in the field away from the dusty dirt road. I could hear in the distance an artillery battery limbering up. The battery blasted evenly, one, two, three; one, two, three. In a second, the retort from the mountains, the echo of the shots, one, two, three; one, two, three. The 105s would have to go to maximum elevation to project over these mountains. They were the sharpest ones I had ever seen. They made the Appalachians look like rolling foothills.

"That's it," the driver said.

"That's what?"

"That's the 8076th. Right there. Good luck, Doc."

The jeep jerked to a halt and I hopped out. Dust covered me from head to foot. A Korean boy about sixteen stood by the tent like a statue and waited. When I looked around, he came my way.

"Hi, Lieutenant," he said. "You the new guy?"

I looked him up and down. A slender boy with black hair and brown eyes, he wore an American fatigue jacket and Korean sandals.

"I'm Choi," he said confidently. "I take you to surgery."

"Where do I put my duffel bag?" I asked.

"No time for bags," he said. "I take bag."

"Where's my tent?" I asked. "I need to wash up before I do anything."

Choi picked up the duffel bag.

"Lieutenant," he said, and he waited.

When he did not continue, I turned to him. His dark brown eyes were fixed on me.

"Lieutenant," he said. "I take care of tent and bag. You take care of surgery."

Yes, it was authoritative. I looked at him closely. He returned the gaze just as closely. Then he smiled slowly.

"Now, I take you to surgery."

I followed him to one of the dark brown tents with the tied-down sides. He was short. I had been told that many Koreans were shorter than Americans. But he carried the duffel bag without any effort, and he appeared strong. He dropped the bag and untied the tent flap and opened it quickly, stood to the side like a doorman, and ushered me in.

I stopped. "Thanks, Choi," I said with deep doubt in my voice.

"You very welcome, Lieutenant," he said with his tight Korean smile.

A dirty wooden board was suspended by a gray string from the tent pole. It served as the address marker of the surgical tent. On it someone had scrawled a greeting: "The Spirit of '76."

The chief of surgery of the 8076th MASH was Maj. John Coleman, who had trained at the University of Louisville. He looked up from the operating table. Two nurses and another doctor surrounded a young American on a litter. They had attached an intravenous to his arm and covered him with a white sheet. One naked light bulb hung over the table. My first sensation upon entering the surgical tent was not the darkness or the smell of dirt and dust mixed with rubbing alcohol and

A nurse scrubbing at the five-gallon can in the operating tent.

soap. The sensation that crawled all over you was the stifling heat.

"Scrub up," Major Coleman barked.

He pointed with a scalpel toward the door, and I turned. A young African American private who served as an orderly took my coat and hat and said, "Follow me, Doctor."

He took several steps to a five-gallon bucket that I had not seen when I entered. It was in a corner, and it was dark even in midday. No light entered the tent from the outside.

"Scrub up here. When you're ready to rinse, I'll pour the water through that bucket."

For the first time I noticed a second bucket hanging from a tent pole. It had holes punched in the bottom of it so that water could run through. I scrubbed, and the private poured the water, and I rinsed and put on a white surgical coat and hung the mask over my head.

The injured were brought in through one end of the surgery tent from a preparation area in the pre-op tent. They were brought on litters and placed on one of the three metal tube tables lined in the surgery tent. Each table had two doctors and two or three nurses clustered around it. Several enlisted personnel assisted the surgery by bringing supplies and necessities. Each of the wounded had been examined before he came in, and the nurse who brought him briefed us on the injuries.

The nurse knew her stuff. She wore olive drab army fatigue pants, boots bloused, and a white T-shirt. A surgical mask covered her face. She looked me over carefully.

"We're glad to have you aboard, Doctor," she said.

I nodded.

"We're way short of doctors."

A second nurse joined us, and we examined a young white soldier with a nasty sucking chest wound. My first thought was that he was younger than my younger brother. His close buzz cut made him look even younger. His eyes were closed and his face turned to the side as if he was peacefully asleep. His gasping chest heaved regularly, then sputtered. I probed momentarily and looked away to prepare for surgery.

"Get used to this," she said. "There's a lot more where he came from."

My immediate thought was that she was testing me.

"You think I've never seen a gunshot wound?" I said.

She shrugged. "Why should you? No one else had before they got here. All we've got here are interns who haven't even seen a child delivered in a city hospital."

We finished that surgery, and another came in right behind it. They placed the litter on the table as I scrubbed again in the five-gallon can.

The nurse crisply explained the wound, and I examined the patient.

"How many you have back there?" I asked.

"We have about a hundred right now," she said. "I hope you like this."

"That's what we're here for," I said with a false bravado.

That evening I broke for dinner. The mess hall, I learned, was over by the five-gallon can. In fact, that was the break room, the mess hall, the scrub room, the dormitory, and everything else. No one left the tent.

"What do you want for breakfast?" the mess steward said.

"Eggs over easy, sausage, and toast," Major Coleman said. "Bring it about zero-four."

"Yes, sir," he said.

Major Coleman looked at me. "You'll get used to it."

By midnight the small of my back was killing me. I straightened up and stretched. A steady stream of perspiration drenched my white undershirt, and the trails of sweat ran down my stomach into my fatigue pants, making a dark stain like a diaper. The nurse occasionally wiped my forehead and neck with a towel so that I could see. The sweat ran into my glasses and from my armpits down my arms into my rubber gloves. If you have ever worn glasses, you know how aggravating a steady stream of sweat into your glasses can be. I had to stop constantly and remove my glasses to wipe the sweat out of them. Periodically, I had to lift my hands over my head so the sweat could run the other way. The ends of my fingers wrinkled from the moisture in the gloves. As soon as we changed gloves, the new ones filled with sweat. Finally, we gave up on changing gloves because the supply was short.

"Don't lean over so far," the nurse said. She was already a veteran. "You have to operate standing straight up. Doesn't tax your back so much."

"Thanks," I said.

I do not know what the army could have done to prepare its doctors for Korea. But whatever it was, they had not done it. The army got caught with its pants down. No one was prepared for this war. Across the military board, the army was napping. World War II combat officers who had stayed in the reserve were called up and sent directly to Korea. Brand new officers who had never seen a day of troop command drew infantry platoon assignments. The West Point class of 1950 saw the lion's share of its ranks go to combat without proper preparation.

The Medical Corps suffered from the same deficiencies. The army had done nothing to prepare the new doctors for combat medicine. Their failure to do any training in the Medical Corps was already the topic of a hot debate in Washington. Congress and the Department of Defense were asking critical and embarrassing questions about the medical training of the doctors, nurses, and enlisted personnel in Korea.

Military medicine differs from civilian medicine in several ways. The civilian doctor spends most of his time and effort on clinical questions: how to diagnose and treat illness. The military doctor must diagnose and treat not only the customary diseases but also the diseases that are peculiar to the combat environment. In addition the military doctor must treat combat wounds, which civilian doctors do not often see. Beyond that, the military doctor must deal with a variety of problems rarely faced by the civilian doctor. In combat, doctors must be concerned with tactical matters, which are generally known as field operations. The doctors must be mobile in the combat environment, set up hospitals in primitive areas, build defensive perimeters, and contend with hostile forces.

They must plan for the transport of all the supplies needed in a modern hospital and for the evacuation of the wounded from the combat hospitals to the field hospitals in the rear areas. And the military doctors must be responsive to the needs and the demands of the tactical command, for their role is not only the provision of medical care but also the larger mission of supporting the combat commander's effort to win on the battlefield.

In military medicine, all doctors become surgeons, treating wounds constantly. Even for those who were surgeons in the civilian sector, the change from civilian to military medicine is challenging. Dr. Edward D. Churchill, a professor at Harvard Medical School, entered the army in World War II as a colonel. Having received no military training before being shipped to the European theater of operations, he learned firsthand the difficulties of the transition. "The teaching of wound surgery to a civilian-trained surgeon is not easy. He starts with an underestimation of the severity of war wounds. A surgeon would say, 'But I've worked for years in Detroit Receiving Accident Hospital. I know how to handle wounds.' But he still would have no conception of the destructive force of high-velocity missiles."

The Medical Corps's view of training showed a disturbing lack of understanding of military medicine as well as of field operations. Although military doctors, perhaps, have always disdained field training and operations, the lack of training had a second consequence: the new doctors were not acculturated to the military medical community. We went into the field blind to the ways and customs of the military and unaware of what we would encounter when we got into combat.

I now know that the army through its officers in Washington contended that we who entered the Medical Corps through the Doctors Draft had a training program. They described the training program in testimony before Congress and in written articles in medical journals. The program for navy V-12s (navy scholarship students like me) was described as follows. The drafted doctors were to report to Brooke Army Medical Center in San Antonio, Texas, on any date between October 16 and November 1, 1950. They underwent one day of processing and three days of training. The program was cyclic so that doctors could appear at any time and begin without delay.

During the processing phase on the first day, each doctor (these were all men) filled out a questionnaire on his medical training, interests, experience, personal desires, and the reasons he should be assigned near his home of record. He received a lecture from an army personnel officer and spoke by telephone to navy personnel officers in Washington, D.C., to ensure that the army made proper assignments for him.

On the second day of training, each doctor received his assigned duty station and was given an opportunity to speak again to navy personnel officers. After those consultations, the doctors began the first of three days of army orientation, which covered army service in the field and in fixed hospitals; training in nuclear, biological, and chemical defense; military correspondence, courtesies, and law; medical supply procedures; military neuropsychiatry; and legal and personal affairs. In addition, those going directly overseas were given a "special class" on that subject, taught by the director of Combined Arms Training at the Brooke Army Medical Center as well as by a wounded Medical Service Corps officer formerly assigned with the 24th Infantry Division in Korea. To wind up the training, the doctors were given instruction on travel problems, pay allotments, insurance, and the execution of powers of attorney and wills.

Even by army standards, this was not much training. The doctors did not stay at Brooke Army Medical Center more than six days before going directly to the station of assignment. In less than six weeks, these doctors had been notified of their induction either through the draft or through Operation NavMed; traveled to Brooke Army Medical Center, San Antonio, Texas; undergone the military training afforded to them; and reported for duty. Neither the draftees nor the 570 navy doctors in Operation NavMed had any military experience other than two weeks for the V-12s in one summer of their medical school training.

That was the army's view of it. The problem with the army's view of it was that it did not happen—at least in my experience it did not. And even if the army's view of it were true, the lack of preparation and training of the doctors was shamefully inept. I say "if it were true" because my experience as one of the navy V-12s drafted in Operation NavMed was considerably different.

The Eighth Army surgeon apparently agreed with my assessment of this matter. In the Annual Report of Medical Activities of the Far East Command for 1952, Brig. Gen. Holmes Ginn reported, "Most of the young doctors coming to Korea have not been given the word on the simple fundamentals of the care of the wounded man, or of the problems involved in the management of battle casualties." General Ginn, after becoming Eighth Army surgeon in January 1952, began an in-country training program for new doctors. That, of course, was too late for me. I was already there.

From the first contact I had with the military when I received my "obituary" at Saint Luke's Hospital in Cleveland, Ohio, I had no training in military medicine or in field operations. I reported as directed to the entrance station in Cleveland, took a physical, went directly to Fort Knox, Kentucky, and moved my family into officers' housing on base. Assigned to the 695th Field Artillery Battalion as battalion surgeon, I was immediately placed on loan to the installation hospital to see the soldiers who came to sick call in the morning. I was quickly recruited for the hospital softball team. After several weeks of sick call and softball, orders came for the Army General Hospital in Osaka, Japan, where my duties were to treat the wounded and sick from Korea. I took my wife and kids back to Portsmouth, Ohio, spent a few days with our families there, and headed west to San Francisco to catch a ride to Osaka.

We flew on civilian aircraft from San Francisco to Hawaii and then overnight to Osaka. On the Northwest Airlines flight, I was accompanied by George Webster and Francis Koobs, doctors from Cleveland who were draftees like me. There was little to do on the flight other than stare out the window at the vastness of the Pacific Ocean. I had a window seat, and as we flew I noticed that several of the rivets were missing from the wing. In the monotony I counted the rivets, much like counting sheep. Over and over I counted the rivet holes. After dark, I slept fitfully in the airplane seat, and at dawn I went back to counting rivet holes. This time I noted that the number of rivet holes had doubled. I called Francis over and showed him. This was of sufficient seriousness to warrant notifying the pilots. We summoned the stewardesses and explained the situation to them. One gasped and turned on her heels and headed up the aisle. The other shrugged with an embarrassed laugh and went on about her business. In a moment, the first stewardess returned and said with a flip of her wrist, "Oh, don't worry. It happens all the time." Both stewardesses did their best to avoid acting concerned about it, so we, considering our destination and the prospects for the next year, disregarded it also. George stayed throughout the war at Osaka in the General Hospital, and Francis went to the front as a battalion surgeon.

At Osaka I ran into an old friend, Dr. John LeBeau, who showed me around the installation. The General Hospital at Osaka was a cluster of

The Japanese waitress "Mary," bringing drinks by the poolside at the Officers' Club, 279th General Hospital, Osaka, Japan.

white buildings on a neatly trimmed campus. The PX was white stucco, the officers' club was white stucco, the barracks and officers quarters were white stucco, and the hospital buildings were white stucco. All this was set against the bright green of the manicured lawns. In the center of the campus was the officers' club, which had a swimming pool and a lounge, and we passed a lot of time with the doctors and nurses by the pool. Our first contact with a Japanese person was the waitress whom we called Mary. I did not learn her real name. She brought American BLTs and hamburgers and a variety of American drinks to us at poolside. She was a cute young woman with a good sense of humor and a reasonable command of the English language. We enjoyed her company.

Osaka was a major evacuation point for the seriously wounded from Korea. It was a huge general hospital with complete medical service facilities for the variety of wounds and diseases found in combat zones. I was sent to surgery and did skin grafting and secondary closures on patients who had already received extensive and, in most cases, hasty medical care in the MASHs and in the field and evacuation hospitals in Korea. On most of the soldiers, we opened the wounds, cleaned them, and closed them with stainless steel sutures just as it was done in the hospitals in the United States. The new doctors did no major surgery at Osaka.

After a couple of weeks, my friend Dr. LeBeau called me and said we had to try out for the hospital softball team. Late one afternoon, we donned our scrubs and went to the nicely manicured softball field near the officers' club. We did not know anyone there. Approximately twenty-five men were on the field. We saw a line near a man who looked like the coach. He had a whistle around his neck and a clipboard in his hand, and he was writing as the men in the line spoke to him. We got in line.

When it was my turn, the man asked my name and unit.

"Surgery," I said.

He looked up from the clipboard. He was a thick man with a salt-and-pepper mustache. He stared at me.

"How long you been here?" he said.

"Two weeks."

"You're not eligible to play," he said.

LeBeau stepped around me. "What do you mean he's not eligible to play?"

"Just what I said. And you're not eligible either."

"Why not?"

"You're not regular army. This league is for regular army officers. It's not for transients headed to Korea."

"What?!" we said.

The coach shrugged. "Think of what it would do to our league if we put you guys on a team and then in a month or so you ship out to Korea. That's not fair to the permanent party people here. You guys mess up our league."

LeBeau was a feisty character. He faced up to the coach and said, "You don't know who you're talking to."

"Who am I talking to?" The coach was just as defiant.

I thought this ought to be good, but I was surprised when LeBeau turned to me and said, "This guy was an All-American football player at Columbia University."

I ducked away in embarrassment.

"Ooo-oh," the coach nodded. "That's interesting. You know something? This is softball. We're not playing football."

LeBeau was undeterred. "We want to play ball. I don't give a hoot about regular army or reserves. We want to play ball."

A smile broke across the coach's round face. "I like that. I like your spunk. You want to play ball? Well, I want you to play ball. I want both of you reservists to play ball. Come to my office tomorrow morning and I'll arrange it for you."

"Where's your office?" LeBeau demanded.

He pulled himself up to his full height. "In the headquarters building. I'm the hospital commander."

The next morning, dressed in our stiffest khakis, we headed over to the white stucco administration building. Several enlisted men were cutting and trimming the grass, and another man was weeding the flower bed in front of the building. There were a flagpole and an artillery piece in the middle of the lawn.

We cooled our heels outside the colonel's office for half an hour before the secretary ushered us in. We stood at the mahogany desk as the colonel continued to work on a stack of papers in front of him. After a moment, he looked up.

"Good morning, Lieutenants," he said formally.

"Good morning, sir," we said.

"Stand at ease," he said.

We already were at ease. After a moment he pushed the papers aside and said, "So you want to play softball?"

"Yes sir," we said.

He stood. "I want you to play softball. But on this installation reservists don't play softball in the hospital league. It's one of the rules. As I mentioned yesterday, reservists aren't here long enough to play on a team, and they usually have a lot of bad habits they bring from the civilian sector in the States. I'm sure you understand."

We stood silently.

"But just for you two guys I've made certain arrangements for you to play. Normally, we don't do this for reservists. But I like you two."

We bit. "Thanks, sir. We really appreciate it."

He reached down at the foot of his desk. "I've made arrangements for you two to play all the softball you want."

He retrieved two softball gloves, a softball, and a bat from beneath his desk and handed them to us.

"Here," he said. "Take these. You can go out and hit to each other all day long. Enjoy yourselves. Now you're dismissed."

LeBeau started to say something, thought better of it, and smiled. We did an about-face and marched from the office. Not only did we not receive any surgical training at Osaka; we did not get to play softball, either. But it made little difference. Shortly after our softball experience, we left the antiseptic white buildings and the manicured lawns and the American sandwiches and beer and the nurses by the pool of Osaka and headed to the hot, brown tents and the muddy roads and the K-rations and the mess hall food of Korea.

Within 180 days of the time I received my first letter from the army, I arrived at MASH 8076, Chunchon, Korea. MASH 8076 supported a U.S. corps as well as a variety of United Nations units. At that point these units were locked in mortal combat with an array of field armies of the Chinese People's Republic, who had begun another of the series of major Chinese offensives of the Korean War.

At four o'clock the mess crew came into the tent with breakfast. When I broke from surgery and made it to the five-gallon can, the nurse handed me a sausage on toast and a cup of coffee. I had to sit down, so I went to one knee and then onto the dirt floor of the tent. The ground was wet from the overflow of the scrub buckets. Legs crossed Indian style, I wolfed down breakfast. With a groan, the nurse sat next to me. She ate quickly. I saw her for the first time without a mask. She was a cute red-haired woman a couple years younger than my twenty-eight. She also was a lieutenant.

"Where you from?" I asked.

"Portland, Oregon," she said. "You?"

"Portsmouth, Ohio. Down on the Ohio River." I paused. "How long you been a nurse?"

"Longer than you've been a doctor." She wiped her mouth with her fingers. "I'm sorry," she sighed. "I didn't mean that the way it sounded. I'm just tired."

I shrugged. We finished our breakfast in silence.

"How are we doing back there?" I asked, nodding to the prep tents. We were washing at the five-gallon can.

"Fine," she said. "They're coming in as fast as we can take them."

"What happened?" I asked.

"I don't know. One of them said a Chinese regiment counterattacked and caught them by surprise. Whatever it was, it's still going on. You can hear it outside. We'll see more today and tonight."

At noon the mess hall sent lunch to the five-gallon can. I do not remember what it was, but by that time it made no difference. We slugged it down and wished for more. None of us had showered, so we all smelled like billy goats. I could hardly keep my eyes open.

"Drink more coffee," Major Coleman said.

"When's our shift over?" I asked.

He smiled. "When the last litter comes through that tent flap back there."

I glanced at the tent flap that led to the pre-op tent.

He patted my shoulder. "That could be days from now."

"Are we it?"

"We're it," he said. "There are three surgeons here, and you see every one of them in this tent."

"We don't take a break?" I asked.

"If you need it," he said. "Sit down here by the five-gallon can. But remember, while you're napping there are men dying out there on litters waiting for you to get up from your nap."

Granted, time was short and morale was low. The challenge for the army was to retrain the doctors assigned to the combat zone. Some years later, in an interview with army historians, the chief surgeon at Walter Reed, Dr. Sam Seeley, reflected on the predicament of the drafted doctors' lack of military medical training and experience. He contended that it was essential for the new doctors to "unlearn the very excellent and beautiful principles necessary in civil practice and learn the rapid and adequate sort of care of massive wounds, massive trauma."

That perspective was valid to a degree. But it also reflected the army's bankrupt attitude toward the Medical Corps and its soldiers in the field. Our lack of training was not restricted to medical treatment of war wounds. Officers in the field in Japan and Korea often had no field training whatsoever. This situation was a part of the acrimonious debate within the Congress and the Department of Defense concerning the type and extent of field training required for doctors.

Dr. Alexander Boysen, who was captured by the Chinese in 1950, was disgruntled about the lack of field training. He said to the Conference with Repatriated Personnel that if medical officers had "had any field training, a good number of men and equipment could have been saved and gotten out. They could at least have known something about the tactics being used." Another ex-POW, Capt. Sidney Esensten, stated to the conference, "I went to the Medical Field Service School in 1947 and I feel that it was a complete waste of my time.... I didn't learn anything about taking care of people in the Army; and I didn't know what a gun looked like; I didn't even know how to head up a medical unit."

Col. Crawford F. Sams, staff surgeon for the Far East Command, who, before General MacArthur's relief, was in line for the position of surgeon general, added fuel to the fire in an appearance before the Armed Forces Medical Policy Council on June 18, 1951. Sams questioned the military training and effectiveness of the Medical Corps in Korea. Sams's own son, a doctor, was killed while defending his aid station against a Chinese attack on the 2d Infantry Division. Sams claimed, after an inspection tour of frontline medical facilities conducted at General MacArthur's request, that nearly four thousand Americans had died in aid stations before they reached the hospitals because of defective evacuation caused by lack of field training. The culprit, Sams claimed, was the army's medical policy of specialization and professionalization, which had pushed aside traditional training in the military field operations needed to provide medical services in a combat environment.

Our younger men [the doctors] were thrown into combat without a day's [field] training—similar to taking a boy out of a drugstore and saying, "I'll give you a gun—go fight the Koreans." We did this to our young doctors. They were pulled out of the specialty programs, arrived in Japan, because we had nothing else; given field equipment which they had never seen before, told they were going to be assigned to field units the names of which meant nothing to them. These young men, within five days after their arrival, were being shot at by the enemy. ... That, I think, was one of the most disgraceful things in the military service. And still, a year later, we are almost in the same fix insofar as the men who are physically in the forward echelons are concerned at this time.

Sams's charges were echoed by Dr. Charles Mayo of the Mayo Clinic, who had conducted an inspection of the medical facilities at the request of the secretary of defense. Both men claimed that the deficiency was not the technical medical care being provided but the lack of knowledge and understanding of military field operations and the techniques of evacuation from the front lines to the MASH. The army had gone astray in its focus on civilian specialization and its downgrading of military and field

medicine. Civilian medicine had no parallel to the military task of treatment and evacuation of the wounded.

I tend to agree with Crawford Sams. But he was a career soldier and
I was not. In MASH 8076, very few soldiers, officer or enlisted, had any
military field training. When I arrived, the unit was right where it was
designed to be—backing up the infantry on the front lines. Yet no one
had thought to place a defensive perimeter around the MASH. The North
Koreans began to follow the medical evacuation lines to infiltrate through
the U.S. lines. The infantry battalions were levied to send soldiers they
did not need to man the perimeter of the MASH. Who do you think they
sent? The worst soldiers they had. They just made things worse. Among
our own enlisted personnel, we had some pretty tough guys from Ohio,
Kentucky, and Tennessee, who went out to the perimeter and started from
scratch. They figured out how to defend our position, and we were a lot
safer after that.

No one had ever shown any of us the first military manual on how
to do things militarily. We just had to figure out the best way to do it and
get it done. Then we taught the next guys who came to our unit, and they
taught the next guys. That's the way the MASH worked. We did that with
medical things also. The first doctors figured out the best way to do it,
then taught the next doctors how it should be done.

Forty-eight hours after I had arrived at MASH 8076, I stood at the five-
gallon can and scrubbed. I was asleep. The private shook me and said,
"Doctor."

I did not respond. I was washing my hands.

"Doctor," he said.

I did not respond. Let him talk all he wants.

"Doctor," he said and he pushed my shoulder slightly.

"Yeah, yeah," I said as I came out of my slumber.

"Follow me, Doctor. I'll show you back to the table."

"Can you get me another cup of coffee?" I asked.

"Yes, sir," he said. "Whattaya have in it?"

"Anything. Just make it strong."

By late 1951, a year after the war started, the Medical Corps had instituted a five-week field training program for new doctors. But there was

debate over whether the five-week training was adequate. The Medical Corps seemed unable to come to grips with the idea that combat conditions require a doctor to be a soldier also. In a 1954 study of "lessons learned" conducted by the Army Medical Service Graduate School at Walter Reed Army Medical Center, field training was still viewed as teaching a person "how to don and wear his military uniform and how to properly execute the miliary salute which, of course, is always executed in the position of attention and never with a cigarette or pipe in the mouth. . . . It may be noteworthy to relate that some knowledge of the conduct of proper military discipline and authority will prevent suffering and may save lives."

I think that says much about our attitude. The career soldiers, from our perspective, tended to be concerned with how to wear the uniform and salute, and then they looked for some connection to the prevention of suffering and the saving of lives. That is fine for soldiers who are spending their time and careers in garrisons in the rear echelons of the army. To us in the MASH just behind the front lines of combat, to us in the summer of 1951, the methods of delivering the best medical care possible to the fine young men who were giving their lives at their country's request eclipsed everything else.

Seventy-two hours after I had arrived at MASH 8076, I had lost the sense of feeling in my feet. I do not think I had spoken to anyone nor had anyone spoken to me for at least twelve hours. Major Coleman was still at the table next to mine, and the others were at their tables, but they were also incommunicado.

When the next litter came in, I scrubbed and was led back to the table by the young private.

"Have you had any sleep?" I asked him.

"We rotate," he said.

He had placed his hand under my arm to support me and guide me to the table.

"How long do you sleep?" I asked.

"Two or three hours," he said. "Sometimes more than that."

At the table, the nurse explained the wound. Before I examined, I looked at the nurse. "Scalpel, please," I said.

"You haven't examined," she said.

"Scalpel," I said.

Reluctantly, she handed a scalpel across the table. I fit it in my hand like a hunting knife and bent over at the waist and ran the scalpel down the front of my right boot and cut the boot laces at each cross until the boots fell open. I stood and took a deep breath and placed my hand on the litter to steady myself until the dizziness cleared. Then I bent over again and ran the scalpel along the laces of my left boot until each crossing lace was cut.

"Doctor," the nurse said. "Doctor, are you all right?"

"I'm fine," I whispered.

"Private," she shouted to the orderly. "Private, get over here."

"I'm fine," I said.

She seemed to be quite upset about all this.

"What is it, Doctor?" the private asked. He was not sure about this either.

"I'm fine," I said, "My feet are tired."

He bent over and looked.

"Let me help you with your boots," he said. He lifted my foot like a blacksmith taking the hoof of a horse, and he pulled one boot off and then the other.

I breathed a great sigh of relief.

"Let me get some water for you," the private said. "We'll put cold compresses on your feet while you stand."

When I looked down, I noted that my ankles were swollen to twice their normal size from standing at the operating table for three days.

At the beginning of the war, General MacArthur's Far East Command had no surgeons completely trained or certified or with extensive experience in military medicine to assign to the newly formed MASH units. The first officers assigned to the MASH units had been called from civilian residency programs.

We all knew that the army method for training was "on-the-job training." Sam Seeley, the chief of surgery at Walter Reed Army Hospital, looked at this philosophically when he was interviewed some thirty years later. "There's only one way to learn good surgery," General Seeley said. "And that's to get bloody wet." It should be noted that Seeley was not English. He meant that "experience teaches"—in this case doctors were to get literally "bloody wet" from the work in the operating tents.

In the combat conditions of Korea, however, "on-the-job training" meant doing whatever was necessary to survive. Once in Korea, there was no time for training. MASH 8076's annual report for 1950 stated in the paragraph headed "Training":

During the majority of the time, the personnel of the hospital have been working. Because of the steady influx of work, "on-the-job-training" has been the source of knowledge acquired by personnel. It is believed that "doing" plus an occasional helping suggestion is the best way of learning under field conditions. . . . During the periods of time when the hospital was not abnormally busy the personnel are occupied with inventories, policing and improvements of all kinds.

What was meant by "on-the-job-training" was going directly into surgery and learning by trial and error. General Seeley meant his words literally. "Doing" surgery was the army's idea of training. He was right. We did not have time for training. We were too busy treating the young kids who were coming into the MASH. I can say without hesitation that I never once, in my entire time in the army, read an army manual, saw a training film, or received formal instruction on military medicine or field training.

Our superior officers in higher headquarters knew this. The army recognized that very few doctors in the civilian sector had any knowledge of the proper early care of war wounds. This generalization, according to Col. John M. Salyer's report to the Army Medical Service Graduate School in 1954, applied even to the most "outstanding" surgeons in the "largest and best" university hospitals in the United States. Dr. Salyer stated that the new surgeon would progress from "a very inadequate wound surgeon to one that could perform excellent surgical work independently within a period of 3 to 4 weeks." When the truth came out, that was the army's idea of preparing its doctors for combat.

In the first months of the war, the annual report for the Far East Command stated that the doctors' lack of experience posed "a serious handicap to their medical mission and a threat to their very existence in the combat areas in Korea." One surgeon reported to Dr. Seeley of his lack of preparation in military medicine: "I don't ever want to be caught again as ignorant as I was about the conduct of the Medical Department activities in a theater of war and not know what to do. I was strictly a professional man and I just wasn't capable [of performing as a doctor in combat]."

By the time I got there in the summer of 1951, the original officers were gone and had been replaced by other doctors who were procured by the Doctors Draft Act, because of the army policy of rotating officers from the combat zone. Nearly two-thirds of all doctors in the Korean War were drafted, and 90 percent of the Medical Corps officers in Korea during the year 1952 were draftees.

The only times I left the operating tent during those first eighty hours after my arrival at MASH 8076 were to take a smoke break or to "make rounds" in the post-op tent. The first smoke break blended into all the others over the next months and rests in one indelible omnipresent image stamped in my memory. I have that image of the night etched into my mind, an image of standing outside the tent on "break" and looking up at the stars. These images, vividly impressed upon me by the awful repetition, have dogged me in my deepest, coldest dreams through the next decades of my life.

We would stand outside the operating tent and look up at the clear, cold sky, and the cool air chilled the sweat that had been absorbed by our T-shirts. It was the clearest, crispest sky I have ever seen. It is what I imagine Montana or Wyoming would look like, where you could stand all by yourself and look out into the expanse of the universe and feel that you could reach out and touch the stars. The cool night air was a great relief from the stuffy heat of the operating tent. I loved the Korean night.

In this image, we stood together outside the tent, several doctors and several nurses and sometimes the enlisted personnel and occasionally a few of the Koreans. In my dreams, Choi, the Korean boy, was there, laughing and joking, like a little brother. And then, always, there was the restful peace and clarity of the night for a few more moments. It was a time when you wanted to whisper or just be quiet.

Suddenly, all the cool peace and quiet darkness burst into a delightful fireworks display when the Chinese launched their flares. The night lit up like the day, and through the eerie flare-induced light came the shrill bugles of the Chinese infantry. It was the way they attacked: Light up the night and fill it with the chilling sound of bugles followed by the terrifying shouts and screams of thousands of Chinese attackers. It worked that way. The Chinese flares stole from us our vision of the beautiful night and gripped our insides as nothing else ever could.

Shortly after the screams, invariably, the frantic flashes and deadly tantrums of American artillery and heavy weapons fire erupted like thunder and lightning across the mountains and valleys, and the tracer rounds crisscrossed the battlefield and ricocheted in large arcs like rainbows out into the darkness. Waves of Chinese had gotten out of their defensive positions and into their own light, only to be met by the most advanced of American technology operated by our boys from Iowa and Oregon and Maine and Florida and New Mexico and Alabama and Texas, who turned the primordial beauty of the Korean mountains into the vast killing fields of a modern war. Each time we stood and watched silently in the eerie light, our night vision spoiled, and we knew with that absolute certainty that you have only in dreams that it would be merely minutes before the casualties came and we would be jerked from the peaceful silence and the refreshing beauty of the night back into the hectic, screaming, groaning, shouting, blood-splattered hell of the MASH operating tent. It is at that time that I usually wake up, at the time when the orderlies carted that first mangled body, spread-eagle—like a crucifix—on a litter and covered in white, blood-stained sheets, through the tent flaps and dropped it on the operating table in front of me.

The other times that we left the operating tent were to make rounds in the post-op tent. An image of making rounds sticks with me, but it occurred several months later near the Hwachon Reservoir. During a marathon operating period, I went back to the post-op tent to check on the surgery patients. Two post-op nurses were greatly distressed as they circled around an Ethiopian infantry colonel and touched him gingerly on the shoulders as if to guide him back to a cot. He had a white bandage wrapped completely around his head.

The colonel, a tall, handsome man, refused further treatment. Politely but forcefully, he said in clipped, British-accented English, "I must find my driver and leave the hospital immediately."

A fretful young nurse, twenty-four or twenty-five, with motherly anxiety, said softly to him, "I'm sorry, Colonel. You can't go. You're in no shape to leave this hospital."

"I have to return to my regiment. They need me."

The nurse looked to me.

"Colonel," I said lamely. "You would be much better off in here. We can get you fixed up before too long."

He looked at me blankly, then smiled graciously. "Thank you, Captain, but I must go now."

"You need to stay, Colonel," I said more forcefully.

He turned to me. "Captain, in a couple of hours my men are going up a mountain on the west side of the Punch Bowl. Many of them will be killed. They need me to be there much more than I need to be here. Captain, when my men go up that ridge, I intend to lead them."

Despite our best efforts, the colonel put on his combat gear, called for his driver, and left the MASH. The United Nations troops had pushed the Chinese back into North Korea, and the forward edge of the battle area lay along an east-west line across the peninsula just above the 38th parallel. There was a sag in the center of the line south and east of the impenetrable Chinese staging area called the Iron Triangle. Gen. James Van Fleet had ordered X Corps to launch Operation Touchdown to take the sag out of the line and pressure the Chinese in the Iron Triangle. In the middle of the sag was a valley that looked from the air like a huge bowl. Through the journalists who reported on Operation Touchdown, the world came to know that area as the Punch Bowl. MASH 8076 had arrived at the Hwachon Reservoir to provide medical support for Operation Touchdown.

After seizing the Punch Bowl, X Corps then turned to the ridges that surrounded the valley. First the 2d, 24th, and 25th Divisions with United Nations support conducted a series of assaults which climaxed at the battle of Bloody Ridge. Casualties were extremely heavy. From Bloody Ridge the Americans turned their lethal attention across the valley to the big ridge. The Chinese were dug in and waiting. Now all politics, economics, cultures, and philosophies dwindled to simple irrelevance. It all boiled down to this: square off toe to toe and see who could kick whom off that ridge.

For what seemed like days, as we cared for the casualties from Bloody, the incessant whine of airplane engines followed by the repeated roar of high explosive bombs deafened all as sortie after sortie of air force fighters and bombers slashed relentlessly at the Chinese bunkers in the boulders above. The army unleashed an awesome artillery preparation of the battlefield, which denuded the ridge of every living thing except the Chinese and North Koreans. Smoke and dust rose in angry protest like the ejaculation of ash from a shuddering volcano.

And then, as always, the mission passed to the infantry. Supported by armor, up the rocky ridge they went like worker ants. In that splendid, tense silence before the battle, the Chinese waited—like a prize fighter in his dressing room—to fight the United Nations troops rifle to rifle, bayonet to bayonet, knuckle to knuckle, tooth to tooth. Some of the most vicious fighting of that vicious war unfolded in the next thirty days on a mountain that came to carry the revealing name Heartbreak Ridge.

The Ethiopian colonel, out of a sense of honor, did not want to miss that fight. I have thought about him often over the years. I have seen his face and heard his voice. I have felt in my own heart his expression of honor and duty. Truthfully, I have wondered about his sense of duty and his courage. But that sense was universal. We saw it again and again among the soldiers on both sides of the fight. The colonel must have died on Heartbreak Ridge. Had he been only wounded, he would have returned to us. There were many wounded. Perhaps he lived. I don't know. But I know that he has lived on very vividly in my memory.

Eighty hours after my arrival at MASH 8076, Major Coleman came to my operating table. He was as worn as I was.

"That's it for now," he said. "Go get some sleep. Choi, the Korean boy, is outside, and he will take you to the officers' tent."

"What time is it?" I asked.

"I don't know," he said. "I don't wear a watch in surgery. The sweat ruins it."

"Is it day or night outside?"

"I don't know that either. It doesn't make any difference."

Both of us turned to go to the five-gallon can. As we stepped forward, we bumped into each other. Suddenly, we laughed.

"After you get some sleep, come to the headquarters tent. We have to get you in-processed."

The private took me by the arm and pulled me toward the five-gallon can. I could not have made it without him.

As I stepped through the tent flap, John Coleman said to me, "Welcome to the 8076th, Doctor."

3 THE MASH IN ACTION

When I came out of the operating tent, Choi was there. It was daylight, about four in the afternoon, and he waited. Even in the heat of the summer, he wore the rumpled army fatigue jacket over his strong shoulders and an army fatigue cap over his jet-black hair.

"Hi, Lieutenant," he said with a Korean accent. "You come with me."

"Where?" I said.

He had started to walk away but turned and gazed at me with an amused smile that we would come to know well. He would shake his head and we knew he was thinking, "These Americans are a strange lot."

"Where you think? I take you to sleeping tent."

And again he was off, his short slender legs chopping on the brown Korean dust. I followed without another word. I knew that saying anything more would be useless. I just followed along. Twenty-five yards from the operating tent were three brown tents with wooden doors. A dusty walk lined with small white stones and tent pegs directed us to the tent flap.

Choi opened the flap for me and popped to the side like a doorman; smiling, he bowed and, with a sweep of the arm, ushered me in.

I hesitated before I entered. Inside the cots were scattered. The heat rushed out the door.

"I fix for you," Choi said proudly.

My duffel bag was folded at the foot of my bed, its contents placed in a footlocker. A bed table with a water glass and a pitcher separated my cot from another. One of the cots was occupied, and I could hear the deep, regular breathing that marks the sleep of the exhausted.

Without a word, I sat on the cot. White sheets and two olive drab army blankets made the bed. It was hard like a wooden bench.

"Nice?" he said.

"Nice," I said.

"You sleep," he said. "I wake you for chow."

"Thanks," I said, and I swung my swollen legs up on the cot and lay down in the heat. I looked at the dark brown ceiling of the tent and, in spite of the previous eighty hours, my eyes were wide open.

This was not my idea of the army. My idea of the army was Walter Reed in Washington or, in the worst case scenario, an assignment as a battalion surgeon on loan to an installation hospital. That was our picture of army life when the war started: a nice easy job pulling a rotation in some quaint army hospital. Little did we know what we were in for when we headed for Korea. Little did we know that the MASH was made for mobility, vicious combat, and improvisation. That was the story of the MASH in action.

Evacuation of the wounded from the combat site to the hospital was always one of the foremost problems facing doctors in wartime. The primary goal of the doctor—and of the tactical commander—was to treat the wounded soldier and return him as quickly as possible to his unit. That kept the strength of the combat units high and reduced the need for inexperienced replacements. Both medical officers (concerned with bed space in the hospitals) and personnel officers (concerned with the replacement chain) worried about the duration of recovery and the time needed for evacuation.

As a result the concept of tactical mobility for surgical units was not new. Medical personnel have always recognized the importance of removing the wounded from the field of battle and conveying them by the quickest possible means to the rear area for medical care. Litter carriers, horses, ambulances, boats, and railroads have all been used to evacuate the wounded for emergency medical care. From early times tactical units have taken medical support with them on combat maneuvers to provide immediate care until the wounded could be evacuated.

The MASH was an outgrowth of the experiences of warfare in this century. World War I had medics and doctors in hospitals and platoons of ambulance drivers to get the wounded from the battle lines to the medical care provided in stationary hospitals in the rear. Fredric Henry, in Ernest Hemingway's A Farewell to Arms, was an ambulance driver in the Italian army. Novelist F. Scott Fitzgerald drove an ambulance in the U.S. Army. The methods of evacuation were tenuous as were the methods of treatment in the hospitals in the rear. In World War I the nonfictional counterparts of Fredric Henry loaded tents and equipment into the backs of the ambulances and followed the infantry and the artillery as close to the front as they possibly could. The French addressed the question by providing mobility in medical care. In the first six months of the Great War, the French devised a motorized hospital to follow the troops to the front and provide medical care to stabilize the seriously wounded before evacuation to the rear echelon hospitals. After the first year of the war, the battle lines stabilized into vast networks of static trenches, and the drastic need for mobilized medical care lessened.

World War II brought a new set of problems for doctors: the infantry and the armor had become highly mechanized. Tanks, artillery, and motorized infantry carried the fight rapidly and violently across the battlefield. Fixed hospitals could not get up and move. Medical units were not nearly as mobile as the infantry and armor units. As the tactical units blitzed across the battlefield, the wounded had to be evacuated farther and farther to receive medical treatment.

The answer was to change the method of medical care delivery. In World War II emergency medical treatment on the front lines improved vastly, and at all levels immediate aid and preparation of the patient prior to evacuation boosted chances for survival and quick recovery. Litter jeeps and field ambulances made the evacuation more rapid. Field surgical hospitals were attached at division level in the European theater, and the surgeons themselves were moved as close to the front as possible. Although the surgical facilities were not as mobile as the maneuver units, the interval from wound to emergency surgery decreased dramatically.

An integral part of the evacuation of the wounded was the provision of surgical care at the earliest possible time and place. If the hospitals were able to move behind the maneuver units, surgeons could provide immediate care close to the site of injury. The field surgical hospitals run by field hospital platoons near the division clearing stations greatly improved emergency surgical care. The surgeons in the field hospital platoons provided the first surgical care to the most severely wounded with the objective of keeping them alive and preparing them for further evacuation and more comprehensive treatment in the rear. Those who did not require immediate surgery to preserve life bypassed the field hospital platoons and went to the evacuation hospitals for emergency surgery. The surgical patients ended up in general hospitals far in the rear for more comprehensive treatment and recuperation.

The Sicily invasion provided the catalyst for the use of a mobile hospital. Isolated by the ocean, which rendered evacuation to general hospitals difficult, and bogged down by the mountains, which hindered evacuation from the battlefield, the tactical units had to improvise to care for the wounded. The field hospital platoons and the division clearing stations teamed up to provide immediate surgical care very close to the front lines. Field hospital tents were erected at the clearing stations, and MASH-like organizations brought the medical care to the battlefield.

As the war progressed, organizations called medical groups were assigned to corps level with the mission of evacuating the wounded from division clearing stations. The medical groups directed the wounded to hospitals in the evacuation chain according to "surgical lag" or "surgical backlog," both terms used to reflect the time required for a hospital to complete the surgical requirements on the patients present. This permitted medical groups to sort patients according to the severity of the wound or by the type of wound. The goal of this sorting was the elimination of backlog and the smooth and efficient flow of patients from the battlefield to the permanent hospitals in the rear.

By the last year and a half of the war, the provision of surgical care and the elimination of "surgical lag" had become fine-tuned by the widespread addition of auxiliary surgical groups, teams of designated medical personnel that could be assigned temporarily to particular hospitals, primarily field hospital platoons, based upon the need of the hospital. Each team consisted of doctors, nurses, and enlisted members capable of accomplishing a variety of types of surgery. The teams were augmented by another component of the auxiliary surgical group, the portable surgical hospital. This "hospital" was a truck-mounted operating room with X-ray and support facilities designed to relieve the field hospitals by taking the overflow. The portable surgical hospital was mobile and well equipped. In addition, during heavy fighting, medical groups were able to move doctors and nurses from evacuation hospitals forward to the field hospitals to assist with the surgery.

The auxiliary surgical groups were an excellent idea, but they had a variety of problems. The surgical teams were under the command of the auxiliary surgical group commander, which caused administrative and command problems at the field hospital level. The field hospital platoons were often irked that they had to provide supply and transportation to personnel not in their command, and the surgical teams in turn often complained that the support they received was what no one else wanted. In addition, the portable surgical hospitals were a great addition, but in many instances the backlog in surgery was due not to lack of space but to the shortage of nurses and postoperative supplies.

After World War II the army went back to the drawing board to iron out the bugs in the auxiliary surgical group concept and to design a mobile unit that could provide immediate surgical treatment to wounded soldiers as near to the front as possible. The immediate aid remained the same. Medics (army) or corpsmen (navy and Marine Corps), enlisted personnel who were trained in first aid, were attached to combat units down to the company level. The wounded soldier, if he was among the fortunate, was treated immediately by a medic or a corpsman. The medics applied first aid to the wounded and began the evacuation process. In the normal configuration of troops, the wounded soldier might then be taken by litter, ambulance, rail, or any other available means to a battalion, regimental, or divisional aid station, where his wounds would be treated by the unit surgeon. Battalion surgeons were generally the first doctors to see the wounded. Because of the limitations of the aid stations and the field hospital platoons at the division clearing station, those requiring emergency surgery or extended care had to be evacuated to the rear areas to a hospital equipped with surgical facilities. Depending upon the availability of ambulances or other vehicles, the terrain, the tactical situation, and the proximity of the hospital, evacuation could take several hours or several days. After surgery, the seriously wounded soldier would be evacuated to a permanent hospital in the communications zone, to a hospital ship, or to the United States.

The army needed a unit—with capabilities greater than the field hospital platoon—to fill the gap in the evacuation chain between the aid stations and the evacuation hospitals. It needed to be an independent unit that could keep up with the maneuver units by using its own vehicles, provide for its own supply by tapping into the area supply channels, and keep track of its personnel administration through its own chain of command. To supply that need, the Mobile Army Surgical Hospital was born in the years between World War II and the Korean War. In 1948 the first MASH was organized in the army. Department of the Army planners designed a sixty-bed unit equipped for surgery and organized with the equipment and vehicles to move rapidly behind the tactical units. The army Table of Organization and Equipment (T/O&E) provided for five such hospitals in the army inventory of units.

The unit, on paper, had:

> fourteen doctors (three surgeons, two anesthesiologists, one radiologist, three assistant surgeons, two internists, and three general duty medical officers)
> twelve nurses
> two medical service corps officers
> one warrant officer
> ninety-three enlisted personnel

Equipped for a new level of mobility, the MASH fit nicely into the scheme of evacuation envisioned by army planners. The structure and mission of the original MASH changed several times over the course of the first eighteen months of the war. In the last half of the war, the tactical situation stabilized, and the demand for mobility no longer existed. As a result the MASH units changed their organization and mission even more during this period. The original idea of the MASH was celebrated in the popular film and television series, and the name MASH came to be applied to a number of medical units that were not, technically, MASH units. During the war surgical sections were assigned to units throughout the theater, ranging in size from battalion aid stations to regimental combat teams to evacuation hospitals. Many were referred to in the common vernacular as MASH. In fact, those units that were by organization Mobile Army Surgical Hospitals retained that designation only for a short period in the war. By late 1952, when the tactical situation had stabilized near the 38th parallel and mobility was no longer a factor in the tactical situation, these units were redesignated and were given other missions. The technical life of the MASH was indeed very short.

When I arrived at the 8076th, rudimentary though it was, this array of tents, jeeps, trucks, clotheslines, improvised field tables, and slit trenches was an advanced specimen in the evolution of the MASH. When the North Koreans blitzed across the 38th parallel on June 25, 1950, the army had five MASH units on paper. None were available to General MacArthur's Far East Command. At Yokohama, Japan, home of the principal medical installation in the Far East Command, medical planners anxiously snatched medical personnel from all over the command to form new units. Three MASH units, high on the list of units to be deployed to Korea, were formed under the tables of distribution (TD) in the 80 series. The designation TD, as opposed to Table of Organization and Equipment, (T/O&E), the designation for the permanent army inventory, meant that they were units created to perform temporary missions and were not intended to see extended service. The prefix 80 meant that they were assigned to the Eighth Army, the major subordinate command of General MacArthur's Far East Command.

In the hectic hours and days after the surprise attack, three MASHs were started from scratch: MASH 8055, July 1; MASH 8063, July 17; and MASH 8076, July 19. Lt. Col. Kryder Van Buskirk, newly appointed commander of MASH 8076, uncertain of what his unit was and what their duties were, found a small office tucked away in the rear of the medical installation at Yokohama, set up a field table and folding chairs, and hung out a handwritten sign that read "8076 MASH." There he waited for his unit to form. The MASH began with a clean sheet of paper. In the next eighteen months, many doctors, nurses, administrators, and planners would paint on that clean sheet of paper their own portraits of what a MASH ought to be.

MASH 8055 mustered only ten doctors and ninety-five enlisted personnel at its first roll call. On July 8, 1950, one week after activation, the unit disembarked at Sasebo for the one-day boat trip to Pusan, Korea, where it immediately supported the retreating 24th Infantry Division. MASH 8063 left for Korea on July 18, one day after activation, and made an amphibious landing on Korea's southeast coast to support the 1st Cavalry Division. MASH 8076 disembarked for Korea on July 25, six short days after Van Buskirk hung out his first sign in the depot at Yokohama for the organization of the unit. MASH 8076 arrived in time to support U.S. forces in the Taegu-Taejon corridor, the main artery that carried the U.S. and ROK retreat to the Pusan Perimeter. A fourth MASH, designated the 1st MASH, a T/O&E unit organized in the United States, deployed in September 1950 to support the Inchon landing. Less than ninety days after the war began, all four MASH units were committed to combat in support of American and Korean troops on the Korean peninsula. All were woefully understrength.

I did not meet Van Buskirk in Korea. He had rotated out before I got there. He stayed, to the best of my knowledge, about six months. But I knew Van Buskirk by reputation. A career soldier, he was by all reports a gregarious sort who liked to work hard and play hard. He was tall and slender and smoked a pipe and smiled and laughed a lot. When the work was done, he liked to stop and have a drink and tell war stories. He was probably what the MASH needed at the beginning—easygoing, flexible, and capable of great improvisation. He left a lot of stories behind. His great contribution was getting MASH 8076 to Korea and operational in a short time. And perhaps a greater contribution was his reputation as a fun-loving, drinking, story-swapping surgeon who cut the trail for many behind him.

In the first six months of the war, nearly all United Nations casualties requiring immediate surgical care were treated in the four MASH units. Because of the high casualty rate, the MASH units, designed as sixty-bed hospitals, were quickly reorganized into two-hundred-bed hospitals. The first step of the casualty evacuation flow remained the treatment by doctors or medics in the battalion aid station. The seriously injured who required emergency surgery were evacuated by ambulance or helicopter to the MASH. In the first days of the war, the MASH units—fourteen doctors and fourteen nurses—averaged as many as 150 wounded personnel per twenty-four-hour period. After surgery and stabilization, the wounded soldier was evacuated to one of three semimobile four-hundred-bed hospitals that were capable of longer-term care. From there the evacuee went to a permanent field hospital, a station hospital, or a hospital ship and awaited evacuation to a hospital in the United States.

In the MASH, mobility was the name of the game. That was a concept we learned well. Put it up, take it down, put it up, take it down. Move it, move it, move it. We, the doctors, nurses, and enlisted personnel, developed a love-hate relationship with the concept of mobility. Moving the hospital was something we had to do that our rear echelon counterparts did not have to fret about.

It had to be done at a moment's notice. When the winds of war shifted, we had to get up and go. On one occasion MASH 8076 received a flash alert of an enemy offensive and a warning order to prepare to move at any minute. As the fighting increased and the roar of automatic weapons moved closer and closer, Lieutenant Colonel Van Buskirk hopped in the jeep and rushed to the regimental headquarters at our immediate

The 8076th in summer 1952. The pre-op, operating room, and post-op wards are in the tin "permanent" building (with the red cross on the top). The tin "permanent" buildings came into use as the war stabilized and the need for mobility decreased.

front. He searched out the Intelligence and Reconnaissance Platoon leader to get more specific information and found him tossing his duffel bag into the back of his jeep.

"Where is the front now?" Van Buskirk shouted over the whining engines of trucks and jeeps and armored personnel carriers.

The lieutenant grinned. "You're standing on it."

Van Buskirk scooted back to the MASH, struck tents, pushed the wounded into all available ambulances and jeeps, and headed south just ahead of the oncoming North Korean troops.

The original MASH had a simple flow to it. It was all tents, tents everywhere, tents for eating, sleeping, operating, drinking, tents for each and every thing, every day of the week, every week of the month, every month of the year. Nine tents, improvised in MASH 8076 into detachable tent sections, were placed together at one end of the MASH encamp-

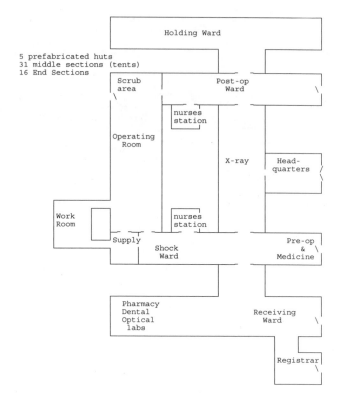

Figure 1. Diagram
of MASH 8076.
Reproduced based
on schematic filed
in the Annual
Report of 8076th
MASH for 1950.

ment to serve as a receiving area. From receiving, the wounded soldier
would go to another set of nine tents, which served as the preoperative
ward. The surgery tent (three tents placed together) was at the end of the
preoperative ward and connected it to another set of nine tents that
served as the postoperative ward. These tents, pre-op, surgery and post-
op, formed a U shape. From the post-op ward, the soldier was taken to
one of two sets of nine tents that constituted the holding wards. This
made an easy and orderly flow of patients for surgical care and preparation for removal to the more permanent evacuation hospitals. Other
tents, separate from the tents used for patient flow, housed the headquarters section, the registrar, central supply, the laboratory, and the pharmacy.

The annual report of MASH 8076 for 1951 configured the tents as
shown in figure 1. This configuration allowed the mobility so desperately
needed for the delivery of immediate surgical care. The detachable tent
sections could be taken down easily, loaded into the backs of trucks, and

moved with the tactical units. The entire hospital was moved in two phases. In the first phase the laboratory, the pharmacy, and the admitting function of the receiving ward were moved into the pre-op ward. Those tents were then taken down, loaded, and moved to the new location. At the new location the tents were used to form the U of the pre-op, surgery, and post-op wards so that the hospital could become operational and begin to receive patients at the new location. At that point, two hospitals were functioning. The old location continued to operate until the patients were evacuated; then we struck its tents, moved to the new location, and added its tents as the receiving and holding tents around the U already in place. The complete relocation could be accomplished in a twenty-four-hour period.

I say it could be done in a twenty-four-hour period. We never would have done it that quickly. But in the MASH we were never alone. There were always Koreans around: refugees, orphans, the homeless, the lost of the war. Choi was one of them. Choi came to MASH 8076 after his family was killed in the war. Perhaps he had helped the guy I replaced. I don't think I ever asked him. He was just there, and as far as he was concerned, I did the surgery and he did everything else. When we got ready to move, Choi took down my cot and packed my goods and put them on the trucks.

"You take care of patients," he would say. "I take care of you."

"I can take care of my stuff," I said at first.

"No," he said firmly. "Your time important. My time is to make your time good."

They were always there. When we struck tents, the Koreans came from everywhere to do the work. We paid them for it or we gave them food. Some we looked at and gave medical care. They would follow us to the new location, set up the tents, and then fade away until the next time. Oh, we had Koreans who were with us always, who stayed right there in the compound and did the dirty work. Finally, we just gave them a tent and they went everywhere with us.

Choi would sleep in the Korean tent sometimes. Sometimes, when we operated in the surgery tent all night, he would be in my tent when I returned. He would sit at the foot of the bed, not on the bed but on the ground at the foot of the bed. He would have the lantern going and a cold drink, a beer or a mixed drink, or a sandwich and sometimes even a glass of milk and a plate of cookies if he could get them from the mess hall.

"I make sure you get back all right," he would say and smile that tight Korean smile.

I would sit on the bed and groan and unlace my boots. Quickly, he would grab the boots and help me get out of them. He would take them, and by the time I woke the next morning, they would be cleaned and placed beneath the cot.

At first I said, "You don't have to clean my boots."

"I clean boots. I good at that."

"Thanks, Choi," I said.

"No thank me," he would say. "I thank you."

And then he smiled that boyish Korean smile, and that was the end of the question.

The construction of the MASH units allowed for few of the niceties taken for granted in rear echelon and U.S. hospitals. No bright lights lit the operating rooms, no sterile hallways connected the tents, no multicolored lounges allowed the medical personnel to relax. The MASH tents were dark and cold in the winter, dark and extremely hot in the summer.

All this was done within the sound of the guns. The MASH was designed to move with the tactical units. The retreat to the Pusan Perimeter turned around and became an offensive after the Inchon landing. The MASH units moved quickly but were always in danger of being in the midst of the fighting. The policy of MASH 8076 was that the nurses stayed with the units at all times regardless of the proximity of combat. The hospital could not be operational, Van Buskirk argued, without the nurses. MASH 8055 began with another policy—leave the women behind when the fighting was fierce. The necessity of medical care in intense combat quickly changed that policy.

In the MASH we had to be ready for anything from massive trauma from a gunshot wound to dysentery—all this in the midst of continual relocation. On one of the frequent tactical movements, MASH 8076 was moving on the Main Supply Route from Chunchon to Hwachon just east of the major Chinese staging area in the Iron Triangle when the supply route was clogged with traffic. The lack of mobility on the MSR made the convoys easy targets for Chinese artillery. We sat on the sides of the roads in these traffic jams and talked or dozed or wrote letters or hummed. Some liked to crawl in the back of the empty ambulances and sleep during these moves. One particular dentist, a good-humored fellow named Rice, was well known for sleeping on one of the ambulance cots during the movements. We all had nicknames, and his, of course, was Rice Paddy. He was an African American who was a favorite of all in the unit. Rice Paddy, like the rest of us, had a great fear of being ambushed on these moves, and we accused him good-naturedly of hiding in the ambulances to keep out of the ambushes.

On this move, Rice Paddy retreated to the ambulance and stayed there even though we were stalled on the MSR. As we sat in the sweltering heat, Rice Paddy was nowhere to be seen. After we had been there several hours in a traffic jam that would have done honor to New York City, an armor unit trudged up the MSR behind us and fell in line. They were an impatient lot, and they swung their turrets and main guns back and forth like huge elephants swinging their trunks.

In the boredom of the wait, the thought struck us all at the same time. The ambulance that served as the sleeping car for Rice Paddy was the last in the line. Immediately behind it was the lead tank of the armored unit. We left our vehicles and surrounded the ambulance.

On signal, we banged on the sides of the ambulance and shouted in our loudest voices, "Ambush! Ambush!"

The back door of the ambulance flew open, and Rice Paddy, half-clothed and still sound asleep, leaped out to what he thought was safety. Suddenly, in midair, he stopped still, his eyes no longer closed but open as wide as they could be. Confronted by the angry main cannon of a Patton tank, Rice Paddy faced what was surely instant and sudden death. He leaped to the ground, covered his head with both arms, and, as they say, hugged mother earth for all he was worth. Only when he recognized that the deafening noise was laughter rather than machine gun fire did he peek up to see what had happened. He was good-natured about it as was everyone else, because we knew that all of us would have done the same thing.

On a move one afternoon toward the Hwachon Reservoir, we were again in the back of the convoy stalled on yet another dusty, small, twisting MSR. After several hours, a soldier searched us out and shouted for a doctor. He reported that a Korean needed medical help near the front of the convoy. I put on my fatigue jacket and helmet and followed him up the long line of vehicles stuck in the traffic jam.

"What is it?" I said.

The soldier walked faster and shook his head. "You have to see it to believe it."

At the front of the line was an old rickety truck and several Koreans who wailed and shouted and walked in circles around the truck. Several American soldiers and two MPs were trying to talk to them. They could not speak Korean, and even if they could have, these Koreans were too worked up to understand.

An MP turned to me. "You a doc?"

I said I was.

He pointed to the inside of the truck. "They need you in there. Quick."

I eased over to the truck and looked in. On the back bench seat of the truck was a woman lying on her back with her legs spread wide. Her agonized screams were the wails of a Korean woman in labor.

I took off my helmet and my fatigue jacket and said to the MP. "Get me all the water you can and go back there and get a couple of nurses."

The 1951 annual report of MASH 8076 stated laconically: "There was one obstetrical case. A Korean boy was delivered at Chunchon on 15 August 1951."

I did my first child delivery right there in a vehicle on the Main Supply Route leading to Heartbreak Ridge. After the baby was delivered, the supply route reopened and the U.S. troops moved on. A new life had impeded for several precious hours the inevitable march to death.

From deployment on July 25, 1950, to the end of the year, MASH 8076 moved seven times. It became operational at Miryang, Korea, on August 2, 1950, and stayed at that location until October 5, 1950. This was the time of the defense of the Pusan Perimeter and the Inchon landing. According to the annual report of MASH 8076 for 1950, during that period (roughly sixty-four days) 5,674 patients were admitted to the sixty-bed hospital. The highest number of surgeries performed in one day was 244. The greatest number of patients treated in one twenty-four-hour period was 608. The highest patient census at one time was 427 (for a sixty-bed hospital). From October 5, 1950, to January 1, 1951, the MASH moved six more times and its twelve doctors and seventeen nurses treated another 3,334 patients. In 1951, according to the annual report of MASH 8076 for 1951, 21,408 patients were admitted to MASH 8076 and treated for everything from gunshot wounds to frostbite to syphilis. In the first five months of the year, the unit moved eight times. In the first

The 8076th moving north.

year of the war, MASH 8076 moved at a rate of once every three weeks and still maintained a steady patient flow.

This, of course, gave the MASH hospitals an air of transience. The flow of litters through the operating tents was constant. Patients moved in and out; many of them were unconscious and never knew they had been there. The impersonal nature of this movement of patients was known in World War II also. The patients in World War II quipped that the initials M.D.U.S.A (Medical Department, U.S. Army) actually stood for "Many Die, You Shall Also." No doubt many of the soldiers in Korea had the same thought.

The rate of movement did not slow down until the tactical situation stabilized in the winter of 1951-52. During the time I was there, we moved irregularly and more often than we would have liked. The constant movement had a tremendous impact upon the unit—as anyone who has ever been in that position well knows. There is no continuity to anything. The patients came through the MASH at an incredible rate; you treat one right after another. Most of them you never see again because they are evacuated as quickly as possible to another, more permanent hospital. You may see a major medical problem—an injury you have only read about; you may have never even met a doctor who has seen that type of injury—

and work on the patient for one hour or eight hours. It may be one of the greatest medical challenges of any doctor's career—and there were many of those. When you go to post-op for follow up, the patient has been evacuated already. Many cases we would follow through the grapevine. Doctors in the hospitals behind us would let us know how the patient did after he was evacuated.

The rapid evacuation coupled with the continual tactical relocation of the MASH dissipated any kind of permanence and continuity. That and the repeated turnover of MASH personnel resulted in a real sense of isolation. In MASH 8076 that sense of isolation translated into a sense of uniqueness, an "all-for-one-and-one-for-all" camaraderie among the doctors, nurses, enlisted personnel, and many of the Koreans who followed us and lived with us. We felt that it set us apart from all the other doctors and nurses, all the other hospitals, and all the other units, regardless of type, in the U.S. Army.

One of the things that have been lost over the years since the end of the war is the appreciation of the sheer ferocity of the combat. The staggering numbers in the annual reports listed above indicate the massive casualties of the combat. When I got there, we had heard the stories. But you had to see it to appreciate it. The stark reality of the horrors of combat saturated the sensitivities of the doctors and nurses of the Army Medical Corps assigned to the combat units. Our Medical Corps peers in the rear echelon hospitals observed the scrubbed and silent patients in the antiseptic venue of the General Hospital. We—and I include the battalion surgeons who were with the tactical units; they saw it before we did—encountered the awful carnage in the field as we rubbed shoulders with the combat soldiers and their wounded comrades. We saw the agony of the squirming and crying young American men chewed up in the ferocity of this savage war who were deposited on the operating tables of our MASH. The reality of combat came to the Medical Corps as a result of the mobility of the MASH. We were not the first by any means to witness the mayhem of the battlefield. The stories of Clara Barton and Florence Nightingale—as well as some excellent memoirs of doctors and nurses from World Wars I and II—remind one that medical personnel have shared the frontline experience throughout the history of warfare. But the mobility of the MASH separated the combat doctors and nurses from their counterparts in the rear echelons in a new way that resulted in the separation of our attitudes toward the army and the war.

It took its toll on all of us. I don't know about Van Buskirk. I don't know how he responded to the carnage. When I got there, his first replacement was still in command. Lt. Col. John L. Mothershead had been in command about six months. He was a good soldier, but I think the war had gotten to him by the time I arrived. He was a good tactical commander; he knew how to move the MASH, how to handle the military minutiae, to file reports, to answer inquiries, to say the right things to the colonels and generals up the chain of command who would, only occasionally, come to the MASH and then stay for only a short time. But Mothershead stayed away from the surgeons. Although he was a doctor, he had very little to do with medicine. He stayed in his tent much of the time and left the surgery to the young guys, the new guys, the draftees.

I can understand all that now. At first I thought a doctor should be in the operating room. We had Medical Service Corps officers (nondoctors) who did the administrative work. My friend Joe Jacko was one of the best in the army. Leave the administrative stuff to them and let us get on with the business at hand. There was plenty of it.

Right from the beginning, the fighting was savage. We all knew about the marines. On August 17, 1950, the marines, counterattacking the North Koreans west of the Pusan Perimeter, outmaneuvered a pocket of enemy soldiers and laid a fierce base of small arms and rocket fire upon them. Hundreds of North Koreans broke ranks and fled in disarray onto the banks of the Naktong River and tried to cross to safety. The marines called for close air support. The vicious turkey shoot that followed has been well documented. After being kicked all the way down the Korean peninsula, the marines finally had their turn. The marines had the North Koreans in regimental strength fleeing in the open. Marine Corsairs strafed, napalmed, and bombed the defenseless North Koreans at will. Marine pilots repeatedly and relentlessly vented the frustration and the wounded pride of the entire U.S. Armed Forces on the enemy below. Hundreds of North Korean soldiers died in a matter of minutes.

Later that same day, marines came upon an American medical aid station that had been overrun by the North Koreans earlier in the week. The wounded who were being treated at the aid station had been bayoneted or shot in the head, or both, by their North Korean captors. The

North Koreans had wired the hands of the medics behind their backs and shot each medic in the head.

In the same maneuver, the marines came upon an American private from H Company, 5th Cavalry, whose company had been overrun several days before. The North Koreans had stripped the American prisoners, searched their possessions, taken the pictures of their wives and girlfriends from their wallets, and herded the unarmed men into a large gully. Standing on both sides of the gully, the North Koreans fired their burp guns into the gully until they thought they had killed all the Americans. Several soldiers survived by playing dead and rubbing blood from wounds over their heads to appear dead. Five survivors from H Company led the marines back to the place of the slaughter. One of the marines later described it as follows: "The boys lay packed tightly, shoulder to shoulder, lying on their sides, curled like babies sleeping in the sun. Their feet, bloodied and bare, from walking on the rocks, stuck out stiffly. . . . All hands were tied behind their backs, some with cord, others with regular issue army communications wire."

In the Pusan Perimeter, MASH 8055 had its first taste of combat. Capt. Oree Gregory, a MASH nurse, wrote in her diary for July 23 and 25, 1950, "I will never forget those casualties [who were coming into the MASH by vehicle from the Perimeter just to their front]. In all my seventeen years of experience I've never seen such patients, blind, or with legs and buttocks blown off. Many died despite skilled surgery." She added a note on the conditions of the day: "The July heat was intense and the flies swarming around were green, large and heavy."

When MASH 8055, called Double Nickels, made its first move, it came upon a scene of civilian slaughter. Col. Chauncey Dovell, Eighth Army surgeon, reported in an interview fifteen years later that thousands of women and children had been buried up to the neck and beaten to death. Bodies had been thrown into the local well. The air was filled with the stench of rotting flesh. Small pieces of flesh and body parts floated in the water and came up in the buckets of water retrieved from the well.

Ferocity was not the sole domain of the Americans and the North Koreans—we knew that well because we often saw the results. The Turks and the Ethiopians were well known for their skill in combat. According to Maj. Gen. (Ret.) James A. Farmer, later the adjutant general of the state of Mississippi, who was an NCO in a tank battalion of the 25th Division at Bloody and Heartbreak Ridges, "the Turks and the Ethiopians were the toughest soldiers alive. The Turkish soldiers liked to use their knives. When a Turkish soldier took out his knife, he didn't put it away until someone got stabbed. Same with the Ethiopians. They did not like to fight during the day. At night, they would cross the lines and search out Chinese encampments. They would cut the heads off the sleeping Chinese, all but one. The one left would wake up in the morning and find all his comrades without their heads. It had a substantial psychological impact. The whole time I was in Korea, the only time I ever felt secure was when I was near the Turks and the Ethiopians."

In September 1951, after the 8076th had reached the Punch Bowl, Dr. Charles Mayo, a consultant to the Department of Defense, toured the medical facilities in Korea. We were surprised by his visit. Dr. Richard Lovelace, his assistant, who later founded a well-known clinic in Arizona, was with him. We were used to the higher-ranking officers and the reporters coming to a safe area in the rear and sending messengers forward to ask us questions. The visitors and the officers rarely came to the front. Dr. Mayo gave the reasons for the reluctance of the visits in his autobiography: As he "inspected a front line [medical] station the post was being shelled at quarter-hour intervals and there were several hits during the time I was there."

As doctors and nurses in the MASH, we saw these incidents close up. We heard the gunshots and often the shouts of the men in the fighting. In our interaction with the soldiers, we heard the accounts of what had happened only minutes and hours before. These conditions, which we did not share with the rear echelon doctors, separated us from them and made us see things differently than they did.

One of the marks of the MASH was improvisation: we did whatever needed to be done to provide medical care to the troops. The premature birth of the MASH in Yokohama was occasioned by serious complications in labor. All personnel were new to the unit. All equipment had to be drawn and packed for deployment. The doctors and nurses were entering a new experience in which we would have to build or improvise nearly everything we used.

In this environment, the doctors did whatever had to be done. When the 8076th arrived in Miryang, Korea, and unloaded its equipment, the officers discovered that the operating tables had been left behind in Yokohama. They scrounged several sawhorses and placed boards across them to form a makeshift table. The litter that transported the patient was then placed on the makeshift table and served as the operating table. Little did they know that this "oversight" would lead to a lifesaving innovation. Many who came into the MASH were wounded badly enough to need immediate surgery. Carting them from litter to vehicle to litter to operating table to litter to cot in the post-op ward placed a great stress upon the seriously wounded. Later, when helicopter evacuation was prevalent, the doctors fixed the operating rooms so that the litter on which the patient was carried from the battlefield was used as the operating table. The patient stayed on the same litter from the battlefield, during the transport on the helicopter, through the MASH, and all the way back to the evacuation hospital. The use of this technique was not only more efficient but also reduced the stress on the seriously wounded and reduced the likelihood of fatal complications.

In the operating tents, the doctors worked until everything was done. Lieutenant Colonel Van Buskirk wrote, "Everybody worked around the clock without orders of any kind. . . . You would nap between cases. You would go to sleep at midnight and sleep until you were needed and someone woke you up. The nurses worked every bit as hard." Surgical supplies were short; every item had to be conserved. Van Buskirk stated that "nurses would give doctors hell if they so much as wasted a suture." When the operating tent lights provided in the army issue light kits did not produce sufficient lighting for surgery, doctors improvised by rigging tin cans and mirrors to focus the light on the surgical areas.

Improvisation was a standard in job descriptions also. Every doctor, regardless of his specialty or training, became a surgeon. No one, but no one, wanted to be a battalion surgeon. We had all heard the story that the first nine doctors, all young interns, who arrived for service in the Eighth Army, informed the chief surgeon that they were specialists in tissue pathology and unable or untrained to perform other duties. The chief surgeon chuckled and promptly informed them that they had just been promoted to battalion surgeons. Eight performed well, the chief surgeon reported, but the ninth, upon his first encounter with combat, "went wild as a jackrabbit. . . . We had to evacuate him the same day as a psycho." That was more in line with what we came to expect from the army.

MASH 8063 learned of a limitation of this constant improvisation the hard way when they sought a way to dispose of amputated limbs. There were no incinerators or waste pickups as there might be in a large civilian hospital. The limbs were placed in a bucket outside the surgical tent. Periodically, several enlisted men buried them away from the MASH. On one occasion, a provisional cemetery was made in a ravine on a hill behind the MASH encampment. Much to the consternation of all in the MASH, during a harsh rainstorm in the middle of the night, gushing water filled the ravine, uncovered the limbs, washed them down the hill, and deposited them in the open areas around the MASH tents. In the morning, the startled enlisted men discovered the limbs, called the Korean augmentees, and ordered them to rebury the limbs in a deeper grave.

As we moved from location to location behind the combat units, we always had an eye out for buildings, any building, four walls and a roof that did not leak too badly. An old building, a schoolhouse, a convent, a hospital, a factory, any old building was a welcome sight—it made an excellent improvised operating room. That meant we could move directly into the existing structure without having to put up the tents.

Many times MASH units moved into abandoned buildings. In MASH 8076, it seemed that we were rarely so fortunate. Only once in my memory did we use anything for an operating room other than an army issue tent. I guess it was just our luck, but others were blessed with buildings and we were blessed with tents.

We had to improvise in our treatment, also. The MASH units were responsible for treatment of all the wounded who were brought to its tents. That included the United Nations troops as well as the North Koreans and the Chinese. American doctors found things among these troops that they did not often find in the bright hospitals in the cities of the United States. In the first months of the war, Lieutenant Colonel Van Buskirk operated on a stomach wound to a ROK soldier. Dr. Van Buskirk made an incision from above the navel downward to the pubic area. He intended to clean the abdominal area and suture the internal wound to stop the bleeding. During the operation, he placed his hand beneath the soldier's intestine to support it while he worked on the wound. As he did, he felt something crawling into his rubber glove and, quite alarmed, he reflexively jerked his hand out. To his great shock, a smiling nurse informed him that it was only a stomach worm that had crawled into his glove.

I heard that story about Van Buskirk. I was not there when it happened. But what I know is that every time you opened an incision on many of the United Nations troops, worms would crawl out. They were everywhere. Most of the Korean troops and many of the UN troops had intestinal worms that are rarely found in the United States. These worms thrive in countries where human manure is used to fertilize crops and where people farm the crops barefooted.

Some of the troops did not like our treatment. We had to improvise with them, also. In the 8076th, a Chinese soldier who had been taken prisoner came in for surgical care. After the operation, he was taken to post-op for recovery. A MASH nurse tended to him as he came to. When he recognized where he was, he looked at the American nurse and immediately spit in her face. Ed Ziegler, our aviation officer, was present in the post-op tent. When the Chinese soldier spit on our nurse, Ed immediately and instinctively belted him across the face. I know Ed well, and I know that he is not the kind who would do that without provocation. No one in the operating tent blamed him one bit.

That was the MASH in action: mobile, in the midst of the vicious combat, improvising for all we were worth. All those things about mobility and the closeness of the violence and the improvisation we had to learn firsthand while we were there. No one could teach us. Not the soldiers, certainly not the doctors in the rear echelon hospitals, no one except the doctors and nurses before us and, of course, our own firsthand experience. Our own experiences, our own actions, may have been the single most important thing that made the MASH what it was in the first year and a half of the war. I have thought about it much since that time, but I have been able to talk about these aspects of it only sparingly.

Our primary concern was to take care of the patient regardless of the circumstances. Sure, we often felt as if we were out there all by ourselves. We often thought about our peers back in the warm, clean hospitals who could wear clean scrub suits and see in the bright lights of the operating room and eat with regular utensils off plates at real tables and take R&R and enjoy some free time in the lounge. We often thought about our peers who did not have to move their tents continually or to hear the gunshots and the groans or to duck when the artillery came close.

But we knew we were there in the MASH for a special purpose. We felt as if nothing else mattered. We felt as if no one else in the world saw things the way we did. But that's why we were there: to get results the best way we could. To us, the wounded were not statistics. They were the young men of the world. And our job was to give them the best medical treatment our experience and training could possibly provide. The doctors and nurses who did the surgery in the 8076th MASH did exactly that.

4 THE MECHANIZED ANGELS

The wounded came to us every way they possibly could. It was always a race. Some came in army ambulances driven helter-skelter the few miles over the hills and gullies and dusty roads. Some hitched rides on the backs of jeeps or trucks that had delivered cargo to the front and had been commandeered to backhaul the injured or the prisoners or those replaced for rest and recuperation (R&R). Some of the wounded scooted off the hills on litters lugged by weary, staggering comrades. Some walked under their own power or with improvised crutches or on the shoulder of a friend. All were bloody and in need of immediate surgical care.

When I got to MASH 8076 in 1951, there was another way that the wounded were transported to the hospital: they came by helicopter. We knew when they were arriving because we got a call first. Sometimes we were relaxing in the officers' tent or playing cards or passing the football. We might be in the midst of surgery or making rounds or in the mess hall. The Koreans were there, Choi and the others, and the nurses and doctors and the NCOs, and we would hear the helicopters coming. I remember that Choi would often run from the operations tent where the Koreans and some of the soldiers passed the time by listening to the radio traffic from the front. They sat and listened much as kids in the United States would sit, all ears, in front of a radio and listen to a major league baseball game. Choi would try to make out what was being said through the static of the radio and interpret for the other Koreans so that they could all improve their English. They would hear the accents or the idioms and giggle at things they had never heard before. We would hear them whisper to each other later and giggle and mimic. "Y'all," they would say, or "You'ns," and they would repeat the chatter they had heard on the radio.

Then Choi would sprint along the path outlined in white rock the way the Koreans liked to outline paths, and he would shout, "Cop'n, Cop'n," meaning "Captain, Captain," and he would find me wherever I was and tell me that the wounded were on their way. He would run, like Paul Revere, at top speed through the mess hall or the officers' tent, the flaps of his hat fluttering like small wings, his chest heaving, his mouth shouting directions. One unit or another had engaged the enemy and needed helicopters to transport the dying. We could hear the whir of the helicopter blades just yards away as they warmed up the engines to fly their missions of mercy. And then they were off, to return only minutes later with their precious cargo. Choi and the others would stand around the landing zone and wait in great and somber anticipation. The rest of us would go to the operating tent and begin preparations.

The *thump-thump* of the rotors broke the tension. The medics and the orderlies would leave the tents and scan the skies until they saw the helicopters, little specks in the clouds. The helicopters descended into MASH 8076 for touchdown at our landing zone. Sometimes, when the loads were heavy, Choi and the other Koreans helped carry the wounded from the helicopters to the in-processing tent for movement into surgery. It was always an exhilarating—if deadly solemn—experience to hear the wounded arrive. You became very still and your blood throbbed in your head and you wanted to do something, but you had to wait. And then they came, and the work began.

The use of the helicopter for medical evacuation was one of the major advances in emergency medical care pioneered in the Korean War. Nearly every major medical center in the United States today is equipped for helicopter transport of patients from accident sites or crime scenes for emergency medical care. With names like Lifeline, Lifeflight, or AirStar, these modern "medevacs" can trace their lineage to the helicopters used in the MASH units of the Korean War.

In World War II air evacuation began with the activation and limited use of the air ambulance company. After the war, in a time when the army could study tactics and plans in the sterile environments of the Command and General Staff College and the War College, the army recognized and studied the use of the helicopter to transport the wounded from the battlefield to the hospital.

Although the helicopter made its debut in World War II, it saw broader—if still limited by today's standards—action in Korea. Korea was helicopter country: the entire nation was marked by poor roads ruined by tank traffic, railroads with bombed-out track and bridges, mountainous terrain with ridges up to six thousand feet. Conditions deteriorated

An H-13D delivering a patient to the MASH 8076 landing zone.

in rainy weather, which washed out roads, and winter weather, which covered roads with snow and iced over bridges. Tactical positions in those mountains became impassable for ground vehicles. The helicopter was the only solution.

In Korea the term *air evacuation* included the entire plan to evacuate the wounded from the theater of operations. First, evacuation within Korea meant carrying the wounded from the battle lines to the surgical hospitals. Second, evacuation meant the movement of wounded patients from the surgical hospitals to the field hospitals or evacuation hospitals. Third, evacuation meant flying the wounded in fixed-wing aircraft from Korea to the hospitals in Japan and from Japan back to the United States. All of these were important functions in the medical evacuation schema. In the MASH we saw the first category, the removal of the wounded from the battlefield to the surgical hospital. It was an inspiring sight for all concerned. Even though the vast majority of patients were still transported on the ground, the presence of the helicopter, specialized though it was, changed the face of medical care on the battlefield.

The first use of the helicopter for medical evacuation in Korea was during the battle for the Pusan Perimeter. Evacuation in this case meant flying patients from the MASH to a field hospital in Korea and later back

Medics loading a "head" patient onto the litter bearer of an H-13D for evacuation to a field hospital.

to general hospitals in Japan. On August 3, 1950, at the Taegu Teachers College, the location of MASH 8055, a Sikorsky helicopter landed in the yard of the school, a building that was being used as an operating room. Two of the serious patients from the post-op ward were carried to the Sikorsky on litters and strapped to the helicopter behind the pilot's seat. There was a pilot and one passenger, Eighth Army surgeon Col. Chauncey Dovell. The wounded were flown from the precarious location of the MASH to the more secure 8054th Evacuation Hospital in the port city of Pusan. Several months later, during the Chinese New Year's offensive, Lieutenants Willie Strawn and Joe Bowler, both flying H-13s, transported four recently wounded soldiers from aid stations at the front to MASH 8063, thus flying the first medical evacuation missions in history. The Third Air Rescue Squadron, an air force unit whose mission was to rescue downed pilots, began to use their helicopters to transport wounded soldiers from the field of battle. Many more medical evacuation flights followed. Later, in Vietnam, such flights came to be known simply as medevac. In Korea we referred to that part of medical evacuation, from the frontline aid stations to the MASH, as copters.

When I arrived in Korea in 1951, the 2d Helicopter Detachment was attached to the 8076th. Later, the 2d was replaced by the 8193d. Each detachment had four helicopter pilots and four mechanics, headquartered with us in the MASH. They moved when we did, they ate when we did, and they worked when we did. I must say that, for the most part, they were a remarkable collection of men. Lt. Col. Maurice Connolly, the third commander of MASH 8076, wrote with great understatement in the annual report for 1951 that the pilots provided "an invaluable and dramatic function for the unit. Their intrepid spirit in picking up patients at forward areas has undoubtedly saved many lives."

The morale factor was a major advantage of helicopter evacuation. Troops could be in the operating tent of a MASH within hours of being wounded. Dr. Elmer Henderson, president of the American Medical Association, toured the Korean theater and reported on the "President's Page" of the *Journal of the American Medical Association*, "I talked to many of the wounded, and all of them were outspoken in their praise of the medical treatment they were receiving." One lieutenant told Henderson, "Doctor, I was wounded when a mortar blew up. I was taken to the First Aid Station in 5 minutes, and within 55 minutes I was on a plane heading for a hospital. When they take care of you like that, a man doesn't mind fighting."

By contrast, local Korean villagers carried the Chinese wounded on litters from the battlefield. Medical supplies were extremely short. Given one day's rations, the Chinese wounded hoped that they could find a hospital before the locals dumped them and headed home. Often, the wounded were left on the battlefield without weapons or food or medical care. It seemed that when they went to the front, the Chinese were on their own to fight fatigue, hunger, and death. When the going got tough, as it did for both sides in Korea, lack of medical support weighed heavily on the minds and morale of the Chinese soldiers.

But for the American wounded, the hope and promise of immediate evacuation and medical treatment was incarnate in the helicopter. Like the MASH they served, the pilots became larger than life in the eyes of the soldiers. They not only served a specific function in the unit, but "their intrepid spirit" also constantly boosted the morale of the doctors and nurses and the wounded themselves. The pilots were the life of the party in the garrison and the cavalry on call for the wounded and dying. Tireless, they were always ready to go.

The pilots, like everyone else, rotated through Korea and through the

MASH. When I arrived, the pilots with the 8076th were James E. "Chick" Childers, Henry "Hank" Lamar, Dayton Warren, and Bill Wiltse. All were young officers raring to get into the air. While I was there, Archie Breedlove, Ed Ziegler, Jim Knighton, and Louis Hamner rotated through. In late 1952 and early 1953, Don Armstrong, Jim Spaulding, Harry Townsend, and Eswick Newport came to the 8076th. They were not only great soldiers and great pilots; they came to be good friends of all the doctors and nurses in the MASH. In my opinion they were the primary reason that the mortality rate among the wounded in the Korean War was only 50 percent of that in World War II.

Ed Ziegler was typical of the pilots who went to Korea. A veteran of World War II, Ed went back into the army in 1949. He underwent six months of fixed-wing training at Connelly Air Force Base, Texas, and was awarded the wings of an air force liaison pilot. At the outbreak of the Korean War, he went to helicopter training, then directly to Korea as one of the first fifty rated helicopter pilots in Korea. Assigned to the 2d Infantry Division, he soon became the division commander's personal pilot. After six months he switched to the 8193d Helicopter Detachment attached to MASH 8076 at the Hwachon Reservoir.

The pilots often kept the doctors and nurses from getting a radical case of tunnel vision. They did the little daily morale boosters that do not look so important to the detached eye or so beneficial from the vantage point of the 1990s. But the pilots did many things that made us laugh and made us forget for a moment the situation we as soldiers and as Americans were in.

They made things lighter when there was nothing but darkness all around us. "Keep in mind that you can't take that many well-educated, highly intelligent people and restrict them to live in an area the size of a football field and not expect some very odd and unusual things to happen," Ed Ziegler wrote years later. "Not all the events shown on the *M*A*S*H* series took place, but I do know that many of them were true, because I had an input to the series for two years." Ziegler and others were consultants for the television series.

Jim Knighton was responsible for one of the lightest of those moments in Korea, an incident that suggested the shower tent scene in the film *M*A*S*H*. We had moved into a new encampment and had some down time before the wounded began to arrive. We liked to read or talk or play cards or have a drink during that time. Some bathed or cleaned equipment or wrote home. The enlisted personnel had situated the shower tent on the perimeter of the configuration of tents so that the women, during their allotted time in the tent, might have a morsel of privacy. Jim came over the pass between two large hills on a flight pattern into the landing zone designated for our helicopters. He was flying without cargo and strayed slightly out of the pattern. We heard him coming, so we stepped out in the cool evening breeze to watch Jim make his landing. He was an excellent pilot. Suddenly, the aircraft lost altitude and went nose up almost into a stall attitude. The engines whined as Jim pumped the power to them in an effort to regain altitude. No doubt he had been caught in a downdraft caused by the wind whistling through the mountain passes. Jim continued to skid over the MASH tents like a huge dragonfly hovering over a country pond on a hot summer afternoon. He came to a hover a few feet above the shower tent. Then, just at the strategic time, the tail rotor dipped under the strain of another huge burst of power and the helicopter shuddered. Jim seemed to regain control of the aircraft, and it began to climb slowly. However, unfortunate though it may have been, the downdraft caught the tent beneath it and sent it flying across the Korean countryside. There, in plain view of nearly two hundred doctors, enlisted men, pilots, mechanics, cooks, Korean augmentees, and anyone else who wanted to look, stood a half-dozen naked nurses who, one moment before, had been enjoying a shower in the shower tent and who now were exposed fully and grasping recklessly for anything to cover their bodies.

Jim protested again and again that he had no intention whatsoever of disturbing the shower tent. "I just got there," he said palms up with an exaggerated shrug of the shoulders. "I didn't even know where the shower tent was."

We looked past his denials and caught him smiling when we asked a very simple and straightforward question: if he did not know the location of the shower tent, why did he make such an obvious path for that one tent and hover over it until it was blown away? Jim had a very innocent smile.

Jim Knighton survived the war but was later killed at Fort Benning, Georgia, during a night takeoff when his twin engine aircraft lost an engine at a critical altitude and crashed to the ground.

If the shower tent stunt happened today, in peacetime, the perpetrator might be court-martialed. But for that moment, in a different time and a different place, it relieved the great tension—at the expense of the nurses—and made most of us forget the stress for a short second. But the nurses themselves, in the midst of the tension, could laugh at the moment—and could laugh with and at us over the situation. They did not complain though they had every right to; they did not quit when many would today. They were big enough to put the incident in context. That is what made the MASH what it was. Hard as it may seem to understand today, interludes like that were great blessings for all concerned.

Lt. Col. Kryder Van Buskirk wrote in the 1950 annual report of MASH 8076, "Too much cannot be said in praise of the helicopters stationed at the hospital who brought seriously wounded patients from inaccessible areas and evacuated seriously wounded casualties from forward medical installations, thereby providing a quick, smooth comfortable evacuation from forward areas to the hospital with a minimum of shock and delay."

Economy was the byword of helicopter evacuation: economy of time; economy of expense; economy of use; economy of personnel; economy of material and facilities; and as a result, economy of lives. Granted, the role of the helicopter was very limited when compared to its role in Vietnam or in the army today. In 1951 most of the pilots and helicopters were being used to help the tactical commanders carry the war to the enemy. They provided the eyes and the ears and the strong backs to see and maneuver about the battlefield. The tactical commanders themselves were just learning the benefits of the helicopter.

Ours were the pilots, few though they were, who would carry the wounded. From beginning to end, the medical evacuation by helicopter was, by necessity, designed for economy of time. It was time that was so precious, and it was time that the helicopter gave the surgeon, precious time to treat the wounds before the patient was too far gone. At places like Heartbreak Ridge, the terrain was so rugged and the fighting so intense that it took American medics hours to move the wounded down the ridge to a first aid station in preparation for transport by ambulance to the MASH. But the helicopter could bypass all that and cover miles in no time at all. On one occasion, a corps surgeon called the 8193d Helicopter Detachment with a message that a soldier had been seriously wounded and was expected to die within the hour. Because of the weather and the terrain, they could not move him by ambulance or litter. The unit called for copters, but the cloud ceiling was right down on the ground and all air traffic was socked in. The corps surgeon left the decision whether to fly to the pilots.

The pilots plotted the unit's location on their maps and knew that they would never make it through a pass just south of the pickup point. They directed the unit by radio to take the soldier through the pass to a point on the south side where the helicopter could land. Flying at an altitude of fifty feet, rotor blades in the clouds, they landed at the proposed location and awaited the delivery of the wounded soldier. When several soldiers arrived, they loaded the patient and the helicopter lifted off. The helicopter was on an incline, so instead of going up it eased down the road to gain speed (translational lift) to help gain altitude. But a wire had been stretched across the road. It caught the helicopter at bubble height, took out the radio antenna, slid up over the bubble, and hit the mast. The helicopter slowed as it stretched the wire until it snapped and the helicopter—as if shot by a slingshot—raced along the roadway and gained altitude. Without further complications, the crew made it back to the MASH. The entire mission took forty minutes. The patient lived.

The helicopter provided economy of dollars. The H-13, the military counterpart of the Bell 47 built at the end of World War II, was the helicopter used for medical evacuation in Korea. It was eight and a half feet high and had a rotor span of just over thirty-seven feet. The workhorse of the copters, it had the horsepower of a pony. Driven by a 176 horsepower Franklin engine, the aircraft (said the manufacturer) would fly at about 100 miles per hour for a maximum range of 250 miles. In practice, it flew at 60 to 70 miles per hour. Later, the H-13 engine was beefed up, and gas tank modifications increased the flying range for medical evacuation. The designation was changed to H-13D. Later still, helicopter evacuation was done by the H-13E, an upgrade of the D model. The H-13E had real problems with the Korean climate. In the extreme temperatures of the summer and the winter, it would not hover at altitudes over six thousand feet—the altitudes near the tops of many of the ridges—and would not carry a full load. At the end of the war, the H-19 was introduced into the Korean theater. The H-19 carried eight litter patients and showed its stuff in the combat parachute assault conducted by the 187th Regimental Combat Team near Munsan. After the jump, two flights of the H-19 evacuated fifteen casualties.

Three helicopters and an ambulance evacuate the wounded from the 8076th to the 121st Evacuation Hospital.

The H-13D cost the government $34,000. On one hand, that was much greater than the $4,621 for the field ambulance, but the army had considerably fewer helicopters than field ambulances. On the other hand, the H-13D was much cheaper than other helicopters. (During this period the army let bids for the H-25, capable of carrying three internal litter patients. Some bids were as high as $340,000.) When computing the cost of operation of the H-13, other factors had to be considered. Crew and pilot training, aircraft maintenance, delay in the usage due to site selection, slow loading or unloading, and grounding due to inclement weather or darkness decreased the cost-effectiveness of helicopter usage. Yet even with added expenses, the H-13 helicopter was a bargain for the army.

Command and control economized the missions of the helicopters in Korea. The helicopters first were under the operational control of the

Eighth Army surgeon. Requests for use of helicopters had to be routed to his office for clearance. In September 1950 the Eighth Army was reorganized and I and IX Corps were added. As the corps configuration developed, the corps surgeons were given control of the approval and assignment of missions for the medical evacuation helicopters. Helicopter evacuations were normally approved for the most serious wounds or for the injured soldier whose wounds would be aggravated by riding in an ambulance. The corps surgeon approved any injury where death was imminent.

Requests for helicopter evacuation of wounded still had to go through the cumbersome route to the corps surgeon's office, but this configuration was very important because it kept the helicopters from being used for other functions. The convenience of the helicopter in Korea—and later in Vietnam—meant that it was in constant demand for every mission and detail from flying the commander back to headquarters to carrying souvenirs to the rear. Without the restriction of assignment from corps level, these helicopters, like all the other helicopters in the army, would have been constantly busy with other missions and would not have been available for medical evacuation when we needed them.

In reality, the air operations section of the corps surgeon's office commanded and controlled helicopter use. When a soldier was wounded, medics applied immediate treatment and took him, one way or another, to the aid station, which was generally manned by a battalion surgeon. The surgeon, or the medics in the absence of the surgeon, reported the injury up their chain of command and asked for a particular type of evacuation. The request for air evacuation went over to the corps surgeon. The corps surgeon's air operations office acted much like a dispatcher. Each MASH supported at least one corps level unit. The corps surgeon's air operations office would task the MASH helicopter detachment supporting that corps to send a copter. In fighting with light casualties, the wounded could be routed across corps lines to a specific location. In heavy fighting, the calls for copters stacked up, and one by one, the injured were shuttled to the nearest MASH.

The pilots tried for the most efficient use of the helicopter on each run. A copter run began with the pilots, and it was serious business. Flying the helicopters, not necessarily a medical function, had its tactical difficulties. The copter pilot had to go to the front to pick up the wounded. Pilots selected landing zones, read markings for them, landed in live-fire areas, and coordinated with artillery and air strikes prior to entering a combat area. Audio and visual communication with ground units became especially important in combat operations. As the helicopter approached the battalion aid station to pick up the wounded, it was an easy target for the Chinese and the North Koreans. The pickup had to be synchronized and swift. The medics on the ground set out a flare of prearranged color when the helicopter approached. It had to be done quickly because the smoke would attract enemy guns.

When the helicopter arrived, the patients had to be ready for transport. The helicopter could not sit on the ground in a combat zone for very long without drawing enemy fire. Beyond that, we did not want to tie up helicopters waiting for personnel to be prepared for transportation. The helicopter could be carrying someone else who was ready to be evacuated. As soon as the helicopter hit the ground, the medics carried the wounded on a litter, placed the litter on the helicopter just above the skids, and strapped it down. The helicopter lifted off immediately. All this had to be done as quickly as possible and was often done under direct enemy fire. In Vietnam this rapid landing and takeoff came to be called a dustoff.

Like the doctors and nurses, the pilots found themselves restrained by rules made by people who had not been in combat. Medical evacuation by helicopter, like the MASH itself, was new in combat and was being tested all the time. Bad weather was always a problem because the pilots had to fly by visual flight rules. On their maps they marked the exact altitudes of the hills, passes, and obstacles on their proposed routes so that they could fly with their skids skimming the ground to stay out of antiaircraft range.

Flight rules and rules of engagement are carefully studied in peacetime. In combat they are not as easily defined or described. The prohibition against night flying and bad weather flying was a sound rule but not always a clear-cut one. Calls came in at dusk or before dawn or in a gray drizzle or light snow. Someone had to make the decision whether to fly. Our pilots, to a man, were brave but not foolhardy. They flew whenever the possibility arose. On one occasion one of our pilots flew out at dusk, picked up two wounded soldiers, and came back in the dark. The MASH, of course, was blacked out, and in the pitch black darkness of the moonless night the mountains were indistinguishable from the clouds.

A helicopter landing in the smoke of a grenade, which marked the pickup point for the wounded. Below, a smoke grenade from a ground unit marks the landing zone for pickup of wounded soldiers.

The pilot was unable to see his instrument panel—or anything else. He radioed ahead and told us he was on his way. It took both hands to fly the helicopter. The pilot placed his pen flashlight between his teeth and scanned the instrument panel and his map in the seat beside him in order to negotiate his way to the landing zone.

The maximum efficiency of use resulted in an unexpected advantage on the front end of the evacuation. Helicopter evacuation required a much closer selection of evacuees than did evacuation by field ambulance or litter. The battalion surgeon or the medic on the scene decided quickly who was to be evacuated based upon several criteria: the extent of the wound itself, the availability of aircraft, the number of casualties, and other means of evacuation available. Priority went essentially as follows: (1) soldiers in shock or continuing hemorrhage; (2) traumatic amputations; (3) open fractures of long bones, complicated by shock; (4) apparent extreme arterial damage or wounds treated with a tourniquet; (5) extensive muscle damage; (6) abdominal wounds; (7) sucking chest wounds; (8) less severe chest wounds; (9) thoracicoabdominal wounds; (10) face or neck wounds with impaired breathing; (11) head injuries in coma; and (12) suspected gas gangrene. These patients, by any method of evacuation, were directed to the MASH for immediate surgery. Those who were to go by helicopter often received closer attention in preparation for the trip.

As a result of the better preparation that was required for helicopter evacuation, these patients were in better condition when they arrived at the MASH. The gravest threat in many serious wounds in Korea was shock. As it worked out, the additional preparation for helicopter transport improved the chances of avoiding shock as well as trauma during transportation. Before any evacuation the patient had to be completely prepared: all medical care possible should have been given, including stabilization of all wounds, complete security of the patient to the litter, adequate attention to blood pressure, adequate sedation for pain and shock, chest wounds tightly bandaged, and breathing airways cleared and secured against blockage by bleeding or vomit. With this preparation, the helicopter not only moved the patient faster but got him there in better condition.

Even with good preparation, the flights did not always go smoothly. The pilot was required to control the aircraft in flight at all times. That meant that the patient had to be immobilized and tightly secured to the litter. The litters were loaded on the outside of the helicopter, one on each side. Balance was essential. On one occasion, one of our pilots picked up an unconscious ROK soldier with a severe head injury. He was placed on the litter and loaded on the helicopter. Each patient was secured by two seat belts, one across the knees and the other across the chest. The flight route was over the Hwachon Reservoir. At full altitude, the pilot felt a tremor and looked to the skid. The Korean soldier had climbed up out of the litter and had his hands inside the bubble trying to get into the helicopter. An H-13E requires the use of both hands and both feet—no autopilot. With no place to land and no way to leave the controls to get his passenger back into the litter, the pilot cut the power to the engine. The sudden drop, worse than a lunge on an elevator, froze the Korean on the skid. His eyes got as big as silver dollars and he withdrew back into the litter. He rode the rest of the way with his hands firmly attached to the sides of the litter.

The helicopter provided economy of personnel by permitting the battalion surgeon to direct the wounded to the appropriate hospital and allowing the army to centralize medical personnel in specialized hospitals. Those in immediate need of surgery went directly to the MASH. Those whose injuries required immediate evacuation but did not require immediate surgery could be sent to other facilities. For example, psychiatric patients or patients dying of complications from illness could be sent directly to a field hospital of the battalion surgeon's choice, thus bypassing the MASH. Helicopters made all the hospitals in the combat zone available to the battalion surgeon.

On the other end, the speed and flexibility of the helicopter permitted the Medical Corps to centralize doctors and nurses in specialized treatment facilities instead of scattering them to different places on the battlefields. At the beginning of the war, each MASH unit did general surgery. When I arrived, the 8076th took all comers. As time went on, each MASH began to specialize. MASH 8076 became known as the place to treat extreme vascular injuries. MASH 8055 was known for its treatment of head injuries. If a head injury came to us at MASH 8076, we would give immediate treatment, stabilize the patient, and transport him to 8055. The other MASH units did likewise with vascular injuries, and by late 1951 we were receiving the lion's share of vascular work. MASH 8063 was known for treating unusual conditions, particularly the mysterious ailment that swept Korea in 1951-52 called, for lack of a better name, hemorrhagic fever. In cases of suspected use of biological or chemical weapons, such as nerve gas, the wounded were taken to MASH 8209, later redesignated MASH 8225, a stable unit that did not move like the other MASH units. Others may have gone to an evacuation hospital. With the reduction in transit time from the battlefield to the MASH, the increase in range, and the flexibility of landing, the wounded could go to a specialized treatment facility where he could receive the best treatment available.

It soon became evident that helicopters could be used in turnaround flights from the front to the rear and back, thus economizing matériel and facilities. This happened first among the combat units. The helicopters could carry people and cargo forward, as well as transport commanders to reconnoiter the battlefield, then return people and cargo to the rear. Ed Ziegler was a pioneer in this area as well as in medical evacuation. He was the very first helicopter pilot to deliver requested combat equipment to a unit in contact with the enemy. At Heartbreak Ridge in September 1951, elements of the 2d, 7th, and 25th Infantry Divisions had battled to the top of the ridge and were clearing the Chinese and North Korean bunkers against very stiff resistance. Heartbreak Ridge consisted of three major hills and the ridgeline in between. The middle hill was Hill 931. Chinese bunkers dotted the ridgeline, and from 931 they could place devastating fire on either of the flanking hills. The crest of the ridge was covered with large rocks, which hindered the movement of U.S. troops and protected the Chinese from American air and artillery bombardment. The Chinese had placed enough bunkers in the rocks to protect four hundred to five hundred men. These bunkers were strong enough to withstand direct hits from the American 105s peppering the ridge. During air strikes the Chinese could leave their positions in their trenches and retreat immediately and with impunity into the bunkers in the rocks to their rear. As soon as the threat was gone, they would return to the trenches and continue the fight.

The 23d Infantry Regiment called for flamethrowers to remove the Chinese from the bunkers. Three flamethrowers were taken to the 2d Division airstrip in the division rear. Two parachutes were available for the flamethrowers. The parachutes were attached to the flamethrowers and loaded on an L-19, a fixed-wing aircraft piloted by Capt. George

{}

Daniels. Because a third parachute was not available, the third flame-thrower was loaded on Ziegler's helicopter for ground delivery. Both air-craft took off at about the same time. Ziegler, assigned at that time to the 2d Division, flew low up the Mundung-Ni Valley and up the south slope of Heartbreak Ridge. Making several passes over both friendly and en-emy positions, he spotted a clear area in the saddle between Hills 931 and 851. As the battle raged, green and red tracer rounds from automatic weapons spiderwebbed the contemplated landing zone. Ziegler squeezed his helicopter down into the saddle of the ridge, cut all power, got out, scooted around the front of the bubble cockpit to the door on the right side of the helicopter, opened the door, and removed the flamethrower from the passenger seat.

From a position just down the hill, a young sergeant sprinted to the helicopter, stooped over to avoid the bullets and the helicopter blades, one hand on the top of his helmet and the other swinging his carbine.

"What are you doing out here in the middle of a firefight?" he shouted. "Get the hell outa here before you get hurt."

"Here's the weapon you asked for," Ziegler said.

Ziegler handed him the flamethrower, retraced his steps around the front of the bubble cockpit, remounted the helicopter, and lifted off with-out taking one round of enemy fire. While Ziegler was on the ground on Heartbreak Ridge, the L-19 with Captain Daniels at the controls passed high overhead. Out came the first parachute. The parachute failed to deploy properly, and the flamethrower slammed into the ground far away from its intended target. The second parachute wafted across the Ameri-can positions into the Chinese bunkers. Neither could be used by the Americans. The flamethrower Ziegler delivered was the only one put into use that day on Heartbreak Ridge.

Flamethrowers became the center of attention when used on the battlefield. The enemy, for reasons of self-defense, wanted to knock them out as soon as possible. Ziegler learned from the unit that the young ser-geant who took the flamethrower was killed in combat later that day.

Maj. Bob Boatwright, an aviation officer with the 2d Division, put both Captain Daniels's and Lieutenant Ziegler's names in for the Distin-guished Flying Cross for the flamethrower mission. The 2d Division Awards Board returned the paperwork with a notation that both offic-ers could not be put in on the same form. Instead of rewriting the forms,

Major Boatwright crossed off Ziegler's name and resubmitted the award for Captain Daniels only. Since the end of the war, Captain Daniels has received the credit for the delivery of combat equipment, the two flamethrowers, to a unit in direct contact, even though the flamethrower used was in fact delivered by Lieutenant Ziegler.

"I figured out that the top of Heartbreak Ridge was not where I wanted to spend the day," Ziegler moaned later, with his typical good nature. "I never did figure out how come the pilot of the L-19 [Captain Daniels, who dropped the flamethrowers that missed the drop zone] got the Distinguished Flying Cross and all I got was three lines of print in a newspaper."

Major Boatwright was a bit more accurate than Captain Daniels. Later, during the same battle at Heartbreak, Major Boatwright got two confirmed kills. He was asked to airlift K-rations to a unit on the ridge. The rations, crated in light-colored and textured wood and wrapped in wire, were loaded in the back of an L-19. Major Boatwright swooped low over the drop zone, and his crew chief pushed the crates out as hard as he could. The crates arched down and overshot the drop zone, exploded end over end, and sent splinters and cans in a fan-shaped pattern right into the North Korean bunkers. U.S. infantrymen confirmed that two North Koreans were killed.

The helicopters were constantly in the air in the medical units as well as the tactical units. Resupply was a secondary mission to evacuation, but it was almost as important. Economy was the watchword. Each time a helicopter evacuated a soldier to a field hospital, it would return with supplies. Medical supplies could be lifted to units in the field upon request. Items such as whole blood, plasma, medicines with limited expiration dates or unusual storage requirements, and replacement equipment could be taken to the units in the field by helicopters retrieving the wounded. During the heavy fighting, we were constantly in need of blood. Often the helicopters ran the mercy mission to the field hospitals to retrieve blood for a patient who was undergoing surgery at that very instant.

The use of helicopters for these missions allowed the army to centralize the supply effort. Distribution of blood and medical supplies required a complex network. Decentralization to the unit supply room so the supplies were on hand was crucial but often counterproductive because of lack of immediate need or lack of storage facilities. Movement of blood and supplies by helicopter allowed centralization of supplies in a rear area facility with refrigeration and humidity control to preserve blood and medicine. With the helicopter, these supplies were only a radio call away.

When the helicopters transported the wounded to the MASH and could fly no longer because of nightfall or weather restrictions, our pilots did not call it a day. They did not mix martinis when there was work to be done. They continued on wherever they were needed. The work of the pilots and the surgeons was inseparable. They helped us and we helped them. We always worked as different parts of the same unit. Eight-hour flying days were common, and in the evenings the pilots often went into the operating tents to assist in any way they could.

"Sunset was always a welcome sight, although the suspension of flying did not end our days," Ziegler wrote later. "In the evenings we would fetch and carry for the doctors. I always visited the troops that I brought in, to see if they needed anything, to write letters for them or just shoot the breeze with them. One of them named us 'The Mechanized Angels.' They loved to talk to 'copter pilots. . . . I liked that."

That's not to say that the pilots—and the rest of us—did not relax when we had the time. On one occasion, Archie Breedlove and I and another doctor were on our way to the movie tent when a nurse notified us that a soldier had been admitted with acute appendicitis. We insisted that Archie accompany us to the operating tent for the simple reason that if we could not see the movie, then Archie should not see it either. Archie removed the patient from the ambulance, carried him to the operating tent, and sat with him while an anesthetist administered a spinal. As we removed the appendix, Archie described the operation in minute detail to the conscious young soldier, who was relieved that his great pain had subsided. Archie then transported the patient to the post-op tent, helped bed him down, and turned him over to the post-op nurses. The three of us then went about our original mission. We entered the movie tent and found an empty bench. The first scene of the movie flashed on the portable screen. Eighteen minutes had elapsed!

I enjoyed the helicopters and the helicopter work. I liked getting out in the field and riding with the pilots. Sometimes I thought I could be a helicopter pilot first and a surgeon second. At one point Archie Breedlove set out to teach me to fly a helicopter. He gave me lessons on the ground, showed me the instruments, such as they were, and explained the stick and the pedals and how they worked. We inspected the aircraft according to the manufacturer's specifications. Then came the big day when I would fly the copter myself. I thought I was doing pretty well. I did exactly what he said. We inspected, we got in, we warmed up the engine. My nerves twitched as the rotors began going faster and faster, louder and louder. The helicopter lifted off the ground very nicely. As soon as we got a few feet in the air, we started spinning very slowly as if the center of the copter was on an axis. I squeezed the stick. I pressed the pedals. It did no good. The more I tried to stabilize the copter, the more we spun.

"Give it more rotor speed," Archie shouted over the engine noise. I gave it more rotor speed. We spun even faster.

"More rotor speed," Archie shouted again. I really gave it more rotor speed and it really rotated faster and faster. The helicopter was like a big top, spinning and spinning only a few feet off the ground, and there was nothing I could do. Finally, we got it under control and back on the ground. The experience convinced me that I was a surgeon rather than a helicopter pilot.

The pilots would relax among themselves, too. The detachment was often required to fly to corps headquarters for aviators' business. This meant an early morning run over the mountains in a fixed-wing aircraft. On one occasion, during the previous evening the pilots had relaxed a bit, perhaps a bit too much. The liquor began to flow freely, and the pilots spent much of the night drinking and socializing. The flight time came around quickly, and the pilots assembled on the flight line at dawn. The effects of the previous hours were evident on all. In absolute silence, they flew by helicopter to division headquarters to pick up an L-19 for the rest of the flight. At division headquarters, the preflight checks were done on the fixed-wing aircraft in continued silence, and the luggage was loaded easily so as not to disturb anyone. The aircraft was a four-seater with a small metal door on each side. The pilots entered the aircraft and in a throbbing silence lifted off. The pilot appointed to do the flying, suffering greatly, settled in and lowered his head to shade his eyes from the bright sun. At about one thousand feet, none of them had spoken. The mild turbulence was tough on a morning-after stomach. Then one of the

Dr. Apel in a helicopter.

pilots in the rear seats opened his door and slammed it shut to secure it. Without a flinch, the pilot flying the aircraft slowly lifted his head and, expressionless, said, "Okay, who just got in?"

In addition to the evacuations, the helicopters provided another advantage to the medical corps: we used the copters to make house calls. Often, in the heat of battle, the wounded swamped a beleaguered battalion surgeon or group of medics in an aid station. The battalion surgeon or the medic would cry "Help!" to the nearest MASH, and if possible, a surgeon would come forward with the helicopter. Many times I snatched a kit bag and hopped on the copter en route to the aid stations to provide immediate medical care and additional assistance in preparing seriously injured soldiers for the flight to the MASH.

In midsummer 1951 an element of what later appeared to be a segregated field artillery battalion was operating in the mountains west of us. I am not sure of its designation, but I have assumed all these years that it was a part of the 555th Field Artillery Battalion, called "Triple

Nickels" (because of the three fives in the unit designation), assigned to the 5th Regimental Combat Team (RCT). Triple Nickels was one of the few segregated units left in the army. We were aware of the unfortunate allegations of cowardice early in the war against certain African American units of the 24th Infantry Regiment. Accused of running from the enemy, they had been under the command of white officers the whole time. The allegations later proved to be racially motivated. If the truth were known, a number of American units had retreated in the face of an overwhelming enemy. Later accounts of the actions of the 24th Infantry Regiment revealed various factors that helped explain the defeats suffered by that unit. Lack of courage on the part of the soldiers was not one of them.

Triple Nickels had seen its share of the fighting. Overrun in August 1950, the battalion was reorganized and went to the field again as a part of the 5th RCT working in I Corps. As the United Nations pushed north of the 38th parallel in April 1951, the Chinese launched their fifth major offensive of the war in an effort to collapse the United Nations line and push all the way to Seoul. In the vicious assault, the UN troops fell back. Two ROK divisions dissolved. The 24th Infantry Division and the 1st Cavalry Division tried to fill the gap. Across the entire peninsula, Americans were in retreat once again. The 5th RCT was in a long column of UN troops moving south. The convoy included elements of the 3d, the 24th, and the 25th Divisions as well as the Commonwealth Brigade (Canadians, Indians, ANZACs) and the British Brigade. Triple Nickels was sandwiched between the 3d Battalion, 5th Infantry Regiment in the front and the 1st Battalion, 5th Infantry and 2d Battalion, 5th Infantry Regiments behind. It was after dark when the Chinese ambushed them. It was perhaps one of the most vicious assaults of the war.

Triple Nickels took the brunt of the Chinese onslaught that night. The 1st/5th and the 2d/5th, both infantry and armor, tried again and again to break through the Chinese ambush to rescue Triple Nickels. The artillerymen, for their part, lowered the cannons and fired at point-blank range into the oncoming Chinese and fought toe-to-toe throughout the night. Eventually, the infantry got through, and what was left of Triple Nickels escaped with the infantry. Triple Nickels lost more than one hundred men that night, and the 5th RCT altogether lost nearly eight hundred men. It was not until June 3, 1951, nearly six weeks after the ambush, that elements of the 24th Infantry Division, fighting their way north, came upon that gruesome ambush site and found the remains of Triple Nickels.

A few months after Triple Nickels was ambushed in the fifth Chinese offensive, MASH 8076 received a call for assistance from the field artillery battalion operating in the mountains west of us. We first recognized that something was wrong when we heard the frantic radio communications from several corps units calling for reinforcements, air support, artillery support, helicopter evacuation, and surgeons to assist with the wounded. We stood silently and somberly in the operations section and listened as the battle unfolded. The field artillery battalion was among those pleading for help. The radioman shouted over the small-arms fire and the static that the Chinese were in their perimeter. Grenade and mortar explosions drowned out the frenzied young voice. Bugles blared in the distance, and the deep and deafening roar of the American 105s fired at point-blank range broke into the transmissions.

"Send helicopters and doctors," the voice shouted. "We need them now."

We had been alerted for possible movement to the north, and the Koreans and enlisted personnel had begun to strike tents. Dayton Warren was one of our pilots, and although I had been with the 8076th only a month or so, he and I had come to be friends. We had flown together on several occasions and had many things in common. Dayton was tall and slender with short-cropped hair. He was conscientious, and his mind was always looking for ways to get things done.

He looked at me and said, "Ottie, you ready?" It was not a mission I was excited about. When we left the tent, we could hear the guns to the north and the west of us. Down in the aviation section, all the helicopters were warming up. In minutes we were airborne over the steep, dark mountains toward the reported location of the field artillery unit. Dayton contacted the unit by radio and asked for a more specific location. When we reached the area, we were unable to locate the unit. Circling the mountains, we searched but saw no signs of combat. We tried again to raise the unit by radio, but there was no answer.

We came over a mountaintop just as dawn was breaking and saw a green meadow near the crest of the mountain. One soldier sat in the field. There were bodies all over. When we landed, the blasts of a blazing firefight, the bugles of attacking Chinese, the thuds of mortars, the shouts of men in mortal combat, all had ceased. An eerie silence enveloped the field.

The soldier sat with arms wrapped around his knees and his head bowed between his legs. As we approached, I could see the man was near shock.

"Where are the wounded?" Dayton shouted.

With a slight nod of his head toward the slope of the mountain, the soldier said, "They're all gone. They're all gone." He dropped his head again between his knees and said, "They're all gone."

Dayton and I glanced at each other. That could mean several things: they had retreated, they had been captured, or they had been killed.

"I'll go look," Dayton said, and he pulled his pistol from his flight jacket. I followed him over the slope. There we found more bodies. The unit that fought there, judging by the bodies in the field, was an African American unit. It appeared to be a battery-sized element. I have no idea how many may have escaped or been captured. The soldiers were spread on the slopes beside the road where they had perhaps sought cover from an ambush, circled their unit, and defended to the death. In the center of the circle were flaming equipment and several charred and mangled artillery pieces that appeared to be 105s. Interspersed among the bodies were Chinese soldiers. They were all dead: the artillerymen, the Chinese, the medics, the cooks, the drivers, the mechanics, the ammo bearers, the radio operator, the officers, all had met their deaths in that field on a mountaintop in Korea. We returned to the meadow and the helicopter. I tended the young soldier in the field. We loaded him in the helicopter, lifted off from the meadow, and flew a course over the battlefield. All the soldiers were gone. We were no help on that day. We evacuated the young soldier to the 8076th and then back to the psychiatric section of a field hospital. We reported to our superiors in the chain of command what we had seen and returned to our sections in the 8076th for the movement north with the rest of the United Nations Command.

Dayton and I did not know whether this had been a Chinese ambush or an American advance or just what the circumstances were that brought those units together on that mountainside. All we could see in the dawn silence were lifeless bodies and smoldering equipment. Neither Dayton nor I ever learned for sure the unit's designation or affiliation.

There can be little doubt that the Chinese knew of the allegations of cowardice aimed by certain white officers at the African American units. Based upon the positions of the bodies and the number of Chinese dead left in the field that Dayton Warren and I saw that morning, there had been a real knockdown-drag-out there. If the Chinese had been expecting an easy go of it when they ambushed these artillerymen, they picked the wrong outfit. They locked horns with an American unit that did not know the meaning of retreat. These young soldiers had not budged an inch.

The pilots with the 8076th were indeed intrepid. They were the lifeline between the battlefield and the operating table. They were strong and brave and risked their lives many times to help the young men in the field. We saw in these pilots the same courage we saw in the young men they brought to us. I considered it an honor to serve with them. It was an honor that our peers in the fixed hospitals in the rear did not have.

At the time, flying medical copters was not as glamorous as flying fixed-wing or rotary-wing combat missions. Those pilots were in the thick of the fighting, and they certainly did the job. The army and the nation owe them a great debt of gratitude. Ed Ziegler, Archie Breedlove, Jim Knighton, Dayton Warren, and all the others knew that they had a silent mission that would not even be recognized by the public until decades later—and then only through a film and a television series. They had the mission to come to the battlefield like mechanized angels and carry away the dying and the wounded. It was a thankless job, but they did it well.

"I made several very good friends while flying for the MASH," Ed Ziegler wrote later. "Perhaps we aviators weren't members of a flight crew who could paint fancy pictures on their aircraft or little bombs denoting missions but I'd like to think that what we did was just as important to the mission as an air crew [in combat]. I am proud to say that I was a part of that mission."

We who served in MASH 8076 also were proud to say that these pilots were a part of that mission.

5 WHERE WE LIVED

Korea was a young person's war. In 1950 the cadre of the army was left over from World War II and, like the army's equipment, had aged markedly in a few years. The officers and commanders at the beginning of the war were, by army standards, quite seasoned. Gen. Douglas MacArthur hovered near seventy at the time of the Inchon invasion. Maj. Gen. Edward "Ned" Almond, MacArthur's chief of staff, was fifty-eight years old. Gen. Walton Harris Walker, commander of the U.S. Eighth Army at the outbreak of hostilities, was born in 1889. Down through the corps, divisions, regiments, and battalions, the commanders and staff personnel were, in 1950, older than their counterparts have been in any other war. But the people drafted to fill the ranks, as in many other wars, were the young from the schools and the streets of the civilian world.

The Medical Corps was no different. The rank and file doctors and nurses had been discharged after World War II, leaving behind only a skeleton crew of the white-haired battalion. After the doctors' draft, the new rank and file of the Medical Corps hailed directly from the medical schools, the nursing schools, and the teaching hospitals of the United States. As I looked around, I saw doctors and nurses, lieutenants, captains, and majors who were new not only to the army but also to the profession of medicine.

I remember well my good friend from Cleveland, Jimmy Jones, who, drafted suddenly and unexpectedly from a residency, followed the same route to Korea as I did. We worked together in the Department of Surgery at Saint Luke's Hospital, and our families socialized as young doctors' families do. Jones was assigned to the 8063d MASH, but in the summer of 1951 the war reunited us. The 8076th moved south to Chunchon and pulled in next to the 8063d MASH to regroup and redeploy. As the Koreans and enlisted personnel dug trenches and pounded tent stakes, the doctors and nurses assembled and checked the surgical equipment and examined the patients who had moved with us. We were told that the 8063d was right next to us, and during a break I went outside and looked down the road. A lone figure sauntered up the dirt and mud road toward us. As he came closer, I recognized the gait of my friend Jimmy Jones. We had a delightful and unexpected reunion there on a sunny afternoon as we leaned against a rusted-out old fence gate on the road between the two MASHs. We swapped stories and experiences, and we laughed about our mutual predicament. When we were in the promising antiseptic halls of Saint Luke's Hospital in Cleveland only two years earlier, who would have ever thought that we would meet like this in Korea, that we would be working in tents, that we would be wearing uniforms rather than civilian suits, that we would experience more surgical cases in one year than we could have in fifteen or twenty years in the civilian sector?

I have seen my friend Jimmy Jones many times since Korea. He became a professor at Case Western Reserve and a practitioner at Saint Luke's. We meet at seminars and other medical functions, where we sit and reminisce about our experiences in Korea. Each time we go back to the subject of the television series *M*A*S*H*, and Jimmy says the same thing. He looks at me with a twinkle in his eye and says, "Ottie, I'm not sure about this. I'm not sure which one is which. I can't make up my mind whether I'm Hawkeye and you're B.J. or whether I'm B.J. and you're Hawkeye."

We have laughed about that many times because it was not until the novel, the film, and the television series that the general public knew anything about the MASH. Since the success of the film, we have been asked many times about our experiences and asked to compare them to the public image created on the screen. I often answer facetiously that most of what was depicted was wrong, but not all of it. I say "not all of it" because several of the episodes in the series *M*A*S*H* were based on my personal experiences as I related them to the writers of the series— so I knew them to be accurate. On a number of occasions, the story consultant, Jay Folb, who was located at the studio in California, called, and each time we chatted at some length. Our conversations were always enjoyable and upbeat. He was excited about the MASH and appreciated learning about its history.

In reflecting on experiences in the MASH, my view, like everyone else's view, is tainted by the television series and, to a lesser extent, by the novel and the film. These creative works received much acclaim and had a committed following. In all honesty, some of what was depicted ad-

Dr. Jimmy Jones,
MASH 8063.

dressed issues similar to those we faced in Korea. None of it, however, portrayed the situation exactly. Art is always an interpretation rather than an exact depiction. In the case of the film and the television series, the interpretation is several times removed from the reality it purports to depict. The reality of the situation is interpreted first by the person who experienced it and then, one after another, by the writer, the director, and the actor. The artistic presentation is always four or five times removed from the reality.

Many things about the experience cannot be portrayed on the television screen, just as they cannot be fully explained in print. That has to do not only with interpretation, but also with the fact that our view of the MASH is a transient view, a view focused on the immediate environment and blind to the overall picture of the war. It is much like a tackle on a football team trying to explain the game afterward. He was right in the middle of it: he sweated in it, bled in it, ached in it; he experienced it firsthand. But his view of the game was limited by his participation. He could not see the touchdown pass because his face was buried in the chest of a defensive lineman as he pass blocked. He could not see the running back making the great moves because his face was in the mud after opening the hole in the defensive line so the back could make the run. Those are transient views, and each person who experiences a war has that limited view. But the transient view is very accurate in its own way.

The film and the television series focused much on the social lives of the MASH personnel. That was only one small portion of the total experience for those who were there. For me, reflection on the social aspect of the MASH experience is difficult for several reasons. It happened in our youth before our attitudes and philosophies of life were fully developed. It happened in the horror of a vicious war. It happened far from home, where you can be absolutely lonely in the midst of crowds. These factors shatter the neat categories of life we have adopted by virtue of our circumstances as twentieth-century Americans. I make this judgment as an observation of life rather than a critique of social values. But our present condition always affects the interpretations we have of life and of the MASH.

American social views have changed since the Korean War. The film and the television series reflect the irreverence and the social attitudes of a segment of the American population in the Vietnam era, some decade and a half after the Korean War. By "irreverence" I mean the disdain for authority rather than what some might consider in the film a cavalier attitude toward women, African Americans, and organized religion. The film, released in 1970, contains a great deal of hyperbole common to that medium in the late 1960s and early 1970s. The film industry had just broken into the overtly sexual script, and *M*A*S*H*, like many other films of that time, focused on that aspect until it was grossly out of proportion. But part of the tension with authority portrayed in the film and the television series is universal to military situations and was present in Korea, and part of it is unique to the Vietnam era. All of it is filtered through the lens of cultural interpretation, which makes it more difficult to deal with the social aspects of the MASH.

As I think back upon the way we lived with each other in the MASH and compare it with the film and the television series, vast gaps open in my memory. I have to say that I made lifelong friends in the MASH. And I have to say that we had some enjoyable times. But like the tackle on the football team, we did not watch from a distance. Our faces were always in the chests of the wounded or searching among flesh that looked like spaghetti for arteries to save or muscles to reattach or shrapnel to remove.

We did not have time for many of the social situations that were later portrayed. We were busy. The war moved, the MASH moved, we moved, and in all that mobility the war, the MASH, and we, individually, changed and continued to change. The best way to put it into perspective perhaps is to think of the changes you would have to make if you knew that for the next year all the aspects of your life, eating, sleeping, bathing, were to be in a tent, that the temperatures would swing from zero to well over one hundred, that you would walk on muddy roads, ride in trucks without shocks, sleep in crowded quarters, and never find a solitary moment, and all that in the middle of a war. In those circumstances only a few considered the social aspects of life a top priority.

Living conditions in MASH 8076 were rudimentary at best. Water, a necessity often taken for granted, had to be carried with the unit by water truck. Drinking water was a precious commodity. We filled canteens and buckets and steel pots (the army helmet) from the water truck. We dared not drink out of streams or lakes for fear of what the North Koreans or the Chinese may have done to them. All personnel lived in tents and used portable showers or cans of heated water to wash and orange crates for bedside tables and makeup desks. But more about the use of water in the MASH in the next chapter. Mud or dust was everywhere. A trip from tent to tent gathered cakes of mud on the bottoms of shoes and deposited the mud on the floors.

We considered our bedding a luxury because it was much better than what the soldiers at the front used: the army sleeping bag. Bedding was most often the old army cot with army blankets and linens. A modern convenience was a small mattress that fit on the cot and made sleeping a little easier. On one occasion MASH 8055 lost all its mattresses and sheets when someone flipped a cigarette into the truck carrying the bedding during a tactical move. They had to go without linens and bedding until they could be replaced through army supply channels. For several weeks the army sleeping bag had to suffice. There were times, however, when the sleeping bag was the bedding of choice. In the brutal cold of the Korean winter, the nurses slept in long johns, flannel pajamas covered by a sweater, stockings, gloves, an operating room stockinette on their head, and anything else they could find and pull on. Thus prepared, they slipped inside a sleeping bag and pulled up several layers of blankets.

Officers' quarters. Note the sleeping bags hung over the clothesline between the tents and the artillery round (white phosphorus) exploding on the hill in the background.

The latrine was little more than a slit trench surrounded by blankets draped between stakes for privacy. It constantly needed cleaning and disinfecting. When we had been in one place for a while, the enlisted personnel would build a multihole wooden toilet over the trench for comfort and convenience. In the cold weather, the latrines created an updraft that was unbearable. Soon after the Korean winter came, each sleeping tent was equipped with one large galvanized iron bucket that sat in a dark corner. Even in warm weather, using the latrine could be hazardous. Two operating room nurses from the 8076th went to the latrine together. The weather was sunny, but the clouds raced by and the wind gusted. Suddenly, a blast of wind caught the blankets, and away they sprawled across the field, dragging the stakes behind them. The two nurses, to their great embarrassment, sat on the wooden toilet in the middle of the open field in broad daylight.

The latrines had to be cared for constantly. Though they began as slit trenches, they were upgraded as time allowed. They were breeding grounds for the scourges of Korea: flies and rats. In the summer months flies were everywhere. They were not flies like we have in the United States. These were the large green kind that buzz with the ferocity of a Russian MIG. Constant cleaning of the mess hall, burial or burning of garbage and hospital waste materials, placement of latrines, and use of DDT kept the flies down to a minimum for part of the time. Fly screens and screen doors were mandatory on all tents during the summer months. The facilities and incoming personnel were dusted with DDT on a regular ba-

Slit trenches, which comprised the "sanitary" accommodations at the 8076th.

sis. During our stay at Chunchon, the MASH received three aerial DDT dustings as a part of the armywide control program.

These measures were aimed at flies but worked for mosquitoes also. DDT checked the spread of malaria so that in 1951 we had only twelve malaria cases—half of those were members of our command. An active campaign against malaria cranked up in the spring and lasted into December. Each person was required to take a daily dose of chloroquine. Two of the 8076th personnel who contracted malaria admitted that they had not taken their regular doses.

Rats were also a common presence in Korea. Control was difficult because of our temporary conditions and facilities and because of the destruction brought by the war. Rats are a symptom of combat. Cleanliness and garbage control, both very difficult in field conditions, were the chief weapons used against this nuisance. Rats were a particular problem during our stay at Hwachon in the summer and fall of 1951. As we stabilized, garbage, our own and that accompanying supply depots and dumps, provided havens for rats. We used traps and poison to keep the rat population under control. In addition, we placed bricks on the floors of our tents, which kept the floors drier and prevented some of the conditions in which rats proliferated. Even with these efforts, rats managed to explore nearly everything we had. An unexpected scream from a doctor or a nurse was, in all likelihood, caused by the opening of a storage box to find a field rat jumping about.

All of our walkways in the MASH were lined with white rocks. The Koreans did that everywhere we went. As soon as the tents went up, the rocks came out and the paths were marked off. At first we smiled about this practice and wondered whether it was a quaint Korean cultural condition: the need to line every path with small white rocks. The first time we went outside a tent at night, however, we learned the utility of white rocks. In blackout conditions it was pitch dark at night. We carried small flashlights, more like penlights, and they had just enough power to illuminate the white rocks so that we could see the paths.

One of the dynamics of any military situation is the necessity for the troops to meet and befriend one another quickly, adapt to the situation, and live and function with rapid turnover. One soldier's friend becomes another soldier's friend upon introduction. Unlike life in the civilian sector, there is little time to get to know one another. That dynamic in the MASH was greatly magnified because of the intensity of the job, the closeness of the living and working conditions, and the rapidity of the rotation.

In 1951 the turnover rate was high. The assigned strength of MASH 8076 was 15 medical officers (doctors), 3 Medical Service Corps officers (administrative officers), 17 nurses, and 120 enlisted personnel. The average tour for a doctor who served in MASH 8076 in 1951 was 10.3 months. The longest stay was 13 months. The overseas tour for doctors was one year. The first three months, give or take a week or two, were usually in Osaka (mine were) or another major hospital. That left only nine months for the doctor to work in the Korean theater. It took nearly nine months to learn the job. Once the doctor became experienced in combat medicine, the rotation date came, and the doctor went stateside with all his experience.

There were three Medical Service Corps officers, nondoctors who served in administrative positions. The average stay was 12 months and the longest tour was 15 months. The nurses' tour was the shortest, and that hurt the most. The average stay for a nurse was only 5.8 months, and the longest single tour was 12 months. It seemed that the nurses were just learning their jobs and getting some experience when they rotated out.

The enlisted personnel did not stay much longer. The average tour

Doctors and nurses of the 8076th.

was 7.7 months and the longest single tour was 12 months. The doctors got to know the enlisted personnel better because they often pulled details, and we would see them in support roles or in changing locations of the MASH.

Not only was the turnover rapid, but also the unit rarely assembled at one time in one place. During my time I do not remember one unit formation at which the entire unit was present. I have seen a picture of the unit in formation, but it was taken after I left on the occasion of the awarding of a unit citation. We usually saw each other in the mess hall, but often, because of a heavy workload, we did not eat at regular times. Doctors and nurses came and went before we realized they were there. The enlisted personnel might be there for a tour of no more than a few weeks before moving on somewhere else. It was entirely possible for a person to arrive and work in a section of the MASH and not be seen by a majority of the doctors for months.

In spite of the turnover, there was a great camaraderie among the personnel in the MASH. That may be a military phenomenon, but I think it appears in the civilian sector also. It is similar to being far away from home and meeting someone from your hometown. On one occasion, when I was on R&R in Japan, I went to a barber shop. After the barber had finished, I left, and on the street I ran into Dr. Jerry Sheets, a friend from my hometown of Portsmouth, Ohio. We waved at each other and shouted quickly about where we were and what we were doing. I learned that he was a battalion surgeon in front of the 8076th and we shared many of the same experiences in this war. After a moment, we had gone our separate ways back to the front. I have seen Dr. Sheets many times since that day and have worked with him throughout my civilian career. But none of those times was as familiar as the time in Japan. The military and war have a way of doing that. Working together in the MASH created that same camaraderie.

The nature of the MASH as an organization was changing also. By 1951 the MASH was a much more complex organization than it was first intended to be. Though it was originally designed to be a small mobile outfit that could follow the tactical units into battle and provide immediate surgical care, a year into the war it had become somewhat of a bureaucratic organization that looked increasingly like an all-purpose hospital.

MASH 8076, like the other MASH units, had two major sections. The first was the Administrative Section, which included the hospital headquarters and detachment headquarters. The detachment headquarters included the guard section, the utilities section, supply, the registrar, the motor pool, mess, the chemical section, the engineer section, the ordnance section, the quartermaster section, the shower unit (a converted delousing tent), the laundry unit, and a signal section that ran a ten-drop switchboard. Among the units attached to MASH 8076 were the helicopter detachment and a platoon of the 584th Ambulance Company.

The ambulance platoon retrieved patients from the front and evacuated them to the rear. Near the MASH tents, they had a tent and a motor pool, which moved with us as we moved. Their mechanics and supply personnel were separate yet operated as if they were a part of our unit. An excellent outfit, the 584th bore the brunt of moving the wounded. Helicopters could not fly at night or in bad weather. Ambulances could navigate the roads under nearly any conditions. Many of our wounded seemed to come in the late afternoon or in the nighttime hours, so movement by ambulance was mandatory.

The second section, the Professional Section, consisted of the Medical Service, the Surgical Service, the Operating and Anesthesia Service, and the Dental Service. The chief of the Medical Service, a position that called for a lieutenant colonel, was responsible for outpatient care, ad-

The motor pool at the 8076th.

missions, the holding wards, the pharmacy, the X-Ray detachment, the laboratory, and the hospitalized patients. The chief of surgery was responsible for the two surgical wards, pre-op and post-op, the care of shock patients until they were transferred to the Medical Services section, the proper handling of all surgical procedures and techniques, and the initiation of requisitions for surgical instruments and supplies. The chief of the Operating and Anesthesia Service was responsible for the functioning of operating tents and central supply. The Dental Service had one dentist who did oral surgery, which consisted primarily of fractured jaws. There was also an Optometric Section consisting of one enlisted man who made new glasses and repaired broken ones. In 1951 he averaged 120 assignments per month.

A year earlier, when the MASH came to Korea, the unit was organized into a Headquarters Section, a Professional Service, and an Administrative Service. The Professional Service Section was the operating ward, pharmacy, laboratory, and X-ray section. The Administrative Service was the detachment headquarters, supply, mess, registrar, and motor section. Everything else we had was added during the year to enable the MASH to meet the demands of the army.

Capt. Joe Jacko, a Medical Services Corps officer, a nondoctor who was in charge of the administrative matters in the MASH, was the adjutant. Joe was a slender fellow who smoked a pipe and had a witty twinkle in his eye. He was an excellent officer and a good friend. He was also in charge of troop morale in the command. That meant it was his duty to arrange for athletic equipment and movies and radios and other things that made life a little easier. The social aspects of the MASH during my stay gravitated around Joe. He was the life of the party. Many times he was the only one who could make life bearable around the MASH.

Joe was responsible for the visitors who came to the MASH. Occasionally, United Service Organizations (USO) shows toured Korea and VIPs (any senior ranking officer or government officer) came to visit the troops. The VIPs, particularly congressmen, came to be an inside joke at the MASH. On rare occasions one of the helicopters would bring a VIP into the MASH. It was a rare occasion because VIPs, frankly, did not like to venture that close to the combat. News reporters very rarely came around. A reporter from the television network NBC, whose name I have long since forgotten, spent some time with us in the Sixth Chinese Offensive, but he was soon on his way to the rear.

Our experience indicated that the news people, the civilians, and the military liked to gather at the rear and stay at the hotels and send messengers up to the front line units to ask questions. Occasionally, when the fighting slowed down, a visitor would come to the MASH by helicopter and spend a short time. The civilians would do their best to keep cheerful smiles on their faces even though they often looked as if they were going to vomit at the sight of the MASH and the condition of the wounded. These civilians would always dress in combat fatigues to look like the soldiers, jump off the helicopter, scoot through the holding wards and, in a flash, jump back on the helicopter and be off. We generally appreciated visitors when they came—except for the military and medical personnel. When the brass and the doctors showed up, we needed an attitude adjustment. Our attitude may have been wrong, but we did not like for them to get in the way.

There were two exceptions during my tour. One was Dr. Charles Mayo, who came to the MASH and spent a day or two with us. He was able to discuss our medical techniques and help with some very delicate surgical matters. The second came quite unexpectedly. A helicopter arrived one afternoon, and we were informed that a visitor was present. It was unusual because the units just in front of us were in contact with the Chinese; that was not the time for guests—neither from their perspective nor from ours. This visitor was not wearing fatigues or trying to look like a soldier. Francis Joseph Spellman, archbishop of New York and vicar

NBC reporter (in shorts) speaking with doctors at 8076th.

to the armed forces, exited the helicopter and walked through the MASH dressed in his Catholic robes, black robes with a red sash on the shoulders and a red skullcap—and this in a place where we had painted over most of the red crosses because they drew enemy fire. Cardinal Spellman, reputedly a man with tremendous influence at the top levels of the U.S. government, did not try to hide from anyone. During World War II and the Korean War he visited the troops wherever they were. His pleasant demeanor and his humility halted the activity in the MASH: everyone, doctors, nurses, patients, and soldiers, dropped whatever they were doing to speak with the cardinal. I am not Catholic, but I greatly appreciated that visit. His mere presence boosted our morale because this man, welcome and comfortable in the highest of international political circles, came to the hot, muddy, reeking tents of MASH 8076 on a mission of compassion rather than self-promotion.

Seventeen nurses were assigned to MASH 8076. The nurses stayed together in a large sleeping tent they dubbed Whispering Manor. I do not recall the exact origin of that term, but it was an apt term because the "manor," it seemed, was always whispering about something. The nurses' tent was off limits to male personnel because there were always nurses in the tent sleeping or relaxing (they worked rotations in the various sections). It would never dawn on any of us that someone might go into Whispering Manor uninvited. Yet on two occasions in 1951 the tent, with nurses asleep inside, was broken into at night by burglars, who stole per-

Whispering Manor, the nurses' tent at Chunchon.

sonal items. The burglars were never caught, but after that we all kept a sharper eye out around the MASH.

All the nurses were young. That was one of the prerequisites of serving in the MASH. Granted, it forfeited the experience of the older nurses. But older women—and men—would have had to be in exceptional physical condition to stand the stress of the living conditions and the strain of the working conditions in the MASH. I am told that after I left, an older nurse arrived in the 8076th. White-haired and with nimble fingers, she was reportedly an excellent operating room nurse and on one occasion, when they found a piano, held the MASH spellbound with a variety of music. I'm sure she is not the only nurse with graying hair to serve in a MASH. But they were certainly the exception.

Not only were the nurses young, but many of them were also very pretty. As soldiers in all armies have known, there is something about women in uniform far from home that makes them even prettier. Our "Hotlips" Hoolihan was a very attractive major named Pagano who served as chief nurse. The "very attractive" part is as far as the resemblance goes. Our chief nurse was not naive or wishy-washy like "Hotlips" Hoolihan. Major Pagano, from New Jersey, was older than the rest of us, probably close to thirty. A short, feisty sort, she was an excellent nurse who ran a tight ship. She had a retiring sense of humor, but when it came to work, there was no bashfulness about her. Everyone knew what she expected to be done. Much like a football coach, she demanded the most of the nurses and yet kept morale high. Like the housemother of a sorority, she counseled, rebuked, disciplined, and most of all commanded the respect of all the doctors, nurses, NCOs, and enlisted personnel in the MASH. Much of the success of the MASH during my tour can be attributed directly to her outstanding administrative and medical skills. She was all nurse and all army and no nonsense.

The nurses in MASH 8076 were from all over the country. Shortly before I left, Lt. Rusty Jordan arrived. A pre-op nurse, she hailed from Georgia and had a great southern drawl. She had a big smile to go with her personality and, after the war stabilized, was discovered by a guy from the Armed Forces Radio Station (AFRS). Before long, Rusty was filling in as a disc jockey on a radio show in which she cooed "Hi, Sugah" repeatedly for a half hour each week. When Rusty rotated back to the States, she was replaced in the MASH by Lt. Dorothy "Ducky" Duckworth, another Georgian. Ducky quickly took over the AFRS show as the disc jockey, and the soldiers heard "Hi, Sugah" throughout Ducky's tour also.

Amy McConnell had the only pressing iron in the MASH. At those times when we got to return to Japan on R&R, we wanted our uniforms and civilian clothes ironed. Amy was nice enough to put the military creases in our pants, so there was always one or two men outside Whispering Manor with a pair of pants folded over an arm. When she was through ironing, Amy would shout at the top of her lungs, "Okay, get in here and get your pants." I do not remember where Amy was from, but she had a terrible time with ice. She could not stand up on ice. She fell down so much that we said she really sat out the war.

Marilyn Brown, a young woman from Oregon, had a great sense of humor and remained friends with many of the MASH people over the years. Marilyn was a smiling redhead whose personality drew people to her. The nurses particularly were fond of her. When Lieutenant Colonel Connolly, the MASH commander, was gone one week, the nurses decided they would all dye their hair red, the color of Marilyn's, and surprise her. During a slack time the nurses sneaked out behind a tent and, in a large group, began to tint their hair. The male officers, of course, observed this activity and meandered over behind Whispering Manor to see what was going on. Before the day was over, everyone in the MASH had tinted his or her hair red. Lieutenant Colonel Connolly was a rather humorless man, and when he returned, he was furious. The entire MASH had red hair—except for one soldier. A light-haired soldier had tinted his hair only to

Lt. Marilyn Brown sunbathing at the beach at Hwachon.

have it turn green instead of red. Lieutenant Colonel Connolly made him wear a hat until the tint completely washed out. His objection was that the wounded would wake up and see everyone about them with red hair. That, of course, was exactly the plan. We hoped that it might add a little frivolity to something that was otherwise without humor.

The next week, a wounded soldier in the pre-op tent looked with great suspicion at the people preparing to render medical care to him. He raised up from his litter and glanced about the tent. He called Amy aside: "Tell me something. Do you have to be redheaded to be in this hospital unit?" Everyone got a big laugh out of it, including the soldier on the litter.

There were also a variety of personalities among the nurses. A tall, slender nurse arrived shortly before I left. She had a roving eye and wit that we appreciated. She always said that when the artillery came in, she intended to jump into a foxhole with all the copter pilots because she did not want to die with a bunch of nurses. The nurses kept their eye on a certain nurse who had that New York model look about her all the time.

They claimed that she came out of the shower tent with makeup on. They called her our GI dress model. As time went by, she got on well with all the people there.

One of the personalities that spread the fame of MASH 8076 throughout the Korean theater was Agnes. I never heard anyone refer to her by any other name. Soldiers came from far around to see her indescribable beauty. On one occasion a tank company and a transportation company came to MASH 8076 at the same time and, in a fit of jealousy, engaged in a battalion-sized brawl in the field outside Agnes's tent. But I am getting ahead of myself. I will speak of Agnes, the friend we left behind, later.

Each time we had the opportunity—and there were not many such times—we relaxed. There were times when we stopped for a drink and laughed as we talked of home and life without the war. Our best place, ironically, was at the Hwachon Reservoir in the fall of 1951. We moved north above the thirty-eighth parallel in the United Nations counteroffensive in the late summer of 1951 and located the MASH on the east end of the Hwachon Reservoir, a huge body of water nearly twenty miles in length. The fighting, which included the battles of Bloody Ridge and Heartbreak Ridge, was to the north of the reservoir. It was extremely hot that summer, often over one hundred degrees, and the fighting was very heavy. We found a place not far from the MASH where the river emptied into the reservoir. The river made a large bend, and the inside bank of the bend was a sandy beach. Shortly after we settled into our encampment, we rigged a barbecue grill on the riverbank and slipped away in the late afternoons to swim and sunbathe. It was a delightful spot where we could relax and enjoy the beauty of the Korean countryside. The pilots and the NCOs, who were excellent scroungers, managed to bring supplies of beer and steaks and hamburgers and hot dogs; we would crank up the grills and cook in the summer afternoons. All of us, doctors and nurses, managed to find bathing suits. Several of the nurses had two-piece suits, which were the rage stateside.

Eventually we built a rickety diving platform on the bank and found some old rubber inner tubes. We rigged several boards near the bank as a dock for those less adventurous sorts who would not brave the diving platform. The Koreans came to the watering hole also and swam with us; Choi found a set of shorts and splashed around and enjoyed the place as

The beauty of the Hwachon Reservoir.

Relaxing on the beach at the Hwachon Reservoir.

Lt. Pearl Taylor and Lt. Helen Rishonowski on the beach at Hwachon.

much as the rest of us. We put up an improvised volleyball net, and everyone played, doctors, nurses, enlisted personnel, pilots, Koreans, ambulance drivers—everyone who wanted to play could play.

Sometimes the pilots would send the young Koreans up the river with empty beer cans to toss into the current so they would bob down to where we were. The pilots would target practice with their sidearms, usually .45s, occasionally .38s. They enjoyed teaching the nurses how to shoot. Most of the nurses were eager to learn, if only to spend some time in recreation with the pilots. On other occasions the pilots would take the nurses up in the helicopters to view the beauty of the reservoir and the beach from the air. Eventually everyone, including Choi and the other Korean civilians, took pleasure rides in the helicopters.

The beach, by all appearances, had the potential for one of those isolated South Sea island experiences: young men and women, far from home, tied to a postcard-pretty location. In fact, some of the men and women did become interested in one another. After the war, the com-

The 8076th Fourth of July picnic at the beach, Hwachon Reservoir.

mander of the ambulance platoon married one of the nurses he met in the 8076th. But our "paradise" was like picnicking at the beach with a huge black cloud approaching on the horizon. No matter how comfortable it became on that beach, we were always glancing at our big black cloud, the omnipresent threat of combat. At any time we could get the call; the helicopters, forewarning us, would rev up, take to the skies, and return with the wounded. Regardless of the circumstances, we could leave whatever we were doing at the beach and be in the operating room ready to receive patients within two minutes. When the fighting began, it was like cramming everything into the picnic basket and running when the bottom dropped out of the big black cloud and you had to sprint for cover to get out of the rain and thunder and lightning.

Because the nurses were the only American females in the combat zone, they were constantly the center of attention—in real life as well as in the film and the television series. They generally got on well with the wounded soldiers. The feminine presence often cooled or cajoled even the toughest the army had to offer. An incident that illustrated the situation was reported in the Osaka General Hospital news. A tough, profane, unpleasant sergeant came into MASH 8076 very badly wounded. He

Georgie and Boy playing on the diving board at the 8076th swimming hole, Hwachon Reservoir.

would not talk to the nurses or cooperate with those who were trying to help. All he could do was growl at people. When it was time for him to be evacuated to the rear by ambulance, Lt. Edna W. Jordan, a young nurse from Gastonia, North Carolina, overheard him say he would like to be transported by helicopter rather than ambulance. Lieutenant Jordan knew that the soldier's temperament had been heavily influenced by his extreme pain. She talked to Archie Breedlove, an aviation officer, and arranged for the helicopter evacuation. Lieutenant Breedlove flew the mission and delivered the unpleasant soldier to a more comfortable field hospital in the rear area. As they unloaded the litter, the soldier called to Archie. "Look, I'm tough," he said. "I am really tough, but that MASH made me see what a heel I am. Please tell them all that I appreciate what they have done for me and give them all my thanks." Tears ran down his cheeks as he spoke. Archie Breedlove delivered the message.

Former patients often came back by the MASH on the way to or from the front to visit the people who had worked on them. Many soldiers dropped in to say hello, just as patients in the private practice of medicine do. People who go through traumatic experiences of surgery often like to keep in touch with their doctors. That is the type of relationship I think a doctor should have with a patient. The patients often saw more of the nurses in the holding wards than they did of the surgeons, and they wanted to say hello to them also. We encouraged this practice for the patients' sake as well as for our sake. It did us good to have people tell us they were grateful for what we had done.

Many people came just to see a pretty face. And I don't blame them for that either. As in any other organization, there were favorites among the nurses. In the times when we were stabilized, particularly after the peace talks began and the front lines were fixed, the nurses were free to go where they pleased in their spare time. They were often asked by other soldiers to join them at division parties or at parties in the rear area. They were free like everyone else to go on R&R to Tokyo or Osaka or wherever they pleased, and many of them did—just as many of the doctors did.

On one occasion the nurses and doctors were invited to a party at 2d Division headquarters. Several of the nurses piled into a jeep driven by one of the pilots and negotiated the Korean roads to the party. The party was long and loud. Most of us made it back, but although the jeep driven by the pilot and filled with nurses made its way out of 2d Division headquarters, it did not appear at the 8076th MASH. The next day we grew more anxious by the minute. Our daily strength report, had it been filled out accurately, would have reflected a number of our officer personnel absent without leave. As we were organizing a search and rescue party, we received a call on the land line that the lost jeep and its passengers were in Seoul. They had taken the wrong road out of division headquarters and ended up in the city.

The nurses, like everyone else, wore the army uniform every day. For the nurses, as for the rest of us, this became tiresome. Civilian clothes felt very good. Lt. Phyllis Laucks of Wheeling, West Virginia, said in the Osaka General Hospital news, "I have never been so sick of slacks in my life." It was a special event for all of us to get out of the uniform and into civvies.

But there were times when the nurses' clothing had another effect on the morale of the command. The laundry facilities with the MASH were good and were reinforced by facilities at division headquarters. The laundry load in a hospital is tremendous. We had to wash all the surgical blankets, towels, surgical suits—everything we used had to be washed. In addition, we had to do our own laundry for our personal clothing. We all put our laundry out to dry. We hung it on clotheslines or over the tent poles or laid it out on the top of the tents. It was customary to see men's underwear hanging out in the sun. No one would take a second look. But we often laughed that bone-tired, war-weary soldiers would march several miles just to glimpse the nurses' underwear hanging on the line.

Matters were not always affable in the MASH. When people are placed in such close confines, they often get under each other's skin. Some of the nurses envied the attention the prettier nurses received. Likewise, some of the men twinged with jealousy when officers from other units invited the nurses to parties—and the nurses gladly accepted the invitations. These matters were sometimes discussed as morale factors during the staff meetings. But such social situations develop in the military workplace just as they do in the civilian workplace. They also appear as petty jealousies over recognition for work done or credit given or over job promotion. Anyone associated with a hospital in the 1990s knows exactly what I am talking about. In the MASH during my tour, the work and social relationships between the doctors and nurses were professional, supportive, and encouraging. There was no backbiting or professional rivalry or double-dealing. Everyone pitched in to accomplish the mission—and hoped that he or she could go home as soon as possible.

Although we saw the results of combat constantly and heard the guns booming at all hours, we rarely engaged in combat ourselves. At one time the North Koreans began to follow the medical evacuation through the lines and back to the MASH. We beefed up our security to keep them out. Occasionally we received incoming artillery or mortar rounds. But for the most part, the combatants were focused on each other, and we simply picked up the pieces.

One of the strange combat experiences of the war happened to us near Chunchon. Our location was in the valley, in the shadow of a mountain. After we had been there a while, at four o'clock one afternoon the air raid alarm activated. The enlisted personnel and the Korean augmentees had built entrenchments around and through the camp, which served as large foxholes for protection against air attack and were to be used as interior defensive positions in the event we were attacked. We had acquired a set of quad-50s: four .50 caliber machine guns mounted in a rectangular configuration, two over and two under, and placed on the back of a jeep. It could be removed from a vehicle and set in a foxhole or antiaircraft position. The four .50 caliber machine guns fired simulta-

neously and could put up a wall of steel projectiles each nearly the size
of a drummer's stick—instant death for small attack aircraft. At the beginning of the war, quad-50s were intended for use as antiaircraft weapons. It soon became evident that they were also vicious antipersonnel
weapons, particularly effective against the Chinese human wave assault.
By mid-1951 the United States had gained air superiority, and the threat
from air attack was not great. We had little need of the foxholes or the
quad-50s. Our biggest worry was artillery or infiltrators.

So it was with a bit of curiosity as well as alarm that we hit the foxholes in obedience to the air alert. When nothing happened, we cautiously
scanned the skies for the North Korean MIGs. Nothing. In a moment an
aircraft appeared over the mountain. It was not a MIG-17. We stared
upward with great curiosity. An open-cockpit biplane skimmed over the
mountaintop, barely missing the peak. The engine coughed over the
MASH, and the plane nosed downward as if he were going to buzz us.
We watched in utter amazement as the pilot made a pass over the tents.
A single Korean aviator, dressed in an old leather pilot's helmet much like
the old football helmets we used as kids, looped away from us and came
for a second pass. By now, we were all standing next to the foxholes, shad-
ing our eyes from the sun as if in salute, and watching the sky incredu-
lously. As he passed us again, we could see his face clearly. He looked back
at us just as we looked at him. He went away from the encampment and
started climbing. He tossed something from his cockpit, presumably a
hand grenade, and it fell harmlessly to the ground and exploded a safe
distance from us. Then off he went, back over the mountain, climbing
just high enough to avoid the peak. It was about all his sputtering biplane
could do.

That evening, an epidemic of Monday morning quarterbacking
swept the MASH. If we had just been ready with the quad-50s . . . One
burst would have chewed that biplane to bits. Whose fault was it that we
did not give him a proper welcome? How did we let that commie get
away? Next time, just wait till next time!

Next time was twenty-four hours later. At four o'clock in the afternoon, the air alarms blasted and we charged for the foxholes. Dead silence was broken by the coughing sound of a biplane engine, and up we
looked to see the biplane barely top the mountain and begin his descent
toward the MASH. He buzzed once as he did the day before, then looped
around and buzzed the second time. We saw his face; he saw each of ours.

Quad-50 antiaircraft emplacement at MASH 8076.

This time we looked him eye to eye. Then, as the day before, he ascended away from us and tossed out his payload, which fell harmlessly to the ground and exploded a safe distance from us.

"Where were the quad-50s?" the first sergeant ranted. "We should have chewed him up. Just wait. Next time . . ."

Next time came twenty-four hours later, at four o'clock in the afternoon. The air alert screamed, and we ambled easily out to the foxholes. In a moment we heard the biplane engine straining to clear the mountaintop, and here came our Korean friend. This time was different. He made the two passes as we watched, but this time he wore a pair of sunglasses and a nice white scarf around his neck. In the breeze, the scarf trailed back from the leather helmet like the tail of a comet, giving him a World War I ace look. This time, instead of greeting him with quad-50s, we waved our hands and shouted greetings as he went by on his first pass. On his second buzz, he dipped his wings to return our wave. On he went, climbing skyward and tossing his payload from the aircraft. We shook our heads and laughed as we strolled back to the tents. In a moment we heard the explosion way out in the field. We did not even look back.

Soldiers of the 8076th in its defensive trenches during an air raid alert.

We called him Bedcheck Charley, and he buzzed every day at four o'clock in the afternoon and dumped his weak ordnance out in the field away from the MASH, where it popped harmlessly like a firecracker. Then, as suddenly as he had appeared, his visits ceased. We felt a bit like a friend was gone. It occurred to us that someone had ordered him to bomb the MASH and continue bombing it until it was no longer operational. In a touch of compassion, this lone North Korean refused to carry out the insane orders to bomb a hospital. Perhaps he reported that his mission was accomplished. Perhaps they knew what he was doing and relieved him of the mission. Perhaps even his military superiors recognized that what he was ordered to do was inhumane and they were touched by a sense of humanity. We will never know. He never reappeared.

The enlisted personnel were a vital part of the MASH. They were constantly present to take care of the administrative matters that made the medical operations possible. In the MASH, as in most medical units, officer-enlisted relations were relaxed. We left the enlisted matters to the NCOs, and by and large they did a good job during my tour. We had some unusual personalities among them. The senior NCO, Sergeant Major Stone, was a flashy figure who wore pistols western style, like General Patton. He performed both administrative and medical duties. His job was to look after the enlisted personnel. His role, like the role of many sergeants major, was broad and often self-defined.

Toward the end of my tour, I was appointed executive officer, a position that should have been filled by a senior Medical Corps officer; but we were short of everything, including senior Medical Corps officers. In fact, I was probably, by that time, the second most senior Medical Corps officer in the MASH. At age twenty-eight I was appointed chief surgeon of the MASH and shortly thereafter took on the ominous title of executive officer. About that time I was also given the nickname Dad, and I am still referred to by that name by some of the MASH members—even by those who are older than I. I would like to think that this term of endearment was given me because of a wisdom much greater than my years. Alas, I think it was given to poke fun at my *lack* of fatherly wisdom and demeanor.

As the "exec" I had to follow up on several of the administrative matters in the MASH. One of those was the operation of the ambulances. We noticed that two of our ambulances seemed to be deadlined (not operating because of breakdown or routine maintenance) at all times. When we asked the details, we were told that minor things were wrong and it would take only days to get them back on the road. It seemed that in heavy fighting all the ambulances were operational, but in slack times they were again on the deadline list. As soon as an ambulance came off the deadline list, another would go on. We continually inquired and did not receive satisfactory answers.

One evening I ventured down to the motor pool to find out what was wrong with the ambulances. The mechanics were sitting outside the maintenance tent drinking coffee and smoking cigarettes. When they saw me coming, they scurried about and seemed to disappear. One embarrassed mechanic greeted me and offered me a cup of coffee. I thanked him and told him that I had come to check on the ambulances.

"They'll be operational first thing in the morning," he promised, and he placed himself between me and the parked ambulances as if to block my path.

"I think I ought to check the ambulances," I said.

"No, no," he shot back, and he scooted along between me and the ambulances. "We'll take care of them."

In a moment, the back door of one of the deadlined ambulances opened, and out stepped a soldier who was buttoning his shirt. Behind him came a young Korean woman who was tidying her skirt. The scene was repeated a moment later in a second deadlined ambulance. It soon became apparent that they were using the deadlined ambulances as mobile brothels, a Korean movable feast, as it were. The stretchers in the back were padded and much more comfortable than army cots. Shortly thereafter, we noticed that the ambulances came off deadline and were operational again.

There were a lot of hijinks among the enlisted personnel. The shower tent always attracted attention. One incident in the film *M*A*S*H* may have been suggested by a scheme carried out in our MASH. In the film, NCOs sold tickets to soldiers to peek through holes in the shower tent and observe a certain officer in the nude.

Several NCOs of the 8076th saw an entrepreneurial opportunity lurking in the folds of the olive drab shower tent and capitalized on it. Sometime after dark, the NCOs stole around to the back of the shower tent and cut two small windows, one above the other, in the tarpaulin. The shower tent was illuminated on the inside by dim overhead lights, and at night it was difficult to see in the dark corners. The NCOs rigged the tarp so that no one could see the windows—about the size of binocular lenses—from the inside of the tent. On the outside, they placed orange crates in a long line so that the anxious soldiers could sit while they waited their turn. Behind the orange crates they placed a wooden ladder so the soldiers could climb the ladder and look through the upper window. Tickets were sold for the enlisted man's viewing pleasure. A dollar and a half bought thirty seconds worth of time at the window. The NCOs had the timing down to an art. The tickets were sold all day long. At night, when the nurses entered the shower tent, the ticket holders for that day quickly formed lines along the orange crates and behind the ladder. An NCO stood on either side of the windows and shooed the viewer away at the end of his thirty seconds.

The enterprise thrived, but the NCOs, businessmen that they were, conjured up ways to boost sales. The first big sales pitch came after some dissatisfied customers complained about not seeing the most attractive nurses. The NCOs instituted a sales drive that involved different-colored tickets. The highest-priced tickets, reserved for the most attractive nurses, were red. Orange tickets were cheaper, but they entitled the holders to view only the plump females. Blue tickets, the lowest-priced ones, allowed viewers to see the more corpulent of the women. This sophisticated marketing plan necessitated a committee of NCOs who would determine which women qualified for the different colors of tickets. That, of course, required a good deal of research.

The second great sales pitch concerned expanding the market to soldiers outside the MASH. In a moment of uncharacteristic chivalry, the NCOs decided that they should share their great blessing with other soldiers but that the program would be run with absolutely no nonsense. The first rule was that all time limits would be strictly enforced. A second rule was that no one was to say a word about any of this. If the nurses found out what was going on, the whole program would be canceled. A third rule was that no one was to show any familiarity toward the nurses in any way, shape, or form. Our NCOs, now perceiving themselves in an entrepreneurial role, became strangely jealous of the rights of our nurses.

Soon, soldiers from frontline units were coming to the MASH in the evenings and hanging around. When the nurses, dressed in robes and carrying towels and toiletries, gathered at the allotted time at the shower tent, eager soldiers marched like ducks in a line toward the rear of the shower tent and everything became very quiet. Not a peep came from the viewing gallery. When the unsuspecting nurses left the shower tent, the soldiers reappeared, breathless, mounted their jeeps, and headed back to their units. The NCOs pocketed the money.

I must confess after nearly fifty years that the officers knew all about what was going on. With a characteristic lack of chivalry, we just kept our mouths shut and ignored the whole thing. Only on a couple of occasions did the nurses inquire about any unusual doings concerning the shower tent. The officers merely shrugged and said the matter would be investigated. The investigations always came up negative, and that satisfied the nurses. The NCOs managed to keep the entire matter absolutely quiet the whole time. I do not know whether the nurses suspected anything or not. If they did, they did not say anything about it. Back in the 1950s, young men in their twenties who were far from home thought this scheme was very funny. The times were different and intentions were different. We have lost much of our innocence about all that. The same scheme was used in peep shows in county fairs, in grade B Hollywood films, and in many college fraternities around the country. Today we are much more sensitive about these things. The young men involved in that—those who lived through the war—are now five decades older and may fail to see the humor in the shower tent scheme. Times change and so do people.

One particular medic from Brooklyn, a real Valentino, managed to keep things lively. On one occasion a USO show came to our area. The show consisted of entirely female entertainers and attracted a great crowd. Afterward, our pilots flew the women to the 8076th to meet the MASH personnel and greet the wounded. The mistress of ceremonies, a very attractive woman, came with Ed Ziegler and explained in a hoarse whisper that, because they had been doing so many shows, she was losing her voice and was delighted to be going to a medical unit so she could be examined. Ziegler assured her that one of our doctors would be happy to take care of her. When he landed at the MASH landing zone, he pointed her to the receiving tent and told her to go straight to the back of the tent, where she would find a doctor. He took care of the helicopter and returned to the receiving tent. He entered the back of the tent to find the medic, Valentino, dressed in white coat and T-shirt, no rank insignia, with a stethoscope hanging from his neck. He had ushered the entertainer behind a divider and had instructed her to remove her fatigue jacket and lower her bra straps. He was in the process of giving her a very thorough examination with the stethoscope.

The Italian Valentino from Brooklyn was a corpsman and a born entertainer. On the cold Korean nights, Valentino would go to the pre-op tent and stand next to the potbellied stove and tell stories to the nurses. The doctors would come out of surgery when they could, and Valentino began a regular show that would often last past midnight. We persuaded him to go through the post-op tent and entertain the soldiers. Soon we had our own USO show. It went a long way to bring smiles to the faces of boys who were seriously injured and deeply depressed. Often we had serious head wounds come into the pre-op ward. A medic would have to shave the patient's head before surgery. Valentino perfected a routine in which he sang and shuffled as he shaved. He did a delightful rendition of "Figaro, Figaro," from the *Barber of Seville* as he clipped away. The patients enjoyed it as much as the nurses.

One night, two Turkish soldiers came into the pre-op tent, one seriously wounded, the other assisting him. The wounded Turk had a scimitar (a long curved sword), and he was not about to surrender it to anyone. When we pleaded with his friend to take it from him so we could work on him, the friend merely shrugged as if he did not understand English. The nurses were very leery about working on an armed person who was not fully coherent for fear that the person, while in a state of half-consciousness, might go berserk with the weapon. The nurses scoured the MASH for patients who could speak French or Arabic or any other language, but the Turks understood none of these. Lieutenant Colonel Connolly was called, and as soon as he recognized the problem, he became very irritated. He ordered an NCO to call the intelligence section at corps headquarters and have them send someone who could speak Turkish. He called for MPs to disarm the Turk. He called for sedatives to put the Turk to sleep. He walked in circles and swore at the situation. Finally, in the height of his frustration, he shouted, "Doesn't anyone around here speak Turkish?"

Valentino popped up. "I do."

Lieutenant Colonel Connolly whipped around on Valentino and ordered, "Well, talk Turkey to him."

Valentino smiled sheepishly and ventured toward the Turk. The tent became very quiet. Patients lying on cots raised themselves on one elbow to watch. The nurses observed this with some trepidation. The Turk's eyes squinted as he surveyed Valentino. His hand eased down to the scimitar. The Turk's friend edged tensely closer to him. Valentino, now the center of attention, stopped short of the cot and faced the Turk as if to stare him down. After a moment, Valentino leaned slightly forward and snapped, "Gobble, gobble."

After a long, tense silence, one of the nurses chuckled, and then another, and then the patients laughed. Lieutenant Colonel Connolly, overwhelmed by the swelling peals of laughter, charged from the tent. Eventually, someone from corps headquarters came down and spoke Turkish to the Turk and disarmed him, and we proceeded to render medical care to him.

There were many humorous times at the 8076th, and there were many good people. My service there was among the most poignant experiences of my life. But it included an element that is missing from the interpretations of the writers, directors, and actors who filmed the motion picture and the television series of the MASH. Those who were there often forget that element, too. At the beginning of the Persian Gulf War, I received a letter from the Department of the Army asking if I was interested in serving as a surgeon. It was, no doubt, a form letter sent to many doctors, but the thought flashed through my mind, the thought of service far away, the thought of another challenge, the thought of doing a doctor's duty. I was, of course, over the age limit. But for a fleeting second as I held the letter in my hands, I entertained the idea of reliving those days in the 8076th. I too had almost forgotten.

I am talking about a sense that was completely lost in the transition from real life to the film and the television series on the MASH. It was lost because it cannot be easily conveyed in those media. To be commercial, the film and the television series had to dwell on the light side and mask the intensity of the human misery. No one will deny that the alcohol flowed. But that has happened in all units in all wars—no more so in the MASH than anywhere else. No one will deny that men and women become attracted to one another in the loneliness and despair of war. Again, that is common to all units in all wars—no more so in the MASH than anywhere else. But like all aspects of war, with time we relegate the misery to the far side of our memories, and we glorify the mythical, the heroic, the things that justify the loss and the pain of conflict. That is the only way we can fight the next war. We forget the human consequences.

In the MASH we saw the human consequences. I have found an old letter to my wife that I wrote on October 24, 1951, during the battle of Heartbreak Ridge. As I wrote to my wife, I gave words to my thoughts during the battle, before the reality of the human misery was but a lost memory.

It has finally quieted down. What a rat race. I had no idea I could get sick and tired of surgery, but honestly I don't care if I ever do or even see an operation again, at this point. This sort of thing makes one so physically and emotionally tired that it really defies description. It makes strong men break down and cry to see these boys come in caked with mud and blood, bled white under it all, all of them in shock of one type or other, saying nothing, asking nothing, and not one out of a hundred complaining about anything, They just lie there and say, "Yes, Sir, or "No, Sir" or "Thank you, Sir" until you want to tell them to yell or cry or do anything but just lie there. God never has before nor ever will again make anything to equal the G.I. They are so wonderful it makes a lump in your throat every time you look at them. I wish every last person in Washington could be compelled to walk through our hospital during a push to see just what these poor guys are going through. But instead they sit back and listen to the stories of the heroes on the front lines taking a whole hill single handedly and telling others what a wonderful thing they have done stopping the Reds in Korea. No one knows what war is until they have seen these hospital tents filled to over-flowing with G.I.'s. All our tents were so full that only one person at a time could walk down the aisles and then we had to put up another tent, put patients in the X-ray tent, all the connecting passage ways and in the Registrars office—any place where there was just a tent overhead was filled. With all the massive injuries we had relatively few deaths among those who reached us. Out of approximately 1519 patients seen during this push only 8 or ten died, that is, at our hospital before evacuation. I could go on and on but enough for this time.

This letter was copied and circulated with a plea for the churchgo-ers and the townspeople to give blood. It expressed my thoughts at Heart-break, and as I read it the memories of the human consequences come back.

I am not speaking now only of the wounded. There were many of those. I am speaking now of the doctors and nurses who came to the MASH. Far and away the vast majority of those who served in the Medical Corps came and served honorably and took home the wisdom and the memories and the anguish that only that kind of experience affords. But the Medical Corps had its casualties; they were in the battalions, in the MASH units, in the evacuation and field hospitals throughout the Ko-rean theater. We tend to forget them or to categorize and dehumanize them. They were not strong enough, we say, or they had problems be-fore they got there. That is the first step in forgetting the human conse-quences.

A very distinct factor in the operation of the MASH and in the op-eration of the army in Korea was illness. Many of the patients who came into the MASH were not wounded but had contracted some disease that made them unable to perform their duties. That is true in any war. The routine diseases of wartime, typhus, malaria, dysentery, frostbite, were rampant among the troops. Common diseases that can be easily treated stateside, like bronchitis, often erupt into serious diseases in the combat zone. A previously unknown and often fatal disease, hemorrhagic fever, a painful condition with headaches and backaches, nausea, and eventu-ally seepage of blood through the skin, swept through the combat zone, and no one knew quite what to do about it. In any war—and Korea was no exception—illness is more prevalent than injury inflicted by the enemy.

One of the reasons that the tour of duty for nurses was so short was illness. When a soldier became so ill that he or she could not function, the soldier was sent to an evacuation hospital. In an environment of irregular hours, sparse meals, and lack of adequate facilities for physical hygiene, it is very difficult to stay healthy. Staying healthy becomes secondary to avoiding combat death. In the MASH, doctors, nurses, and enlisted personnel all worked long and tedious hours, a schedule that for most people lowers resistance and results in some sort of illness. Several times doctors or nurses were summarily shipped back to Japan or to the States because they needed to become the patients.

A few doctors and nurses came to the medical units who were not professionally prepared; such personnel had to be relieved before they did too much damage to the unsuspecting wounded. Others could not cope with the mangled bodies in army tents in the mountains where the temperature fluctuated with the seasons from near zero to over a hundred degrees. They would stay in the battalion or the MASH or the field hospital for a month or two, then overnight would be gone. Some sought refuge in alcohol abuse. Others lapsed into a state of shock when they found themselves among the many wounded and dying. A few doctors became psychiatric patients and were returned quietly to Japan and then stateside.

When I was the executive officer, I had to deal with the personnel problems in the 8076th. One particular officer, a Medical Services Corps officer (a nondoctor), was constantly intoxicated. A congenial fellow, he could not get up in the morning and face the day. He would drink and get boisterous on occasion and punch walls, but most often he would sit down on the ground, back against a tree or a rock or a truck tire, and cry. He did not want to return to the States because he felt that would be interpreted as weakness or failure on his part. Eventually he had to be relieved and whisked away and finally discharged.

I am not speaking of weakness. I am speaking of the human condition and its confrontation with the horror of war. We never said "good riddance" to those who were shipped back summarily to the States. Always a part of our souls went with them. When we, the doctors and nurses, are asked to compare the real MASH to the film and the television series, the casualties may not be the first thing mentioned, but they always linger in the back of our minds. The Korean War produced many causalities both inside and outside the MASH. When we think of the fun we had at the beach at Hwachon, we risk forgetting about the big black cloud on the horizon. When we smile about Bedcheck Charley, we risk forgetting about the absolute terror inflicted by the technology of war. When we are asked about doctor-nurse relationships, we risk forgetting about those who were summarily sent home because of illness or drunkenness or some other casualty and about all those who went home with the imprint of Korea in their psyche. That is what is lost in the transition to film and television.

6 IN THE OR

The nerve center of the MASH, the very reason for our existence, was the operating tent. In the flux of mobility and the rapidity of case flow, the operating room became the test tube for innovation. In addition to helicopter evacuation of the wounded from the battlefield, several advances in emergency medicine came to fruition in the MASH in Korea: the treatment of blood-loss shock, the widespread use of antibiotics, early ambulation, and techniques in arterial repair. Other advances, in the areas of neurosurgery and initial psychiatric treatment, were pioneered in the MASH units. The neurological work was done primarily in MASH 8055, and the psychiatric work, according to my knowledge, was done in conjunction with the evacuation hospitals. Neither of these was done to any extent at MASH 8076. Our MASH, as noted earlier, was known as the arterial repair hospital.

The conditions were ripe for medical innovation. When the peace talks came and the tactical lines stabilized and the war ground into its third year, the MASH settled into a fixed position. The military medical structure took over again, and the spontaneity that spawned innovation was squelched. But in the first year and a half, the MASH pioneered and experimented its way into the annals of emergency medicine. You had to see it to appreciate it. A number of the things that happened were merely improvisation. We had no notion that the changes we made would result in an advance in medical care. Others were ideas we thought through, discussed among ourselves, and planned before we did them.

Many of the advances resulted from the peculiar nature of the mobile war and the rapid flow of the wounded to the aid stations and to the MASH. In World War I the front lines were stabilized and the hospitals were as much as 150 miles from the front lines. Many died during evacuation. In World War II the hospitals were more mobile, but the Medical Corps could not keep up with the tactical units. In Korea, the wounded often got to us before the blood clotted. That changed some of the ideas and the methods of treatment.

The operating tent itself was just a tent that moved along with the ebb and flow of the tactical situations. In the operating tent were three or four surgeons waiting for the wounded. When I arrived, Major Coleman and Captains Scow and Starr were the surgeons. The surgeon I replaced had already left. I had passed him on the road going out of the MASH. Three surgeons manned the operating tent. Shortly after I came, Capt. Albert Starr, a classmate from Columbia, rotated out to reduce the total number of surgeons to three. Albert, from Brooklyn, New York, was an excellent surgeon who later served as a professor of surgery at the University of Seattle. He was replaced by Capt. Donald "Waldo" Schwing, who arrived shortly before Albert's departure. After John Coleman left and I became the chief of surgery, Capt. Bob Meyers arrived. Waldo and Bob were excellent surgeons who fit in well in the MASH. The aggregate years of experience beyond residency of all the surgeons could be counted on one hand. Perhaps the benefit of that inexperience was idealism. They were all young, and they were all eager to become excellent surgeons and to render to their fellow soldier the best medical care possible.

In the operating tent, the surgeons were assisted by the other doctors. Three doctors who were not surgeons were assigned as assistant surgeons. There were, of course, other doctors to fill out the positions assigned in the MASH. Those doctors included practically every kind of doctor found in a hospital, and they worked in their areas when the patients arrived. When the doctors were not working in their own areas, they served as assistants to the surgeons in the operating tent. Even our dentist, Dr. Rice, whom we called Rice Paddy, assisted in surgery in the operating tent. One surgeon worked at each operating table, and another doctor and several nurses assisted in the surgical procedures.

The surgeons gravitated by happenstance toward certain specialties. It was not a planned or orderly assignment but more a specialty of necessity. A surgeon would perform a certain procedure until he became proficient in that procedure. Then, when a patient with that wound came in, if that doctor was available, the patient would informally be assigned to him. This procedure began in the pre-op tent. When a doctor or a nurse recognized a certain wound, he or she would send a message into the operating tent for the doctor who had gained some proficiency. It was literally a shout from one tent to another. John Coleman, for example, out of necessity became interested in and did work on arterial repair. If a patient was admitted with severe arterial damage, someone in the pre-

Major Pagano, the chief nurse, shakes hands with Major Coleman, chief of surgery, as John rotates back to the United States. The other two are Captain Schwing and pilot Dayton Warren.

op ward might literally shout, "Hey, John, can you take this patient?" If John was available, he would take the patient. If he was unavailable, the patient was sent to the next available operating table. In heavy loads, each surgeon took whatever came. It was not a situation in which the surgeon practiced in a specialty. It was the general practice of surgery, in which the surgeons may have found a preference and worked on that preference if circumstances allowed.

There were occasions when patients arrived who were in need of two surgeons. In that case we would double up if we could. If a patient was near death, two surgeons would begin to work on him until he could be stabilized. Then one surgeon would be relieved by another doctor so the surgeon could go to another table and another patient. If the patients were lined up through the pre-op ward, we did not have the luxury to put two surgeons on one patient. We just took them as they came.

MASH 8076 admitted 21,408 patients in 1951, including those admitted for all causes: illness, combat wound, frostbite—any reason a person came to the hospital and was admitted. As in most wars, many

Major Coleman and Captains Schwing, Starr, and Scow play cards outside the bachelor officers' quarters at the 8076th, Chunchon. Ruins of Korean buildings can be seen in the background.

patients admitted were for treatment for something other than combat wounds. In earlier wars the ratio of noncombat injuries or illnesses to combat wounds was three to one. It was not until World War II that preventive medicine reduced that ratio significantly. Of the total number of patients admitted in 1951, 8,675 were admitted for combat wounds or as battle casualties. Of the total patients admitted, 19,143 were evacuated to field hospitals and beyond for further treatment, and approximately 2,000 were returned to duty. From a different perspective, nearly 90 percent of the patients admitted in 1951 were serious enough to be evacuated for further treatment. Of the total number admitted, 188 died at MASH 8076. Of this 188, 138 died of battle wounds, 45 of nonbattle injuries, and 5 of illnesses. In 1951 surgical procedures were performed on 5,176 soldiers (the records did not begin until February 6, 1951). Of those, 4,993 were battle casualties. That averages approximately one hundred surgeries a week for the forty-seven weeks the records were kept. Three surgeons and three doctors assisting the surgeons, working in pairs, operated on those patients.

The surgeries in the MASH were of every conceivable nature. The 5,176 surgeries from February 6, 1951, to the end of the year included 2,538 debridements (open the wound, clean it, and suture it closed) and 1,688 orthopedic procedures. The third highest category was abdominal procedures—538. Modern military technology was capable of causing injury to nearly every part of the body. The use of armor, artillery, and air support made the war more mobile and lethal. Land mines devastated the human body. Armor and artillery shell bursts, and antipersonnel bombs and land mines, cause explosions that scatter shrapnel, small shards of metal, out in a fan-shaped pattern. These weapons were common in World War II but not as accurate or as prevalent as in Korea. Shrapnel went into all parts of the body and severed arteries, pierced muscles, shattered bones and tendons and ligaments, and destroyed organs.

There were, of course, many old-fashioned wounds, usually in the abdominal area. Korea was a place where soldiers could shoot bullets from one mountaintop and hit soldiers on another mountaintop, and the wounds were often localized; there would be a small, neat entrance wound and a large, ugly exit wound. We could repair those very directly without much ado about finding the wounds. They were very evident. Yet, there were still abdominal wounds caused by a variety of methods. A piercing wound in the abdomen meant that we had to make an incision from the breastbone to the pubic bone and repair the intestines. Yards of intestines had to be taken out of the abdominal cavity and the holes from a through-and-through wound, a wound that had completely penetrated the intestine by going in one side and out the other, had to be sutured on each side of the intestine. It took a long time to explore the intestines and find all of the punctures.

The Turks particularly generated a lot of abdominal wounds. The Turks did not like to use modern weapons. They liked to get close to the enemy and use knives and swords and bayonets and scimitars. Those weapons penetrated, punctured, slashed, and demolished the chest and abdominal areas. The Chinese knew how to use knives and bayonets, too, and were not the least bit bashful about it. After the Turks and the Chinese had gone at each other, we were tied up in the operating tent for days repairing intestinal wounds.

The surgical cases, of course, did not come at a nice even rate of one hundred per week. The highest rate of admission was at Hwachon during an eight-day period from October 14 to 21 (during the battle of Heartbreak Ridge), when 1,582 patients were admitted, 1,423 of which were battle casualties. The other 159 were nonbattle injury, illness, combat fatigue, or psychiatric disorder. The next highest sustained rate of admission came at Suwon in the first week of 1951 (the Chinese New Year's offensive).

When a wounded soldier came in, he was placed in line with everyone else. The pre-op ward was often filled, with many in life-threatening situations. Journalist Philip Deane was with MASH 8055 during the period of the defense of the Pusan Perimeter, and he described an operating tent at full capacity in these terms: "The school [Teajon Primary School, where MASH 8055 first set up at the Pusan Perimeter] was a large building whose courtyard was full of vehicles and walking wounded. The smell of disinfectant hung in the air. Inside, litters covered the landings and filled the rooms. Doctors operated in blood-splattered fatigues."

For most patients who were not a heartbeat from death, surgery began in the pre-op ward, but the preparation and prioritization for treatment began on the battlefield. Generally, the patients who came by helicopter were in life-threatening situations. Many who came by ambulance were in the same condition but were located in a place where air evacuation was unavailable. When they arrived at the MASH, they were taken to admissions and then to pre-op. In pre-op the priority of treatment was set again. A pre-op nurse and a doctor, if available, established an order for the patients to enter the operating tent based upon the condition of the patient. Those near death came in first, and the rest were prioritized. Immediate medical attention was given to the patients in pre-op as they waited their turn for the operating table.

In the late summer of 1951, a young man from Ohio entered our MASH with multiple wounds caused by extensive shrapnel injury. I am not sure where we were at the time; I do not remember, but I remember this young man. At least two of his wounds severed arteries, one near the right shoulder and the other in the upper thigh. He had several penetrating wounds in the lower thigh, the abdomen, the upper extremities, and the upper chest. He had a small entrance wound beneath his left armpit. After we opened him up, we found serious injuries to his stomach, spleen, liver, and pancreas that had to be repaired immediately. The trail from the entrance wound had gone downward through his abdomen and out his upper thigh. The exit wounds on this young man created the avul-

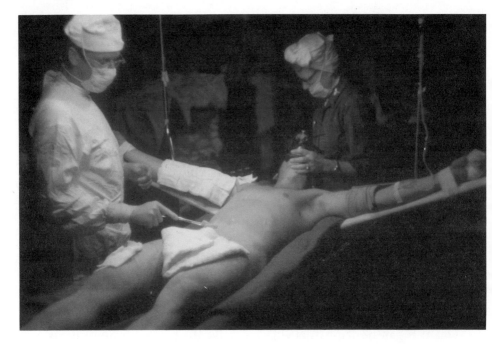

The young man from Ohio. Note the entrance wound beneath the left armpit.

sion of the scrotum and the loss of part of his penis (this caused a great deal of bleeding).

The young man from Ohio, because he was near death, was carried from the copter into the pre-op ward, hastily prepared for surgery, carried into the operating tent, and placed on a table for immediate attention.

The operating tent itself was very simple. All we needed was something over our heads. That overhead cover could be a tent or a building or a hangar. MASH 8055 set up in an abandoned school near Pusan, 8063 used a hangar, and in the 8076th one of the first "homes" for the operating room was a vacant warehouse in which 407 patients could be accommodated at one time. In the months after the Inchon invasion and the subsequent offensive, MASH 8055 found itself in another school in the Pyonyang area. The enlisted personnel and Korean laborers had cleaned the place out. The desks and pictures on the walls all were tossed out the windows. Inside, children's pictures and schoolwork were still tacked to the bulletin boards. During most of my time with the 8076th, our oper-

ating room was in the army issue olive drab tarpaulin tents that we came
to love so well. The musty smell of army tents was with us always.

In the beginning the operating tent was the center of the facility.
Everything else, supply, X-ray, the wards, was placed around the operating tent likes spokes from the hub of a wheel. During surgery, if we
needed a variety of instruments or a special kind of suture or a particular clamp or more blood, the attending nurse would go get it immediately. Everything had to be accessible from the operating tent. Later, when
the mission of the MASH expanded to include medical procedures other
than surgery, those sections were separated from the operating tent and
became nearly autonomous. The surgeons often helped in those areas
when not actually engaged in surgery. Although the sections became
separate, it remained a team effort.

The operating tent contained three operating tables spaced in an
orderly fashion in the center of the tent. The tents did not have tarpaulin floors. Dirt floors worked well in dry weather but were very difficult
in muddy weather. If we stayed in one location for any length of time,
we placed bricks on the floors of the operating tent to keep the floor from
becoming a muddy mess.

The army issued light kits to illuminate the operating tent. These were
necessary for three reasons: first, we had to keep the flaps down to keep
the flies and the mosquitoes and the dust out. Second, we had to regulate the atmosphere in the operating tent; by that I mean that we had to
be focused on the surgery and not distracted by what was going on outside. Third, surgery requires bright lights. The light kits were transported
in footlockers that contained wires, bulbs, and metal lamp shades. The
lights were strung across the ceiling of the tent by attaching them to the
tent poles and centering the bulbs and shades over the operating tables.

The lights, as well as the X-ray machines, the heaters, the office machines, and everything else electric, were, according to the table of organization and equipment, to be powered by one five-kilowatt and one
fifteen-kilowatt generator. We were able to scrounge a thirty-kilowatt
generator to help with the load. The operating tent had top priority on
electricity and lighting. The lights and equipment in the MASH, in contrast to those in other units, had to be operated around the clock. We
needed them in the daytime as well as at night. That meant that the generators had to run constantly. The generators were even more crucial
when we moved. At least one generator had to be unhooked and sent with

the advance party. While it was gone, we had to get by with the amount of electricity the other two could produce.

In weather hovering near zero, the generators were our most important item. But subzero temperatures would cause the oil lines in the generators to become sluggish, and as a result the operating tent lights would dim. We did the best we could. There were times when surgical procedures were begun under the illumination of the light kits, only to have the light kits or the generators fail. The olive drab army issue flashlights came out then, and the nurses and doctors and medics shined them on the patient until the procedure was concluded or the generators came back on.

In the winter months, the 250,000 BTU tent heaters, which had been converted from gas to electric motors, were powered by the generators. They had been very unreliable when powered by gas engines. After they were switched to electric motors, they were coddled like babies—and were nearly as temperamental. When the generators were off and the heaters not working, the temperatures in the tents quickly dropped. Medical personnel put on layers of sweaters and field jackets, and the patients were draped with as many army issue wool blankets as we could find. Light and heat were at a premium throughout the war.

Spotlights are used in modern operating rooms to illuminate the inside of the body after an incision is made. At the 8076th, we rigged our own lights by using a naked light bulb and placing a can around it like a shade so we could direct the light where we wanted it. A nurse or a medic would stand behind us holding the light in his or her hand and would move it as we directed. The light kits were upgraded, but we still did not have enough light. A nurse or a medic would hold a hand-size mirror and reflect the light from the powerful overhead bulb onto the area of surgery as we directed.

Water, nearly as important as electricity, was always a requirement in the operating tent. In addition to the problems of lack of water for personal use, mentioned in chapter 5, the functioning of the hospital required an enormous amount of water. The problem was that water was not available in many of our locations. When we did manage to set up near a town or city that had a water system, the water production had usually been destroyed or contaminated by the war. As a result we had to provide our own water wherever we went. The MASH therefore had a water truck assigned to it as part of the organic equipment. It was kept

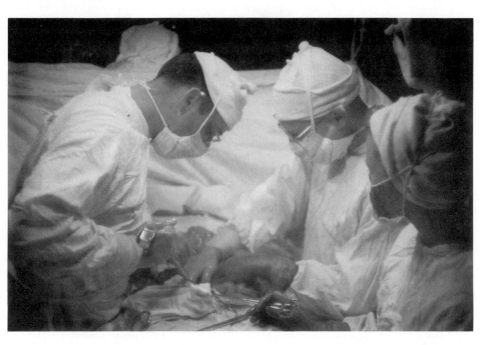

Dr. Apel in surgery. Note the upper right of the photograph. A medic is holding a mirror to direct the light on the surgical area.

in the motor pool and driven by our enlisted personnel. They had a simple but very important mission: keep the operating tent fully supplied with water. Our water truck made runs constantly to the nearest army water point—usually we received this kind of support from the closest combat division—to fill up and return with the water. The enlisted personnel emptied the water into field bladders or other equipment and returned to the combat division water point to get more. If the water point was not available, the drivers had to make the long haul to the nearest corps or field army water point. A plentiful water supply was absolutely mandatory.

The water was used not only for drinking and cleaning, but also for scrubbing in the operating tent. We had field ranges to boil the water for a variety of uses. We needed warm water to scrub before every procedure, and boiling water was used to sterilize instruments. After surgery we often needed the same instruments for use on the next surgery, so they had to be cleaned quickly and returned to the operating tent. We also needed a constant supply of clean bandages, cloths, sheets, and blankets for use during surgery. Even after the 8076th acquired three additional field ranges to help with the load, all the ranges burned constantly to support the operating tent. Additional ranges or other methods of heat were used for the water needed for the mess hall, the shower tent, and the laundry. Others had to worry about that water.

The hours in the operating room were irregular. Our workday would begin when the injuries came and would end when they slacked off. With only three or four surgeons, we were in the operating tent a good deal of our waking hours—and many of our nonwaking hours. The advantage of having so few surgeons (if there was any advantage) was that we could work together informally to cover the operating tent at all times. It was very much like a sports team in which each surgeon had an assignment and could substitute for the others when needed. If someone needed to step out for any reason or was involved with a complex surgical procedure, the others could fill in and carry the load. The better we knew each other, like any team, the better we worked together.

We generally had some notice through the intelligence channels of major offensives or of spontaneous and unexpected firefights. The Chinese routinely attacked at night as if it were a psychological ploy. Each night would involve some degree of fighting. Division intelligence estimates of the number of wounded produced in the offensives, both ours and the Chinese, were very accurate, often missing the actual number by no more than a few percent. Thus we were able to accurately forecast and procure surgical supplies and to plan for patient care in the operating tent.

After the patient was processed through the registrar and admitted to the MASH, he waited in the pre-op ward for an open operating table. The patient was still on the original litter that carried him into the MASH. He would stay on that litter until he reached his final destination. In the operating tent, the "tables" were in fact contraptions rigged to hold the litter. When MASH 8076 arrived in the country at Miryang, Korea, it had not packed its issued operating tables. Sawhorses were scrounged and placed together to make the tables. The patient had to stay on the litter. As time went by, the advantages of remaining on the litter became evident. We had rigged a rack made of metal tubing, contoured to the litter, so that the patient and the litter could be brought into the operating tent and set into the rack for surgery. The metal racks could be adjusted in

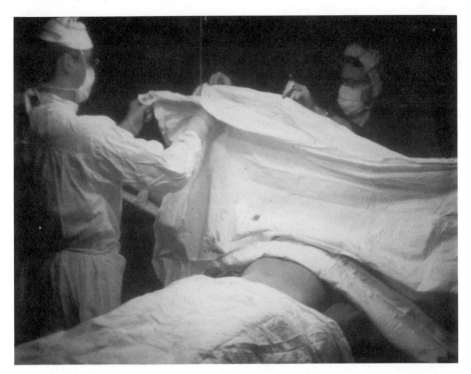

Folding sheets in preparation for surgery in the operating tent of MASH 8076.

two ways: first, to the height of the surgeon to relieve the strain on his back, and second, to turn the patient so the surgeon had easier access to certain parts of the body. MASH 8063 concocted a very similar rack made of footlockers and adjustable in height to suit the surgeon. This operating table innovation avoided the trauma of moving the patient from bed to bed and the effort of changing blood racks; as a result the patient was more comfortable and less traumatized. It also made the surgeon a bit more comfortable.

The treatment of blood-loss shock reached a high level of sophistication in the MASH during the Korean War. Shock is caused by a number of factors, but the type of shock seen most often in combat results from the loss of large amounts of blood. Throughout the history of warfare, medics have tried to treat shock in a variety of ways. In World War II blood-loss shock was treated in three ways: first, morphine sulphate was given to reduce the tension in the patient; second, blood transfusions (plasma and whole blood) were given to replace the lost blood; and third, blood pressure levels were watched closely to prevent the patient from lapsing into shock. In Korea we faced two major problems concerning blood: obtaining an adequate supply of blood to treat the patients and transfusing the blood in a timely fashion.

Korea facilitated two improvements in the treatment of blood-loss shock: the use of type O blood and the use of plasma. These advances were not discovered in Korea—in fact they were widely used in World War II—but the MASH provided the opportunity to perfect the procedures and accomplish the advances. The use of plasma was developed in the 1930s by Russian doctors in experiments on animals. Heralded as a great breakthrough in the treatment of shock, the use of plasma at the beginning of World War II was widespread. Plasma is easy to store, has a long shelf life, does not require typing as blood does, and can be transported easily. The life of a pint of blood was about twenty-one days if properly refrigerated. If the blood began to get stale, as it did after a couple of weeks, the plasma was used instead of whole blood. Plasma was a lifesaver. It could be used in large quantities to raise the blood volume of the patient and stabilize the heart rate and blood pressure. There were drawbacks, however, that quickly became apparent. Because plasma lacks the red blood cells, it also lacks the curative powers of whole blood. By 1943 the army began to use type O blood (universal donor) in connection with plasma for initial treatment of severe wounds. In Korea the advances of World War II were polished and perfected to a new level of proficiency. Following the work done in World War II, plasma was used in the initial treatment to raise blood volume and stabilize the patient. Whole blood was then used for further treatment.

In the pre-op ward of the MASH, nurses and doctors watched the patients closely as they waited for surgery. Nearly all of the patients had been wounded seriously and had lost large quantities of blood. For the most part, the bleeding had been temporarily stopped before they were transported to the MASH, but most of them were in need of some blood when they arrived. The young man from Ohio, mentioned earlier, had a transfusion bottle hooked to him when he arrived at the MASH and was in immediate need of additional blood. We had to have blood in the pre-op ward and the operating tent ready for those patients when they arrived. That presented significant problems for the Medical Corps.

Blood distribution was a major effort in Korea. The elaborate scheme used and perfected by the army in World War II had been dismantled, and in 1950 the distribution system was nonexistent. Because of the mobility of the war in the first year and a half, blood centers had to move with the tactical units. Blood was distributed from a central location, usually the Eighth Army surgeon's office, and sent to locations near the front lines. We would forecast the need for blood, based on intelligence reports, just as the tactical units would forecast the need for ammunition. It was our ammunition in the MASH. In advance of an offensive, it would be shipped to us and kept in the refrigerator.

Much of the blood was given during blood drives in the United States and shipped to Korea. At the outset of the war, the Office of the Surgeon, Far East Command, forecast the demand for blood at approximately one pint per soldier per injury. The forecast also envisioned no requirement for whole blood from the United States. Sufficient amounts of whole blood, according to the Far East Command, could be obtained from military and civilian dependents stationed in Asia. The forecast need for blood was revised upward during the war and came to nearly three and a half pints per soldier per injury. The need for blood from the United States became immediately apparent. By July 1950, when the fighting was heavy around the Pusan Perimeter, the demand for whole blood was critical, and the Red Cross and the American people responded gallantly. Although blood collection programs used in World War II had lapsed, the Red Cross resurrected them in 1950. Whole blood began reaching the MASH units and the field hospitals in August.

As the war dragged on, the success of blood drives in the United States roller coastered. Donations rose with the reports of fighting in Korea and dropped when the publicity of the war trailed off. In 1951 Generals Ridgway, Marshall, and Bradley led a crusade in which the army begged the American people to give blood for the soldiers at the front. The Red Cross set a rather modest goal of three million pints and hoped for much more. That required less than 2 percent of Americans to give a pint of blood each for the war effort. Even with the high-powered campaign, the goal was barely met. Yet, 1951 ended with high donations after a long autumn of battles, beginning around the Punch Bowl. In 1952 donations fell off with disillusionment about the war but picked up during periods of heavy fighting.

At the beginning of the war, one shipment of blood came from a rather unexpected source. After the defeats that backed the United States up to the port of Pusan, the U.S. and ROK soldiers needed blood. The occupation army in Japan appealed to the Japanese people to give blood for Americans fighting in Korea. Long lines of Japanese stood outside the blood bank in Tokyo for the Americans (the occupying army). The blood was flown from the U.S. Medical Laboratory in Tokyo to the blood bank in Korea and helicoptered to the MASH units. An interesting quirk arose at this point. Japanese blood contains less of the Rh-negative factor than the blood of people of European origin. Therefore, Japanese blood could not be used to treat Americans. Japanese blood was used only for Koreans or other Asians. But it did allow doctors and nurses to use other blood for Americans and thus maintain adequate levels of blood in the medical facilities.

Some parts of the body can survive for short periods with the loss of a significant amount of blood. The problem for us involved transfusing sufficient quantities of blood. That meant that we had to maintain a sufficient level on hand and that it had to be given to the patient in a timely fashion. One of the problems with maintaining sufficient levels in the available blood supply was the blood typing. Using the wrong type of blood in a patient can cause disastrous results. In the rear areas, it could be typed and prepared for use and stored in the refrigerator.

The patients who came to us could not wait for us to type their blood—nor did we have the time or the facilities to do it. Many patients were UN troops without dog tags or blood typing. The answer came in the use of type O blood, which will not cause a reaction and can be used regardless of blood type. The MASH received only type O blood from the distribution centers. The other types of blood generally went to the rear area hospitals. With only type O blood, we could use the supply without delay for typing and without worrying about the patient's reaction to the wrong blood type. That made the delivery of blood to the patient much quicker. Both the use of type O blood and the use of plasma solved the problem of maintaining the supply of usable blood for transfusion.

The second problem was getting the blood or plasma into the patients in a timely fashion. The answer came with some experimentation and improvisation. Blood was transported in glass bottles that were hung on metal racks; by force of gravity, the blood dripped through a tube and an intravenous needle into the patient's vein. The transfusion could take up to twenty minutes for one pint of blood. The young man from Ohio was bleeding profusely and needed blood and plasma as quickly as he could get it. At the normal rate of one pint per twenty minutes, he would bleed several pints in the time it took to give him one pint.

At Walter Reed in Washington, Gen. Sam Seeley, chief of surgery, had an idea that blood could be packaged in soft containers and pumped during the transfusion. This idea was one he had mulled over for years. The time for the test came after Pusan and Inchon and the United Nations counteroffensive and the Chinese intervention. Blood was shipped to Korea in plastic bottles, with the idea that it still could be hung from a rack and gravity-fed into the vein. Alternatively, it could be held between a nurse's palms and forced into the veins. This technique was tried in the MASH. A pre-op or an OR nurse could force-feed a pint of blood—which normally took twenty minutes to drip by gravity—into a soldier's vein in five or six minutes.

The use of the plastic bottle in this manner changed the configuration of the operating team. To use blood this way required an additional person at the operating table to monitor the pulse and the blood pressure of the patient, to determine the proper amount of blood to be given, and to administer oxygen when required. The rejuvenating effect of force-fed blood was remarkable. After the successful test in the MASH, the plastic bottles were sent to battalion aid stations and given to medics in the field for immediate use on the wounded. This concept is still in use today in emergency medicine.

In an emergency operation in a modern hospital today, blood is generally available when needed. Six or eight units (pints) of blood are often used in serious operations. To go beyond ten or twelve units is considered perilous. The young man from Ohio was losing blood faster than we could get it into him. During our work on this young man, we used fifty-eight units of blood.

On those occasions when the helicopters brought the wounded from a major battle, the additional demand for blood depleted our supply and required us to divert helicopters from the evacuation mission to the supply mission. The helicopters scurried back to the blood distribution point for blood and plasma and ferried it to the MASH until the demand was met. Once again, the helicopter became the lifeline between the Medical Corps and the wounded soldier.

The nurses notified us in the operating tent that the young man from Ohio was near death and that they were ready to bring him in. We finished as quickly as possible with the patient in front of us and shouted, "Litter!" which was the signal to bring the next patient. Two medics carried his litter into the tent while a nurse carried the blood rack. As long as I live, I will never forget what he looked like. He was covered with a white sheet that was splotched with blood. His arms were extended away from his sides on splints, crucifix-like, so that the intravenous needles would stay in. His face was covered, as we often did to keep the lights out of the patient's eyes. He was unconscious. When we removed the sheet to examine the wounds, he had bandages over much of his body. He was immobile and helpless and pitiful. I remember a sick feeling coming over me: this guy was not going to make it.

We examined him and found a variety of wounds. It appeared that a land mine or an artillery round had exploded near him and sprayed him with shrapnel. He had penetrations all over his body. The most serious wounds, from the standpoint of loss of blood, were the arterial wounds beneath the right arm and in his upper thigh. These wounds had to be addressed immediately for they had brought him as near to death as he could possibly get. The most difficult wounds from the standpoint of time consumption were the abdominal wounds.

As we examined this young man, we quickly formulated a plan. Two doctors, John Coleman and I, would begin the work on him. We would find and repair the damaged arteries. Two more, Waldo Schwing and a nonsurgeon doctor, would repair the abdominal damage. Then John and I would come back and repair the wounds to the thigh, the scrotum, and the penis. In the meantime, the doctors not working on this patient would continue with surgery on other patients as they came.

During our first tour on this young man, John and I opened and examined the arterial wounds in the shoulder and the thigh. They were bleeding profusely, so we packed them off and prepared them for vein grafting. This took several hours of operating time and many units of blood. As we operated, we continually called for more blood.

Waldo Schwing and another doctor then stepped in and worked on the internal injuries. They discovered severe lacerations to his liver, spleen, and pancreas. His stomach had been perforated, and the entire thoracic area, including organs, had to be cleaned and sutured closed. This took several more hours. When they were done, John and I came back and worked on the wounds in the groin area.

During the whole time, the young man lay motionless, spread-eagle on the litter. Several times I thought we had lost him. We constantly pumped blood into him. Several times we barely detected a pulse. His skin turned white from the loss of blood. There were times when we were ready to give up on him, but he kept on fighting. He gave no indication of giving up, so we were not about to give up either.

When we were finished, we were exhausted, as I am sure he was. We shouted "litter!" and one set of medics brought the next surgical procedure while another set of medics took the young man to the post-op ward where the nurses would watch him very closely. It was the closest thing we had to an intensive care unit. We ordered something new for him: substantial doses of antibiotics. This young man's body had undergone an extraordinary degree of trauma. First, the extent of the wounds themselves traumatized him. Then the hours of surgery and the entrance into his body to repair the wounds shocked every living mechanism in his young frame. He was highly susceptible to infection. Frankly, infection was not the chief of our worries with him. We were more concerned about his recovering from the traumatic battle he had just undergone. But in the remote event that he should pull through, we did not want to be defeated by infection.

The MASH provided the laboratory for another major innovation in emergency medicine: the widespread use of antibiotics. Antibiotics were not new to the medical field at that time. Penicillin had been around for a little over two decades and had been first used on a widespread basis in the latter stages of World War II (as evidenced by my experience as an orderly at Sampson Naval Base Hospital in World War II). Other antibiotics had been developed during the World War II period. After World War II, penicillin and streptomycin had been used in civilian hospitals for the treatment and prevention of infection in wounds and other injuries. But other than penicillin and sulfa drugs, which were administered frequently by 1944, antibiotics had not been used on a wide scale anywhere in the world. The major obstacle to greater use of antibiotics was the lack of knowledge of the types and amounts to use. The MASH provided the opportunity to test and experiment with the administration of antibiotics on a large scale.

In the treatment of any wound, the doctor was required to determine the nature and extent of the wound. This determination included a finding of the cleanliness of the wound: the dirtier the wound, the more antibiotics needed. Then it was necessary to determine which antibiotic was needed for this particular wound. Records of the use of antibiotics were kept in the MASH and the other field hospitals and sent with the patient to the evacuation hospitals in Japan and the United States. Studies were done on the effect of the antibiotics in varying dosages. Guidelines for the administration of types and amounts were developed and sent back to Korea for use on later patients. By the end of the Korean War, amounts and types of antibiotics for use in a variety of wounds and infections were established for routine use.

We administered large amounts of antibiotics to this young man and to many others like him. Their treatment of and prevention of infection in his wounds and the surgical procedures gave him a much better chance to survive the gross trauma to his body. This use of antibiotics advanced the field of emergency medical treatment tremendously; the benefits were bestowed on our patients and are still benefiting people entering hospitals around the world today.

Early the next morning, I went to the post-op ward to check on the young man from Ohio. He looked like a different person. His skin was pink. He no longer appeared to be on the edge of death. His vital signs were good and, most importantly, he had a pulse in each of his extremities. That meant that our arterial repair had worked. The blood was once again flowing through the arteries that had been compromised the day before.

In the post-op ward another of the major improvements in emergency medical care took place. I do not know exactly how it came about. I suspect that the mobility of the MASH made it a necessity, but I do not know that for sure. The post-op ward was always crowded and was always susceptible to being relocated as the tactical situation dictated. There were not enough cots, nothing to do during the day, no day room with tables for ping-pong or pool or cards, no coke machine in the hallway or swimming pool outside. There were no televisions or magazines or books or comics to read, as you find today in hospitals or in the waiting areas of doctors' offices. This was a combat hospital without any of the luxuries. As a result of all those circumstances, the patients tended to get up and move around the post-op tent, stick their heads outside when they could, and walk up and down the aisles between the cots. The post-op ward was a big tent with two hundred cots in it and often well over two hundred patients. No private rooms, no double suites: everyone was under one tent. If a patient in one end of the tent snored, everyone, all two hundred plus patients, heard him. This was about as basic as you could get.

We noticed that in the midst of these conditions, patients tended to mend relatively quickly. Initially, we thought there could be several reasons for that. Our primary thought was that most of the patients were young males who were in fairly good physical condition. But that did not hold true for all the nationalities that came to the MASH. As we watched this phenomenon, we began to correspond with doctors in the field hospitals to see whether they had observed the same things. They had. Patients were healing more quickly than we expected.

Our conclusion was that the cause of the rapid healing was what is now called early ambulation. Before the Korean period, patients of this nature would be restricted to bed rest and would not be allowed to move for weeks. During World War II, doctors had observed in the general hospitals in the United States that the soldiers who moved about freely tended to mend more quickly. Doctors also realized that convalescent efforts distracted the patients and made them focus on the future. Soldiers engaged not only in physical therapy but also in educational programs in which they could earn high school degrees. Soldiers were encouraged to socialize, and as one historian points out, the increase of venereal disease in convalescent hospitals during that time suggests that the convalescent efforts allowed the soldiers to regain their strength. The first convalescent ward opened at the general hospital in Battle Creek, Michigan. Others around the country followed suit so that the evacuated patients could begin therapy and start on the road to rehabilitation. But it was not until the Korean era that patients began to move about much earlier, thus increasing the circulation to the wounds and hastening the healing process. This was more than convalescence.

Early ambulation is a concept employed in many kinds of surgery today. Doctors and therapists try to get the patient back on his or her feet as soon as possible after the surgery and increase the chances of a speedy recovery. That situation is unrelated to the recent requirement by insurance companies that patients be discharged from the hospital at the earliest possible date. That is, for the most part, an economic decision and in some cases is a defensible position. Early ambulation is a doctor's decision made with the patient's best interests in mind. The benefits of early ambulation were discovered in the MASH in Korea.

Our young man from Ohio was not on his feet right away. It took him some time to come around. But he was up and he began the early ambulation while in the post-op tent. He stayed with us ten days and was sent back to Tokyo General Hospital for further treatment and recovery. A classmate of mine from Columbia was assigned to Tokyo General, and he wrote some time later that the young man was doing very well and was going home soon to be discharged from the army. It was not lost on us that in earlier wars he would not have made it. Had it not been for the innovations in arterial repair, the treatment of blood-loss shock, the use of antibiotics, and the practice of early ambulation that had come about in the MASH in Korea, he would not have lived through the war. That gave us a great sense of accomplishment.

There were other times, of course, when we felt that sense of accomplishment. Lt. Phyllis Laucks of Wheeling, West Virginia, a twenty-six-year-old nurse who served with the 8076th in 1951, said in the Osaka General Hospital newspaper, "If one measures the amount of work one does compared to the amount of good one does, then being a nurse here is better than in the United States. Every day we can see the thanks and appreciation in the men we care for and every night we can go to sleep with the satisfaction of knowing we have done our best to help." I think she spoke for many of us when she said that.

When criticisms of the Medical Corps were raised in Washington before Congress, politicians often took our side in the public relations fight. Regardless of whether they were sincere or whether they were seeking to gain political favor with their constituents, we appreciated them. Assistant Secretary of Defense Melvin A. Casberg said publicly, "If I had a choice of being shot down and critically injured on 16th Street in Washington, D.C. or in the main line of resistance in Korea, I would have chosen the main line of resistance in Korea. Such professional care we have never had before. We have had top-notch men on patient evacuation with helicopters." I assume he was engaging in hyperbole. No one, given a choice, would choose to be critically injured on the main line of resistance in Korea. But we thanked him for standing up for us.

Other thanks came our way. I enjoyed going to the post-op ward and talking to the soldiers we had operated on. We were there to help them, and it gave me a great sense of accomplishment to talk and joke with and encourage a soldier who had been near death only hours before. I had worked on a young infantry lieutenant from South Carolina. A well-spoken and congenial officer, he had been seriously wounded and had spent several days with us before he was evacuated to Japan and eventually back to the United States. While I was still in Korea, I received a letter post-marked in South Carolina. It put things in perspective. In an elegant script it said:

My Dear Captain Apel,

My husband, Lt. [name given], has written me about his recent injury—about your being so very nice to him, also the nurses. It means a lot to me to know that he had such excellent care. He wrote in detail about the time you spent with him, etc. May I say, "Thank You" with all my heart. It is a wonderful job you are doing & I am sure you will be blessed for it—It seems a terrible sacrifice to make—giving up homes, families, to go to such a forsaken place—but feel that it is a job that just has to be done—we at home who have loved ones so far away appreciate & honor all that you all are doing. This is a simple note—words are not at my command to express my deep feeling of appreciation for your kind-ness to my husband. I work for an Army doctor, reserve, (secretary) so I know a little about doctors.

Thanks again.

[Signed]

I have kept that letter over the years. Perhaps it was a sacrifice, but letters like that one and the opportunity to serve with and help young men like her husband made it worthwhile. They create a bond that has lasted for me over the past five decades.

I also gained a great deal of satisfaction in working with men like John Coleman and Albert Starr and Waldo Schwing and Bob Meyers and the many other doctors who came to the 8076th. I have often thought that every professional needs to go through a basic training in his pro-fession. Soldiers take basic training to learn how to fight as a unit. Pro-fessional athletes take basic training in the college ranks or in the minor leagues. As surgeons, we took our basic training in the MASH in Korea. And just as soldiers do when they go through basic training in the mili-tary, we learned the fundamentals through experience and formed bonds with our fellow workers that have lasted a lifetime. I think back on the operating tent, that musty, olive drab tarpaulin with three makeshift tables in it, and I think of the people and the experiences. In my files I still have an old clip from the newspaper published by the Osaka Gen-

eral Hospital. It is yellow and cracked and tearing where the folds have
been. It's an article about the MASH, saying in part: "Captain Albert Starr
of Brooklyn, New York, who served with 8076th said, 'Patients get no
better treatment in the States than we give them here. Our hospital might
not look as nice as those in the States but every patient we receive, no
matter what his nationality gets the same treatment and care. That in-
cludes the Red PW's that we take care of.'"

In the nearly five decades since that time, I have been in several hospitals and operating rooms. The operating tent in the 8076th did not look
as nice as even one of them. But when I think back on it, Albert Starr was
right. Every patient we received, regardless of nationality, got the same
treatment and care and got the best we had to offer. I think fondly of
working in that operating tent and of working with the quality of doctors who worked there. That gives me a great sense of satisfaction and
accomplishment.

Shortly before I left Korea, I received another letter from the United
States. This one was postmarked Dayton, Ohio, a hundred miles or so
north of my hometown of Portsmouth. This letter, too, was from a wife—
the wife of the young man from Ohio. She thanked all of us for working
on her husband. The mental images of the battle we had working on that
young man quickly came back. She said he had been discharged from the
army and was doing fine. He was working in his father's tavern and playing softball and enjoying life again.

I passed that letter around the MASH, but by that time most of the
doctors and nurses who had worked on the young man from Ohio were
gone. Several thousand seriously wounded soldiers had come through the
8076th since that time, and no one remembered him but me. I folded the
letter and placed it among my personal belongings, and I smile every time
I think about that young man.

7 "WE'RE GOING TO BE COURT-MARTIALED"

Doctors in nearly all the states today are required to take a certain number of hours of continuing medical education annually. That is usually done by attending seminars offered in the doctor's field at the university and research centers around the country. In recent years I have regularly attended three that have become my favorites: the International Breast Cancer Conference sponsored by the University of Miami Medical Center and held in various locations in Florida, a second at the Medical College of South Carolina in Charleston, and a third at the American College of Surgeons meetings held around the country. In 1994 I attended an excellent seminar on surgery at the University of South Carolina. Charleston is a delightful city, and the seminar takes advantage of the beauty and gentility of this southern metropolis. I went in the spring when the flowers and the trees were in full blossom and the southern weather was balmy. I had attended this seminar for several years and had come to know some of the sponsors and the other surgeons. I always enjoyed the presentations and the social gatherings sponsored by the Medical Center. The seminar provided an opportunity for surgeons from around the country to get together and compare notes and discuss problems in the practice of surgery.

At the seminar, Dr. Jacob Robison, a faculty member at the Medical College of South Carolina and an army reserve medical officer, gave a presentation on vascular surgery in the U.S. Army. I had a passing interest in this topic since I had done a good deal of arterial surgery in Korea and had learned that particular facet of my trade in MASH 8076. Over the years, my practice has gone in the direction of cancer research, and I no longer do arterial surgery, nor had I followed closely the development of arterial repair since leaving Korea. It was with some interest and, frankly, a bit of nostalgia that I listened with great expectation to this presentation. I associated arterial repair with the 8076th.

Dr. Robison delivered a very professional and very informative lecture. But my attention soared when he spoke of the history of arterial repair. I was pleased to hear him say, "The Korean War is best known medically for advances in arterial repair. Revolutionary advances in arterial repair were made by doctors in the Army Medical Corps, procedures that broke through the century-old stalemate in arterial injuries and are being used today."

That brought back memories of the 8076th.

With the confidence of a military officer in a briefing, he stated, "Only a total of approximately 200 arterial repair procedures were done in Korea. Arterial repair was an advance of the Korean War pioneered stateside at Walter Reed."

That caught my attention, and I approached him at the break after the presentation and told him that I had served with MASH 8076 and that we had done numerous arterial repairs at Chunchon and Hwachon and elsewhere in the summer of 1951 and throughout 1952.

He told me of his work and discussions with Gen. Carl Hughes, one of the pioneers of arterial repair. General Hughes, then Lieutenant Colonel Hughes, and air force Maj. Edward Jahnke were assigned to Walter Reed Army Hospital in Washington, D.C., during the Korean War and did much work there in the field of arterial repair. Their work relied to a large extent on arterial repair done in the MASH units.

"I wrote a paper on the work we did," I told him.

"Where was it published?" he asked.

"It was a pilot paper," I said. "My professor at Saint Luke's recommended that I send it to the Journal of the American Medical Association."

"Did they publish it?" he asked.

"I didn't send it," I said. After I left active duty, I put it aside and did not look at it again for years.

"If you want me to send any of your material to General Hughes, I would be happy to do that. I am sure that he would be interested in looking at what you have."

"There were several others who did arterial repair," I said.

"I'm sure General Hughes would appreciate hearing from them also," the colonel said.

I thanked him for his time, and when I returned home, I dug out the old paper I had written on arterial repair. The typed pages had cracked and turned yellow. The penciled remarks of Dr. Donald M. Glover, the chief of surgery at Saint Luke's Hospital in Cleveland, had faded but were legible. A letter from Dr. Welsh, commander of the U.S. Army Hospital at Fort Monroe, Virginia, and my commanding officer when I returned from Korea, was still attached to it. I sent a copy to Dr. Robison at the Medical College of South Carolina and several weeks later received a nice letter from him, thanking me and informing me that he had sent the paper to General Hughes. I later received a letter from a professor of surgery at the Uniformed Services University of the Health Sciences in Bethesda, Maryland. He said he would review the material with General Hughes and write again. The paper, and the information contained in it, had been buried in my files for over forty years. (The paper is reproduced at the end of this chapter.)

In the late summer of 1951, near Chunchon, Korea, Maj. John Coleman, the chief surgeon of MASH 8076, sat next to me in a field chair. He had just come from the mess tent, and he held a cup of coffee in his hand. I sat outside our sleeping tent and looked out into the mountains. It was a brief time during the day when we could stop and rest. The sun was high and hot. John and I had worked together since my arrival, and I had come to respect his abilities and his knowledge of surgery. He was not much older than I and had come from a residency at the University of Louisville. We sat for a moment in silence.

"Ottie," John said. "Have you ever seen a vein graft?"

We were still looking out at the mountains. "No," I answered.

"Ever read about one?" he said.

"I read several papers in Cleveland on vein grafting."

He thought for a moment. "We're seeing a lot of soldiers with extreme trauma to their arteries."

I nodded. I knew where he was going. "A lot of severely damaged arteries in the extremities, the arms and legs."

"I think we can repair those with vein grafts," he said. It had the air of conspiracy about it.

"I'm willing to try," I said.

"I've done a couple here," he said. "On North Korean prisoners."

"Here?" I was surprised. The army manual for surgical procedures was a remake of the surgical manual used in the European theater of operations in World War II. It did not include arterial repair. I had never seen a copy of the surgical manual or any other army regulation that said in writing that arterial repair was prohibited, but I was told stateside and in the hospitals in Japan that army doctors were not permitted to do arterial repair. The term *arterial repair,* as used in the army at that time, included vein grafting and was a general term applied to any surgical treatment of severely injured blood vessels. Today the field is called vascular surgery.

"We can do it," he said softly.

"You've done some here?" I asked again.

He nodded. "I've had to do them by myself. No one else knows anything about them."

"You ever do one before you got here?" I said.

"No," he said. "But I read about them in my residency."

"At Kentucky? Did they do any there?"

"No," he said. "It's not every day that you have someone come into a university hospital with wounds from artillery or machine guns."

We laughed. We both knew the problem with vascular surgery. It was brand new in the civilian hospitals, and the army did not allow it. The work in the civilian hospitals was very tentative. Vein grafting had been done, but the pioneers in the field were not very sure about the technique. The art of vascular surgery was in the developmental stage. The army shied away from those kinds of things because the army hospitals (like most civilian hospitals) were not equipped to do experimental work and research as the university hospitals were. Army general surgeons, the few that there were in the years before the Korean War, generally had other things to do (like their civilian counterparts) and did not always keep up with experimental work. At the time John Coleman and I talked outside our tent in Chunchon, the techniques for vein grafting and other arterial repair were virtually unknown in the military medical community outside the work done at Walter Reed Army Hospital.

At the outbreak of the war, Walter Reed was designated by the army surgeon general as the vascular surgery center. Soldiers with severe vascular wounds were evacuated to Walter Reed for observation and treatment. In 1951 these efforts were in their infant stage at Walter Reed. The Walter Reed Surgical Department appointed a Surgical Research Team to study advanced methods in arterial repair. Lieutenant Colonel Hughes and Maj. Edward J. Jahnke, of whom Dr. Robison had spoken, were members of the research team.

There was a great need for arterial repair in the Korean War, but very little was being done. The thought of performing a vein graft was challenging and, from a surgeon's perspective, mind-boggling. At the beginning of the Korean War, the standard army method of treating severe arterial injuries was to stop the bleeding by placing a clamp over the end of the damaged artery and suturing the end closed, a procedure called ligation. After ligation, a period of observation determined whether secondary vessels would develop sufficient blood flow to allow the survival of the limb. If this peripheral blood flow did not develop, the army standard procedure called for amputation of the wounded extremity (the arm or the leg). The methods under experimentation in the research hospitals and the methods we used in MASH 8076 were vein grafting (removing a portion of a vein from elsewhere in the patient's body and inserting it into the injured artery) or anastomosis (removing the injured portion of the artery and suturing the artery end to end).

The army had legitimate reasons for its policy on arterial repair. The problem with arterial injuries dates back to the beginning of warfare. Medical textbooks have called vascular surgery "the most venerable of all surgical specialties for it began with man's first attempts to staunch hemorrhage." The primary problem with arterial repair was the threat of gangrene. The limb had to be amputated before gaseous gangrene set in or the patient risked death. In a combat environment, the priorities were to avoid gangrene and its complications, stabilize and evacuate the patient, and worry about the patient's life rather than his limb.

The obstacles to arterial repair encountered by doctors in a combat environment were several. First, the delay between injury and surgical treatment diminished the possibility of successful treatment. In World War II the maximum delay that allowed successful treatment of a wound that included minor damage to an artery was six to eight hours. The incidence of amputation went up sharply after that period. Second, the type and size of wounds inflicted by modern weaponry created a greater chance of severe arterial damage than injuries inflicted by weaponry used in wars of earlier centuries. Often, exploration of the arteries would reveal profusely bleeding places where sizable pieces of the artery had been ripped away by shrapnel. Repair in those situations was impossible. Third, statistics show that damage to the arteries in the legs required amputation twice as often as damage to arteries in the arms. That was perhaps because of gravity, but the bleeding was more difficult to stop. Fourth, associated injuries often mask arterial damage. In Korea, patients came to the MASH in shock and with damage so severe that the pulse was barely recognizable in any of the limbs. Doctors were often required to explore for arterial damage based upon such symptoms as nerve damage, fractured bones, or lacerations with expanding hematomas. Doctors faced with massive wounds would often clamp the arteries and then tend to other life-threatening wounds. Fifth, large amounts of hemorrhaging into the surrounding muscle and tissue increased degradation and made it difficult to work on the artery.

All these problems focused immediate attention away from arterial repair and toward the most recognizable wounds. As a result of these problems, the primary treatment of severe arterial damage at the outset of the Korean War had not changed from that used prior to World War I. From the military perspective, the old way of ligation and amputation was still a very reasonable and safe approach.

In the five years after World War II, medical research had challenged that approach when treating patients in the pristine halls of the university hospitals. The primary study on arterial repair was done in 1946 by Dr. Michael DeBakey, who at the time was in the army. DeBakey, later renowned for his work in heart transplant surgery, among other things, studied the results of more than two thousand arterial wounds in World War II. This widely publicized (in surgical circles) study provided the basis for study of the problem in the medical schools and research hospitals in the United States. Other studies from World War II were available to those young medical students and interns who were interested in a problem that had little application to private practice in the United States. A surgeon stateside would rarely see this type of problem. But these studies were among those that both John Coleman and I had read in medical school and in our residencies and recalled when we discussed the matter in Chunchon.

The doctors and nurses in the MASH units took advantage of civilian research in the face of the army's prohibitions against arterial repair and planted the seeds for those coming behind us. It was not that we came up with anything revolutionary on our own. We followed others in the civilian sector who had done the theoretical study on the topic. We had the opportunity to put the theory into practice when the wounded came to us in Korea. What we put into practice, many others could use at Walter Reed and elsewhere to the benefit of the army and the wounded.

There is no doubt today that repair of acute arterial trauma was one of the major medical innovations of the Korean War. In World War II nearly half of the cases of arterial damage in extremities resulted in amputation of the limb. During the three years of the Korean War, doctors reduced the incidence of amputation to 15 percent. The work on improvement in arterial repair was done from both ends of the evacuation chain—from the MASH as well as from Walter Reed. The catalyst came from the MASH units. They were the doctors providing the immediate medical care.

Unbeknownst to John Coleman and me in the summer of 1951, arterial repair was first performed in MASH 8055. Dr. Richard Warren, a civilian doctor in the army surgeon general consultant program, visited MASH 8055 in early 1952 and reported speaking with several surgeons who had attempted vascular surgery during the year 1951. He was quoted in an article by Dr. Hughes as saying, "At one hospital approximately 40 vascular repairs were said to have been attempted of which 11 were considered as successful."

The beginning time in the 8076th is vague because our initial arterial repairs were done on Chinese or North Korean prisoners of war and not recorded. That may sound harsh today, but in Korea a number of procedures, not just arterial repair, were tried first on the North Koreans and the Chinese. In addition, because of the army prohibition, the first arterial repairs done on Americans in MASH 8076 were not noted in the charts.

In the summer of 1951, shortly after my conversation with John Coleman, we received several Chinese who had been wounded in a firefight and coptered into the MASH. John was at the next table; I glanced up and he nodded for me to come over. At that time it was very unusual for two surgeons to double up on a patient. I transferred my patient to another doctor and stepped to John's table. The lights were focused on the upper arm of the soldier on John's table. His bicep area looked like spaghetti.

"Get ready," John said. I did. John used a forceps to explore the upper arm. A chunk of this man's artery in his bicep area was missing.

"We're going into the thigh and take a piece of the vein and we'll attach it right here," John instructed. He had the forceps placed next to the artery in the upper arm.

We occluded both ends of the artery with Penrose drains. In a moment we had opened the soldier's thigh to get a suitable vein. The procedure was called a vein graft and consisted of taking a small portion of a vein from one part of the body and sewing it into an artery to replace the damaged part of the artery. The vein had to be very near the size (in diameter) of the artery so that it could handle approximately the same blood flow. We clamped two places in the vein and removed a section the size we needed for the artery in the upper arm. In performing these procedures, we did not have the variety of clamps used today. The clamps available back then were indelicate and when used on an artery or a vein risked scarring or occlusion, either of which would have frustrated the procedure. John and I improvised with a Penrose drain that was looped around the artery or the vein like a noose and the ends tied with elastic occluding tape where the knot on a noose would be. This "clamp" would be much gentler on the delicate vascular tissue.

The vein segment had to be reversed and sutured to the proximal and distal arterial ends of the graft. When you harvest the vein, you have to make sure that it is inserted properly in the artery. A vein has valves in the inside lining to help with circulation. The valves must be situated to help rather than hinder the flow of blood in the arteries. Failure to insert the vein properly would cause serious complications in blood circulation. The Penrose elastic occluding tapes were removed, distal first and then the proximal, and the "clamps" eased off the artery. With some apprehension, we observed the new section of "artery" to check the patency of the graft.

The first thing that I noticed about removing a piece of the vein and suturing it closed was that the suture was very thick and cumbersome for use on small, sensitive areas. The suture's size was called "double-ought," two zeros like the sizing of shotgun pellets; it was used for suturing thick muscle and flesh. As thread is used in sewing cloth, we used heavy suture for heavy material. But we did not have a fine silk suture for sensitive items. We struggled to get the vein ends sutured to the arterial ends. The second thing I noticed was that the surgical instruments were very cumbersome. Like the sutures, they were big and unwieldy in small spaces. They were made and shaped for heavy, rugged work in places like the abdominal wall and not for maneuverability in the small, delicate places like veins and arteries.

This vein graft took us a great deal of time. It was the first I had ever done and one of the first that John had done. I am not sure how I felt about that procedure immediately after we finished. I had that sense of dread that something would go wrong and threaten the life of the Chinese soldier. The next morning, bright and early, we checked the post-op ward. Our soldier looked fine. We checked his vital signs, and they were good. Then, we came to the most significant test. We looked at his upper arm. There were no signs of infection. More than that, he had a slight pulse in his upper arm. That meant that the vein graft was patent and blood was flowing through the artery. But we were not yet out of the woods. He would stay with us for several days to assure that no reaction closed the graft and stopped the circulation. This soldier responded well, and after a few days we brought him back in, felt for pulses, and examined for skin color and warmth. We found him healthy and closed him up. He was then evacuated through the POW evacuation chain, and we never heard of him again.

We then did a number of vein grafts on North Koreans and ROKs and then on Americans. With the Americans, we would send them to Osaka without noting that a vein graft had been done. We then contacted doctors we knew in Osaka to inform them of the procedure and to ask them to check on the patients. After each vein graft, John and I sat down together for an after-action report. We talked about the injury, about our technique, and about the suture and equipment. What could we do to improve the procedure next time? But there was a deeper problem. We both knew that the procedure we had just performed was not to be performed in the army.

Each time we reassured ourselves. John said, "We are both trained surgeons who have worked in the best civilian institutions in the United States. That counts for something."

We set out the pros and cons of arterial repair as we envisioned it. We discussed our conduct from the ethical standpoint of doctors with a duty to help patients. We thought that our failure to use vein grafting on soldiers who needed it violated the Hippocratic oath that we took when we became doctors. To amputate a limb when it did not pose an immediate threat to the life of the soldier bordered—so our private debate went—on intentional malpractice.

Then we came to the question of what other MASH units were doing. We later learned that both MASH 8055 and MASH 8063 had tried a couple, but we were separated by distance and did not get the chance to compare notes with them. Throughout the MASH units, doctors were experimenting with medical ideas they had brought with them from the teaching institutions and civilian hospitals in the United States. Our fear, right or wrong, was that these were things of which the career army doctors had little knowledge. As in most generalizations, we were wrong. There were many fine doctors who were also career army officers. But it was in this instance that the mistrust between the career soldiers and the reservists was most detrimental. Our attitude toward them was that they were "lifers," that they were more soldiers than doctors and that they knew, in actuality, very little about the advances in medicine. Conversely, I think the prohibition against arterial repair arose partly out of the career officer's distrust of reservists who were drafted into active duty. They tended to see us as inexperienced and unaware of the treasury of military medical wisdom. They saw a group of civilians who knew just enough about military medical care to be dangerous to those entrusted to them.

Shortly after John and I began vein grafting, we ordered a finer suture through our own supply channels.

"Can you get us some four-zero or five-zero," I asked the supply sergeant. Double-ought was the thickest, and the thread became finer as the numbers went higher (one-zero was skipped, two-zero, three-zero, etc). Four-zero and five-zero were fine silk sutures that could be used on sensitive tissue like arteries.

The supply sergeant searched the few books he had and came up with a blank. "We don't list that suture in the army inventory," he said. "I'll see what I can do." He was a good supply sergeant, which means he was a great scrounger. If it was anywhere out there, he could find it.

Finding the instruments would be very difficult. We needed a much smaller size instrument with a curvature that would allow us to use it in close quarters. The army supply system offered nothing like it. Again, our supply sergeant promised to do all he could.

Midsummer to Thanksgiving of 1951 saw some of the heaviest fighting of the war. Arterial wounds were plentiful, and John and I continued to perform arterial repair at each opportunity. Then Waldo Schwing arrived. Waldo was at the same level we were. He had read about arterial repair but had never seen it. He was chomping at the bit to try it.

In the meantime, the arterial repairs that we had done were showing up in the evacuation hospitals and in the general hospitals in Japan.

One afternoon, the MASH commander, Lt. Col. John L. Mothershead, called John and me to his tent. John Mothershead was a career officer who preferred the administrative aspects of medicine. He stayed in his tent and commanded the MASH. He did not interfere with the medical care aspects of the operation. Only rarely did he enter the pre-op, post-op, or operating tents. If he mistrusted the reservists, he did not show it. He expected that we would do our jobs and he would do his. We kept an easy peace that way.

Lieutenant Colonel Mothershead offered us a field chair in his tent and asked casually how things were going. We knew, of course, that this was not a social visit. He hemmed and hawed a bit and then blurted out his concern.

"Have you done any vein grafting or arterial repair here?" he asked us.

We hesitated a moment and then responded that we had been doing that for some time now.

"The Eighth Army surgeon's office sent word down through the chain of command that vein grafting is in violation of army policy," Lieutenant Colonel Mothershead said very officially. "They have stated that you are to cease and desist."

A long silence ensued. It was no use to be upset with Lieutenant Colonel Mothershead. He was just doing his job. We thanked him for passing the word on to us and, the message having been delivered, he excused us.

Very shortly after that, our supply sergeant came to the operating tent and told us that he could not find any four-zero or five-zero suture anywhere in the army inventory. He had gone to every hospital in Korea and had contacted friends in U.S. hospitals in Japan. No one had it. Then he smiled. He was not going to let us down.

"Two of my men are going on R&R in Japan," he said. "Leaving tomorrow. I did find out where they can get that suture from a Japanese medical supply place."

The sergeant did not know the cost, so John and I both pitched in all the cash we had on hand and gave it to the enlisted men who were going. One week later, they returned with the suture we needed.

John, Waldo, and I caucused on the message from the Eighth Army. We had recognized when we began that this could develop into a problem. We again debated our course. Nothing had changed on our end, so we committed to continue on our course and to perform arterial repair whenever the circumstances called for it.

At that time we had an unexpected visitor. In September 1951, during the series of battles for the Punch Bowl, Lieutenant Colonel Mothershead called us to his tent again. This time it was a mandatory gathering of officers. Two civilians, Drs. Charles Mayo and Richard Lovelace of the Mayo Clinic, were spending the afternoon with us, and the colonel wanted all the officers to have an opportunity to speak with them. We moved to the mess hall and sat around the tables drinking coffee and talking medicine. In the distance, the artillery boomed into the Punch Bowl and up Bloody Ridge. The Chinese were firing back, and while we talked several rounds landed nearby. It was close enough for Dr. Mayo to mention it in his autobiography.

We enjoyed the afternoon very much, and the talk eventually turned to arterial repair. Dr. Mayo asked point-blank whether we had found an opportunity to perform the procedure. We hesitated. Dr. Mayo was here on a trip sponsored by the secretary of defense. With a sheepish smile, we confessed. We had had, we said, the opportunity to do several vein grafts. He was excited about it and asked many questions. Finally he said, "Do you have any in here now?"

We did not. But he was persistent. He had the glow of a young boy wanting to see a baseball game. "I would love to see one and to see the procedure done."

It happened that late that afternoon, just before Drs. Mayo and Lovelace were scheduled to leave, a soldier arrived by copter with multiple wounds, including a badly damaged artery in his arm. Both Charles Mayo and Richard Lovelace followed us into the operating tent and watched as we repaired the artery by grafting a vein from the soldier's leg into the artery in his arm.

They wanted to talk about it afterward and ask questions and give advice. We went back to Lieutenant Colonel Mothershead's tent, and they talked to him about it. The colonel was reticent about the whole thing. He smiled at the appropriate times, but he was thinking more of the Eighth Army surgeon's office than he was of the Mayo Clinic. Before they boarded their helicopter that evening, they looked at us with that smile that said, "Good show, men." They encouraged us to keep up the good work and assured us they would talk to our superiors up the chain of command about what good work was being done here. We appreciated this encouragement, but unfortunately, praising us to our superiors on this topic was the last thing we wanted.

During a lull in the fighting, John and I decided to take a day or two off and go to Tokyo for R&R. It was the first time I was out of the MASH since arriving. Dayton Warren flew us to Chunchon, and we caught a hop to Pusan and from there into Tokyo. From the air base we got a taxi to a Japanese hotel. When we got out of the taxi, the first thing we saw was a Japanese boy about twelve who approached us and tried to sell us his sister. That is something you often hear about happening in occupied cities, but the reality of it leaves a bad taste in your mouth. It is like seeing pictures of the poverty and degradation in a city as opposed to being there in person. We politely declined, entered the hotel, and took a room.

In our room we found that the bath was a communal affair at the end of the hallway. We headed down the hallway to take a real shower. In the bathroom each of us took our clothes off and hung them on the door and stepped into single stalls to enjoy our first real shower in months. The doors opened and in walked two Japanese women. They had brought towels for us and were preparing to enter the stall to deliver them. You read much about that these days and may not find it surprising. You can even see it on television in prime time. But in the early 1950s, it created culture shock. We quickly thanked them for their kind hospitality, covered ourselves with the towels, and excused them permanently.

One of the sights on our agenda was the Dai Ichi Building, which housed the U.S. Headquarters for Japan and the Far East Command. It had been MacArthur's headquarters, from which he ruled over Japan after World War II. We had heard a lot about the changing of the guard and the ritual in which the Japanese guards lined the streets and turned their faces away from MacArthur when he came by so that none of them could be accused of plotting assassination. Now MacArthur was gone, but we wanted to see the building anyway. It was close to the place where we really wanted to go and for which we had made the trip: a certain Japanese silver shop near the Dai Ichi Building. In the windows were ornate cups and plates and goblets and eating utensils made from silver and handcrafted to the customers' tastes. Many Americans took advantage of that benefit of postwar Japan. Silver items as well as a variety of other household goods were well made and cheap.

John and I entered the small shop, and a bell attached to the door announced us to the silversmith. The shop was dark but very neatly kept, much like an American shop in New York City. We were greeted by an elderly Japanese silversmith. He spoke just enough English that we could tell him what we wanted. After a few moments, he got the main idea but not the details. John and I tried in vain to explain what we needed. Finally, I saw a piece of scrap paper on his counter, and I took out a pen and drew a figure.

"I need an instrument that looks just like this," I said. And on the scrap of paper I drew the instruments we wanted for arterial repair. I drew them freehand and showed him what size we needed. As I drew, he smiled as people do when they are not sure what you are saying because you speak a different language. He looked closely over my shoulder and nodded his head swiftly and said, "Oh, yes, oh, yes, oh yes," signifying that he understood what I meant. He smiled and bowed slightly and told us to come back in several hours. Later, John and I stopped by the silversmith's shop, paid him with funds from our own pockets, and carried out the surgical instruments we would use in the 8076th for arterial repair. The items he delivered to us were identical to the drawings.

Today, one of the instruments we bought in Japan on that trip sits on my office desk as a keepsake. It is a clamp that I drew on a scrap of paper to show the silversmith. It is slightly smaller than a deck of cards and has two separate pieces of silver of equal size. Two bolts protrude from the bottom piece through the top piece and are held tight by wing nuts. The clamp was spread apart and placed over the end of the damaged artery, and the wing nuts were tightened until the two pieces came together and closed the artery to stop the bleeding. The silver fit snugly on the artery without doing any damage to the tissue. When the repair was done, the clamp was removed and the pulse was reestablished.

I look at the clamp fondly from time to time, there on my desk, and occasionally show it to other doctors who ask about the instruments we used. The army did not have one like it in its inventory, so it had no name or identifying supply number. We just called it the clamp.

John Coleman's rotation date was drawing near. I would be named chief surgeon of MASH 8076. The load for arterial repairs was divided between John and me and Waldo Schwing. Before John left, we received another direction from the Eighth Army surgeon's office concerning arterial repair: cease and desist. Lieutenant Colonel Mothershead called us to his tent and asked us again about the situation. Again, we discussed with him our procedures and our thoughts about both arterial repair and the army prohibitions.

This time the colonel shrugged and said that he trusted our judgment in the matter. We were the surgeons, and we had to make the judgment calls in the operating tent. He had much the same attitude we had, an attitude, right or wrong, that permeated all the MASH units and, if the truth were known, would have been shared by any commander in the field. This direction from our higher headquarters, we thought, was much like a desk commander micromanaging the tactics of his field commanders. We were the ones in the field; let us make the immediate decisions on procedures.

Three things happened after that. First, we continued to perform arterial repairs when the circumstances required them. Second, the other MASH units began to send arterial repairs directly to us. They notified the battalion surgeons in the units they supported to copter the extreme arterial wounds directly to the 8076th. Third, the patients on whom arterial repairs had been performed were going back through the evacuation channels to the field hospitals, the general hospitals, and eventually to Walter Reed in Washington.

Lieutenant Colonel Mothershead, soon to rotate out and be replaced by Lt. Col. Maurice Connolly, received another message from the Eighth Army surgeon's office concerning arterial repair. Two staff officers from the Eighth Army surgeon's office, Drs. John Howard and John Davis, would visit the 8076th in the near future. Shortly afterward the two arrived. They were both young men in the rank of major, and neither was a career officer. Howard and Davis spent the day with us and made it clear that they had been sent to investigate and inspect arterial repair procedures done in the 8076th. We showed them through the MASH from the admissions section to the mess hall and sat and drank coffee with them. They quizzed John and Waldo and me about arterial repair, and we explained the full procedure. We showed them examples and talked to them about followup in the field hospitals. We took them to the post-op ward, where they inspected an arterial repair procedure in a soldier waiting to go back to the evacuation hospital.

Toward the end of the day, they became very serious. They explained to us the army procedure in dealing with severe damage to arteries in the extremities: explore, ligate, and amputate. They were very professional. We thanked them for their time and parted with the amenities that soldiers do. "If you're ever up our way, stop by and say, hello." They wished us good luck. Howard and Davis were excellent doctors. Both left the army and had distinguished careers in medicine, one as a professor at the University of Toledo Medical Center and the other in private practice in the Boston area.

At about that time Lieutenant Colonel Connolly replaced Lieutenant Colonel Mothershead, and in the in-processing briefings, we informed him of all the unusual activities in the MASH, including our ventures into arterial repair. Connolly was an administrative man like Mothershead. He wanted to handle the front office and leave the surgery to the surgeons. But Connolly, a rather humorless man, was also a man who did not like for other people, even those in his chain of command, to meddle in his business. MASH 8076 was under his command, and he would do as he pleased. That was my observation. I do not know if he ever passed that message up to the Eighth Army surgeon's office. But on our end of it, he intended for us to do as our professional judgment dictated.

The war was going hot and heavy in the fall of 1951. The young man from Ohio, and many like him, came through our MASH, and we were becoming fairly proficient in arterial repair. We performed these procedures not only on Americans but also on all the other troops who came in. The ROK MASH began to refer their arterial repair work to us, and we spent some time with the Korean doctors showing them how to do vein grafts. We lost count of how many arterial repairs we did because we often sent the international patients through their own chains of command for evacuation. ROKs went to the ROK MASH; British, Canadians, and ANZACs were evacuated through their own channels; Turks, Ethiopians, and Indians went through theirs; and so forth. POWs stayed in our evacuation channel but were kept separate from the U.S. troops. We were unable to keep track of them after they left our MASH. By the time John Coleman left, the number of arterial repairs done in MASH 8076 was over one hundred.

In the winter of 1951, after John Coleman left, Waldo Schwing and I were doing the arterial repairs. A back-channel message came from the Eighth Army surgeon's office, the source of which was not revealed to us. Lieutenant Colonel Connolly called us in and told us that the higher-ups had had a stomach full of this arterial repair business and we were to shape up. He characterized the communication as threatening. Connolly merely shrugged, as if to say, "There, I told you. Now go on about your business."

The surprise to all of us came shortly after that. Maj. Gen. William E. Shambora, the Far East Command surgeon, arrived from Tokyo unexpectedly—at least unexpected by the surgeons. General Shambora was about as high as you could get in the Medical Corps. He was an imposing man physically, short and square like a bulldog, with a bulldog's scowl on his face. By reputation he was very aggressive, very brusque, very hot-tempered. He was followed by an entourage of aides and assistants, and as he walked, they walked behind him; as he turned, they all seemed to turn in unison behind him. The entourage went directly to Lieutenant Colonel Connolly's tent, and General Shambora entered while the others waited outside. Of course, they were only on the ground for seconds before the whole MASH knew they were there. We were frankly somewhat intimidated.

After General Shambora had been in Lieutenant Colonel Connolly's tent for a while, the word came down to send Apel and Schwing up to the headquarters. Waldo and I reported as ordered. They were standing outside the tent when we got there, Lieutenant Colonel Connolly, Major General Shambora, and a bevy of colonels, lieutenant colonels, and majors. From the look on Lieutenant Colonel Connolly's face, the visit had not gone well. The general was scowling, and Lieutenant Colonel Connolly was looking at the ground and kicking pebbles back and forth between his combat boots. General Shambora had that commander's glare in his eyes that could melt Attila the Hun. He said very little to us. We explained to him our thoughts on arterial repair, led him through the operating tent and the post-op tent, showed him what we had done, and told him in each case why we had done it.

At the end of the brief tour, as we approached the headquarters tent, the general looked at us and said, "Do you understand that what you have just explained to me violates army policy?"

We said that we did. We were dismissed without another word, and we returned to the operating tent. The general talked again at length to Lieutenant Colonel Connolly, and they all left before dusk. Connolly wandered down to the operating tent and told us that he did not know what the visit was about.

"Are we going to be court-martialed?" I asked.

He shrugged. "I don't know that either."

Maj. Gen. William E. Shambora (center of photo, facing in the direction of the camera) on his visit to the 8076th. Lt. Col. Maurice Connolly, partially obscured by another officer, has his back to Maj. Gen. Shambora. He has a cigarette in his mouth.

Waldo looked at me and said, "We're going to be court-martialed."

But Lieutenant Colonel Connolly was going to have his say about all this. In the 1951 annual report of MASH 8076, which Connolly wrote, the topic of vascular injuries was addressed under the heading "Outstanding Clinical Experiences, Improvements in Medical Practice and Progress in Fields of Research and Development." The report stated that arterial repair

should be attempted in all instances in which there is at least a possibility of success and where failure to repair the vessel would result in undoubted loss of the extremity. This decision involves mature surgical judgment and is influenced by the time since injury, the amount of concomitant soft tissue damage and the presence of severely comminuted compound fracture in the vicinity of the vessel injury.

The report was sent through the chain of command to the Office of the Surgeon, Eighth Army; the Office of the Surgeon, Far East Command; and on to the Office of the Surgeon General, Washington, D.C. We did not hear anything more from the Eighth Army surgeon's office or from the Far East Command. In 1952, out of the clear blue, the direction came from the Office of the Surgeon, Far East Command, that MASH doctors were free to use whatever arterial repair methods they deemed appropriate under the medical circumstances.

At about the same time, our supply sergeant received notice that four-zero and five-zero sutures (the type required for arterial repair) were now available through supply channels. In addition, medical supply would send the instruments required for arterial repair to each of the MASH units.

The vascular surgery done in our MASH was very successful. From the beginning we recognized that our chances of success were greater in Korea because of the people we were working on. The soldiers were generally young men in fairly good physical condition. In the civilian studies upon which we relied, the patients were older and often not in good physical condition.

I wrote the paper on arterial repair in Korea and at Fort Monroe. I selected fifty patients for discussion in the paper and included in-depth case studies on ten of those fifty. The arterial repair on each was successful. The number of arterial repairs in the 8076th through August 1952 numbered well over two hundred. When I returned to the United States, I sent my paper on arterial repair to Dr. Donald M. Glover, chief of surgery at Saint Luke's Hospital in Cleveland and received a response after I returned to Fort Monroe, Virginia:

The paper is excellent. It is written in good style and tells a worth while story. The material is not entirely new, but its current interest and practical character should make it acceptable for publication. . . . The fact that your experience is more favorable than theirs [some of the studies done in World War II] may be due in considerable part to the earlier time for definitive surgery made possible by better transportation and the position of the MASH hospitals. . . . The way you have set up the paper in the first paragraph it might be acceptable to the A.M.A. Journal or would almost certainly be acceptable to the Ohio State M.J.

When I arrived at Fort Monroe, I had the opportunity to discuss the paper and our work in the 8076th at length with Colonel Welsh, the hospital commander. He was very interested in our experiences from both a professional and a personal standpoint. He made several comments, dated October 24, 1952, on a piece of blue U.S. Government Office memorandum paper: "This is interesting. You are to be congratulated. Suggest publication in the Armed Forces Medical Journal as a preliminary report." Dr. Welsh made some insightful comments concerning followup since some of the patients were still in the army hospitals.

The advances in arterial repair may have happened without the work of the MASH doctors. However, without the environment created by the organization and deployment of the MASH units, this innovation would have been years away. Had any of the circumstances in our MASH not been present, the progress would still have occurred eventually. The circumstances of the Korean War allowed the MASH doctors to act virtually unhindered by the military medical community and to apply the techniques that had been learned, but largely untried, in civilian institutions to a large pool of patients needing that type of treatment.

Lieutenant Colonel Hughes and Major Jahnke came to Korea from Walter Reed in 1952. I remember when they came, but I did not meet them. They were coming to Korea just as I was returning to the United States. The work on arterial repair done in the MASH and at Walter Reed benefited not only the soldiers in Korea but also thousands of people who entered hospitals in the United States and around the world for emergency arterial repair in the next generation. The techniques in arterial repair that were started in the university hospitals after World War II were refined in the MASH units in Korea. Those techniques, rudimentary compared to today's work, have developed into the use of plastic arteries and veins as well as autogenous grafts. The patients of today are the beneficiaries of the advances in arterial repair in the Korean War.

EXCURSUS

This is the paper written by Dr. Otto F. Apel in the fall of 1952, shortly after his return from Korea. It describes arterial repair as performed in MASH 8076.

A TREATMENT OF VASCULAR INJURIES
Otto F. Apel, Captain, MC

The perplexing problem of vascular injuries has been a topic of wide discussion and varied opinions since the beginning of World War II. Within the past 5 or 6 years, attention has been brought to bear on primary repair of injured vessels rather than the commonly practiced ligation. It is the purpose of this paper to present a few of the problems in vascular injuries that we have met at the MASH hospital in Korea during the period from August 17, 1951, to August 1, 1952, and the way in which they were handled. This is a paper directed, in the main, to physicians outside metropolitan areas where surgery is done with what equipment is at hand—much the way the surgery is done in combat zones during wartime. The paper is presented for the purpose of emphasizing the fact that a severed artery does not mean a severed extremity in a good percentage of cases, and that a surgeon with a good grasp of fundamental surgical techniques can handle traumatic vascular injuries and produce heartwarming results.

INDICATIONS FOR SURGERY

At our MASH we adopted a few very obvious indications for surgery when an injured vessel was suspected. A cold, numb, pulseless extremity should always be a candidate for exploratory surgery. An expanding hematoma in close proximity to a large vessel should be explored. If these simple suggestions are adhered to and surgery is done as early as possible following injury, many limbs will be saved that previously would have been sacrificed. The arterial spasm that is seen associated with gunshot wounds closely adjacent to the vessels is a factor to be considered, but the real consideration should be "Is an amputated extremity a good substitute for an exploratory scar on a normal, useful limb?" In our opinion the vascular spasm is a direct result of perivascular injury, and both conditions can be alleviated at the time of exploration. We do not hold with the opinion that conservative management and watchful waiting for an A-V fistula to form is the best possible Rx. The best that can be achieved in this mode of an Rx is an eventual proximal and distal ligation of the aneurysmal or fistulous site and more watchful waiting to see if the collateral circulation established is sufficient to sustain the limb; or an additional major operative procedure of attempted arterial repair or vein graft at a time when healing processes have rendered the site a technical hazard.

TIME INTERVAL

The best possible time for repair of injured vessels is within the first 6 hours following injury. This is our own observation.

If the time interval is more than approximately 8 to 10 hours or the tourniquet has been overlooked in prolonged travel to the hospital, irreversible damage has been done to the tissues of the extremity by anoxia. The Surgical Research Team for Korea has established the evacuation time at 3.6 hours from the time of injury to admission to a MASH hospital. My own cases averaged 4.7 hours: The shortest time was 2 hours and the longest 15 hours.

TECHNIQUE OF REPAIR

Because of limits placed on equipment in a mobile hospital in order to keep the outfit mobile, the ultimate in vascular surgical equipment was not on hand when this series was compiled.

As is fundamental in good surgical technique, an adequate exposure of the injured vessel is essential. The incision should be made along the length of the vessel so that it may be exposed well proximal and distal to the site of injury. The vessel is dissected free proximally and distally so that rubber tapes made from Penrose drains may be placed around the vessel to ensure complete control. This is done *before* the site of injury to the vessel is ever disturbed. In most cases the clot that has formed in the vessel will not be disturbed and good hemostasis is secured. If the clot has been disturbed, manual pressure at the site of injury by an assistant has to be carried out. This is best done by folding a 4 x 4 gauze pack on the end of a sponge forceps, keeping the assistant's hands out of the operative field. The control tapes having been put in place, the injury site may now be inspected. The clot is sucked out of the vessel with a small soft rubber catheter proximally and distally until there is a good free flow of blood from both ends. When this is done, the rubber tapes are pulled taut, securing hemostasis, and the tension on the tapes is maintained by placing a Kelly clamp around them close to the vessel. If there has been a complete transection of the artery, with little loss of substance, so that the ends come together with no tension, a primary end-to-end anastomosis can be carried out. The severed ends of the artery are freshened with a very sharp plastic surgery scissors or a number 11 Bard-Parker knife blade. Then the Carrel type anastomotic suture may be utilized to good advantage because it will facilitate manipulation of the artery with minimal trauma. This is done by placing 3 stay sutures of 5-0 silk arterial suture, at equal distances apart, through both ends of the artery in a way that will cause the knot to be tied on the outside of the artery. These stay sutures are snugged up and tied, making sure that intima opposes intima, and both ends of each suture are left long. Placing a mosquito hemostat on the ends of each of the three sutures makes it possible to manipulate the artery (using the hemostats) so that adequate exposure of the repair site is obtained. A continuous over-and-over stitch is used between the stay sutures, bringing intima to intima, and the needle end of number one stay suture is tied to the free end of number two suture. The same procedure is used between the remaining stay sutures until the entire circumference of the artery has been repaired. When this has been done, the long ends are out and the rubber tapes removed—the distal tape first, then the proximal tape. If there is leakage at the anastomosis site, it can be controlled by an interrupted stitch at the site of leakage.

If the injury to the artery is more than ¼ of the circumference, it is best to divide the artery and reanastomose it as described above. If the perforation is less than ¼ of the circumference of the artery, repair may be accomplished by freshening the edges of the wound and suturing using a continuous interlocking stitch, again making sure that intima approaches intima.

In arterial injuries where there is a loss of substance great enough to produce tension on the anastomotic site, a vein graft should be carried out. The vein best suited to becoming a donor is the greater saphenous. However, the cephalic vein can be used. The section of vein used should be two to three times longer than the length of artery missing, to allow for the contractibility of the elastic tissue in the vein wall. The section of vein is taken after the arterial site is completely prepared to receive it and placed immediately into the site of arterial injury. The ends of the vein graft are reversed. This is done to alleviate the action of the vein valves, if present. The graft is put in place with the same Carrel type suture described above.

When the tapes have been removed and the patency of the vessel lumen assured, the arterial spasm may be reduced by local injection of ½% procaine into the vessel wall. This is done with a #25 hypo needle. Then approximately 50 mg of heparin is injected through the site of repair or vein graft. This would seem to reduce the immediate chances for thrombosis. The operative site is then flushed with warm saline solution. Closure of soft tissues around the artery, especially muscle, is of importance because it is thought that the vein graft or repair site may derive some nutrition from nutrient vessels of the soft tissues. A Penrose drain is placed down to, but not touching, the repair site. Soft tissues are closed with 3-0 chromic catgut and silk to the skin. Immobilization of the part was not done in our cases, because we felt that in the absence of tension at the repair site, limited motion would be of no harm. However, these patients are kept at bed rest for a period of about 1 week with progressive active and passive exercises of the injured limb, if possible, from the first postoperative day.

We believe that the least traumatic type of vessel occlusion possible should be utilized and that the lumen should just be occluded, no more or no less. It is known that crushing of the vessel wall and intimal damage is as conducive to thrombus formation as the site of the repair itself, possibly more so.

POSTOPERATIVE MANAGEMENT

When the patient is first seen in the preoperative section, he is given IV strepto-mycin and penicillin (0.5 g and 500,000 units, respectively) along with the rou-tine shock therapy. Tetanus antitoxin and in some cases gas gangrene routine are started. Postoperatively the patient is started on large doses of antibiotics. Five grams of streptomycin and 600,000 units of penicillin are given every 4 hours.

Sympathetic blocks are used on the cases in which the limb temperature remains decreased below that of the opposite extremity, or when the pulse ini-tially appears strong, then becomes weak. In cases where the pulse does not re-appear at all postoperatively, sympathetic blocks are used almost routinely or as routinely as the tactical situation and patient load permit.

Anticoagulants postoperatively were not used. This was because of the dan-ger of leaking at the repair site and the possibility of hemorrhage from associ-ated wounds.

Papaverine has been used postoperatively and appears to be of benefit be-cause of its prolonged dilatory effect. This drug was not used in any of my cases, however.

The drain is removed in 24 to 36 hours. The wound is inspected at that time, again on about the fifth day, and again when the patient is evacuated. Orders are left with the postoperative nurse to take pulses every ½ hour and to observe care-fully for possible hemorrhage. Progressive muscle tone exercises and limited active exercises are started from the first postoperative day, if the type of associ-ated injuries will permit.

In none of my patients have there been gross wound infections or disrup-tion of repair during the postoperative course at the MASH or in those I have been able to follow in Japan. This period is from 8 days to 6 weeks postopera-tively.

ASSOCIATED VEIN INJURIES

In a great majority of traumatic arterial injuries, the veins are also involved. In most of these the best treatment is ligation. However, in some sites vein repair is feasible and in my mind very worthwhile. These sites are where disruption of venous return will cause death or loss of a vital organ or reduce the patient to a vascular cripple for the rest of his life. The veins that in our opinion should be repaired are the vena cava, the common iliac, the renal vein, and the portal vein. Also the axillary vein at a site where collaterals could not take over and prevent a large, swollen, and limitedly useful arm.

The techniques of repair and management are the same as for the arterial injuries, except for the use of local procaine, which is not used in vein repair. Elevation of the part postoperatively enhances drainage. These venous injuries will be mentioned in the presentation of cases.

CASE PRESENTATION

1. E.C.M., USA, W, 20 years
Wounded in action—gunshot wound of left shoulder. The wound of entrance was just inferior to distal ⅓ of clavicle and the wound of exit on posterior chest wall. The path of the missile was through the axilla. The pleural cavity was not entered. There was a large hematoma in the axilla, and the radial pulse could not be palpated. The fingers were cool and pale. There was normal range of motion of the hand and fingers, but they were numb.

The axilla was explored through an anterior elliptical incision extending from midclavicle to the midportion of the biceps muscle. The pectoralis major was split along its fibers and the pectoralis minor was severed near its insertion to the humerus. The large vessels and nerves of the axilla were exposed and the artery and vein controlled above and below the injury with rubber tapes. The clot was evacuated and a perforation approximately 1½ cm in length was seen in the third portion of the axillary vein. There was a very small tear in the artery at the same level. Both were closed as described above. No sympathetic blocks were used. The pulse was bounding immediately postoperatively.

Time of entry to the MASH was approximately 5 hours after injury. Pressure dressing applied on the lines was not disturbed until operation. The patient was discharged at the end of 8 days. Good pulses, the hand remained warm, and normal sensations returned. No further followup has been obtained at this time.

2. E.S.B., USA, W, 22 years
Wounded in action—gunshot wound of right inguinal region. The patient was wounded at 0730 and admitted to the MASH at 1330. On physical the patient had positive signs for intraperitoneal injury. The dorsalis pedis pulsation on the right was diminished but present, and the right foot was cool. During the preparation for exploratory, the inguinal wound began to bleed profusely. An incision was made over the femoral region and extended to the inguinal ligament. The large vessels were exposed. There was a large hole in the vein at the level of the bulb. The bulb was virtually shot away. The femoral artery was in severe spasm

but otherwise uninjured. The common femoral vein was tied above, the saphenous and deep femoral tied below before the bleeding was controlled. The arterial spasm was relieved by ½% procaine injected into the vessel walls.

At the conclusion of the operation, the right foot was warm and of normal color with bounding pulses.

Postoperatively the leg became moderately swollen but the pulses remained good. The swelling has persisted to the last report on followup, which was 4 weeks after the injury. This is not debilitating, however.

3. R.P., USA, W, 21 years
Wounded in action by shell fragment perforating the right shoulder. The patient was admitted 4 hours after injury. The wound of entrance was at anterior border of the deltoid at the level of the tip of the clavicle and the exit in the axilla posteriorly. There were clinical signs of radial and ulnar nerve damage. The pulse in the radial artery was present but weak. The indication for surgical intervention was an expanding hematoma at the time of admission. The axilla was opened through an elliptical incision at the anterior border of the deltoid extending over the pectoral region. The axillary vessels were exposed and dissected free, and a large perforation was found in the axillary vein. This was doubly ligated above and below. The artery was then inspected and a tear approximately 5 mm in length was found on the posterior aspect. This was closed primarily as described above. No severance of nerves was observed. The wrist was placed in a cock-up splint.

Postoperatively—the radial pulse became bounding, the hand warm and pink immediately postoperatively. There was no swelling of the arm or hand after the third postoperative day. The nerve function did not return on discharge but had slightly on followup 3 weeks later. There was no swelling of the arm or hand at that time, but the patient still carried it in a sling.

4. J.K.P., ROK, 21 years
Wounded in action by gunshot perforating the left axilla. On physical examination there was no radial pulse and the hand was cold and numb. The hematoma in the axilla was relatively small. The axilla was opened through the anterior approach and the axillary vessels exposed. There was a perforation of the axillary artery involving approximately ½ the diameter. The artery was transected surgically and the edges freshened. The ends approximated with no tension. A primary anastomosis was then carried out as described above. The wound was drained and closed routinely. The pulses and color returned immediately postoperatively and remained of good volume to discharge 10 days later. The time interval between injury and admission could not be ascertained because of the

condition of the patient and lack of data on admitting emergency tag. On questioning later, the patient thought it was about 5 hours. No further followup.

5. Chinese POW, age unknown
Wounded in action by gunshot perforating neck of left humerus and left chest. Compound comminuted fracture of humerus. On physical exam there were no pulses in left arm or hand, and the hand was cold and motionless. The axilla was approached through anterior incision, and a large tear of the brachial artery was discovered with loss of substance of 3 cm in length. The vein was intact. The artery ends were freshened and a vein graft was taken from the left greater saphenous vein. This was transferred to the arm and put in place as described above. The axilla was drained and closed. Immediately postoperatively there was a weak pulse and the hand became warmer but not as warm as the normal extremity. The first postoperative day the radial pulse disappeared. The patient was treated with stellate ganglion blocks, but the hand again became cold. The patient expired on the second postoperative day from the combined chest and extremity wounds. At postmortem the graft was normal in appearance and the suture lines were intact, but a probe could not be passed through the distal anastomosis because of a thrombus that had formed at that site. The interval between injury and admission was approximately 15 hours.

6. ROK, 20 years
Wounded in action by shell fragment. Penetrating wound of right upper arm. On examination the right arm was pulseless, cold, and numb. He was injured 3 hours before admission.

An incision was made on the medial aspect of the arm between the muscle bundles of the biceps and the triceps muscles. The brachial vessels were exposed and a large tear with 2 cm loss of substance was seen in the brachial artery. The edges were freshened and it was seen that the ends would not come together without undue tension. The cephalic vein was cut down on, but it was found to be too small. The saphenous was then taken and placed in the arterial defect as described above. The wound was drained and closed routinely.

Immediately postoperatively the radial pulse was good. It remained good, and the hand regained its warmth and motion to discharge 10 days later. The patient was using his arm and hand normally on discharge. No blocks or vasodilatory drugs were used in this case.

7. C.J.S., ROK, 24 years
Wounded in action, gunshot wound of right upper arm. The patient was admitted approximately 5 hours after injury. He sustained a perforating wound in the upper third of the right arm producing a compound comminuted fracture of

the upper third of the humerus. On examination there were no pulses at the wrist and the hand was cold and numb. An incision was made between the bellies of the triceps and biceps muscles, medially, and the brachial vessels exposed. There was a large tear in the brachial artery involving ¾ of the diameter of the vessel. The transection was completed and the edges freshened. End-to-end anastomosis was carried out as described above. The brachial vein was also injured, and this was tied off. The radial pulse was good but not as strong as the left postoperatively, and the hand regained its normal color and temperature. Stellate ganglion blocks (2) were given, and the normal strength pulse returned and remained after the second one. The arm was placed in a plaster Velpeau; on discharge 10 days later, the patient was able to move his fingers freely and had normal color and temperature in the fingers. The radial pulse remained good and strong.

8. W.D., USA, W, 22 years

This patient sustained multiple injuries caused by shell fragments. There were neck and tracheal injuries, a penetrating chest wound, a penetrating abdominal wound, and a wound in the upper third of the right thigh. The presentation will be limited to the extremity wound, though two other major operations had to be performed on the patient as well as the vascular exploration.

The right foot was cold and pulseless. A linear incision was made over the femoral region of the thigh and the femoral vessels exposed. A linear tear was discovered on the anterior aspect of the superficial femoral artery approximately 1 cm in length. This was sutured as described above without transection. The pulses came back to normal immediately postoperatively and the foot and leg regained their normal temperature. On the first postoperative day the pulses in the affected limb became somewhat less strong and the foot was slightly cooler than its mate. Paravertebral blocks were done, and the pulses regained their normal strength and remained normal after the second block. This patient was followed in Japan and the limb was perfectly normal at the last report 6 weeks after operation. Time interval from injury to admission was 3 hours.

9. D.N., USA, 23 years

This patient was wounded by direct artillery burst on his aid station. He sustained a penetrating wound of R.L.Q. and was admitted 4 hours after injury. On examination he presented positive signs of intraperitoneal hematoma filling the entire right gutter and pelvis. This was explored over the path of the iliac and a large tear was found in the common iliac vein extending from the bifurcation of the vena cava tangentially down to the bifurcation of the internal and external iliac veins, where the shell fragment was lodged. There was also a 2 cm linear tear in the iliac artery at that place where the fragment was lodged, half in the artery and half in the vein. The vein was clamped proximally at its junction with the vena cava. A ligature could not be placed around the stump without going entirely around the vena cava, so the clamp was left in place. The internal and external iliac veins were ligated distally. The artery was repaired as described above without transection.

The pulses came back strongly immediately postoperatively and remained good. The leg became swollen and remained so. The clamp was removed on the fifth postoperative day without untoward results. On followup in the evacuation hospitals in Korea and Japan, the pulses continued good and the swelling persisted at last report 4 weeks after injury.

10. ROK, Civilian, 35 years
Sustained through-and-through gunshot wound of left shoulder. There was no radial pulse and the hand was cold at time of admission 2 hours after injury. On exploration there was a 2 cm tear in the distal portion of the axillary artery at the junction of the posterior humeral circumflex artery. The injury involved $2/3$ of the circumference of the artery. The artery was transected and end-to-end anastomosis done as described above. The pulses returned, as did the temperature of the hand. On the fourth postoperative day, however, the patient developed typical causalgia symptoms, which persisted to some degree at discharge 2 weeks after injury.

SUMMARY

A discussion of the problems involved in vascular injuries has been presented with emphasis on management and immediate repair. The types of injury have been reviewed and the surgical treatment suggested.

Ten cases have been presented, nine of which have had encouraging results. No amputations had to be carried out. The purpose of the paper is to stimulate interest in immediate surgical repair of major vascular injuries, with a view toward fewer resultant amputations.

8 THE FRIENDS WE LEFT BEHIND

In the spring of 1952, the USO advertised the coming performance of Danny Kaye and his traveling show. Flyers came in the military mail. Armed Forces Radio dotted its daily menu of the new songs and the jazz of the swing bands of the forties with excited utterances of comedy and music from the great Danny Kaye. An air of enthusiasm surrounded the Danny Kaye show. It was like working hard every day knowing that you are going on vacation, and that sense of relief lightens you when you leave work Friday afternoon. The Danny Kaye show gave us a carefree feeling of escape from the tedium of the war.

We loaded in jeeps and deuce-and-a-halfs (two-and-a-half-ton trucks used to carry cargo and troops) and joined what seemed to be half the U.S. Army on the tank trails out of the mountains and down to the IX Corps headquarters area. The MPs directed traffic into large fields, where we parked. We walked to an open field that served as an amphitheater around a hastily built wooden stage. Streams of soldiers poured into the field with that same atmosphere of anticipation, as if we were crowding into a college football stadium on a sunny Saturday afternoon. A sea of soldiers and sailors buzzed together in the bright sun. Units sang their songs while we waited for the show to begin.

When the public address system blared with the voices of the warm-up show, presented by a trio of young women, we could see in the audience hundreds and hundreds of smiling American faces. The green uniforms melted into a solid fairway across the open field, and the music cranked up, and the crowd swayed with the entertainers on the stage in front of us. As we looked about, all were Americans. There were no visible Koreans or Africans or Europeans. Once again, this was an American show. That is not a complaint. I was very happy for a touch of the States. I had been overseas about a year, and I missed the United States; I missed home and I missed American life, songs, music, and language. The Danny Kaye show brought us to a refreshing oasis of Americana; we appreciated it from the bottom of our hearts.

In a strange way, the Danny Kaye show brought my thoughts simultaneously to the war in Korea and to home in the States. Americans have certain body movements and styles of clothing and manners of speech that identify them as Americans. In that huge audience beamed the faces and the language and the music of America. As we yearned for the comfortable environs of the States, we had that troubling sensation of contrasting the familiar images of home with the harsh and obscure culture of Korea. We were fighting thousands of miles from our cities and our streets; and as we basked in the respite of the throbbing music and the familiar vernacular of the American entertainers, we had to reflect on the purpose and direction of the war. Why were we there in a foreign land? And when we thought about that, we had to think about Korea and its people. They were suddenly elevated to something higher than mere shadows in a puppet land that responded instinctively to American economic and military superiority.

Perhaps it was the Danny Kaye show, or perhaps it was the nature of the stabilization of the war that was taking place at the time the show arrived, that caused me to think again about the world beyond the MASH. In early 1952, after I had been in Korea long enough to think about my approaching rotation date, I received two letters from Washington. The first asked that I extend my tour in Korea for four months. The peace talks were beginning, and the army was trying to stabilize transfers. The second letter offered me a regular army commission (I, like most doctors, had a reserve commission). Although flattered by the offer, I refused the regular army commission. The decision on the extension was not easy. The additional four months would make my tour with the 8076th a little over twelve months. I surprised even myself by delaying that decision.

In early 1952 the lines began to stabilize north of the 38th parallel. The fighting was as heavy and as vicious as during the first half of the war; but instead of engaging in broad tactical strokes across the entire peninsula, the adversaries were bogged down in a slugfest that contested mere yards of terrain. In May 1952 the United States moved to the south end of the Iron Triangle in an effort to roust the Chinese out of their impreg-

The Danny Kaye Show. Note Danny Kaye (standing) in the middle of the photograph.

nable staging area. It was one of the bloodiest months of the war when the Chinese and the United Nations troops clashed near Chorwon at the southern entrance of the Triangle and fought the fabled battles on Old Baldy and Pork Chop Hill.

Earlier, in the late summer and the fall of 1951, we had settled at Hwachon. That was the period of our heaviest workload. Fortunately, we did not relocate for the remainder of the year. Although the stabilization did not ease the caseload for us, it reduced the amount of time we spent in relocating the MASH to follow the tactical units. During this period we began to look up from the operating table and see the war in its international perspective. We had soldiers from a number of different countries in our MASH over the year 1951:

Australia	56	Netherlands	52
Belgium	2	New Zealand	11
Britain	337	Philippines	30
Canada	16	Thailand	20
Colombia	213	Turkey	31
Ethiopia	148	ROK	818
France	232	ROK augmentees	898
Greece	12	POW	874

We heard that the Norwegians were planning to send a MASH to Korea as a part of the United Nations effort. There was a great deal of anticipation in the Medical Corps about the arrival of the Norwegian MASH. As far as we could tell, very few Norwegian or other Scandinavian troops were involved in the war. We were eager to see what a Norwegian MASH looked like and welcomed the opportunity to serve with Norwegian doctors and nurses.

Eventually, several Norwegians came to the 8076th to look over our shoulders and learn the operation of a combat MASH. They were a gregarious group, and we enjoyed working with them. They went through our facilities from beginning to end and made notes and drew schemes of tents and operating tables and supply areas. We talked with them and taught them some of the lessons and shortcuts we had learned through hard experience. It was a rewarding time for us to exchange with them ideas and concepts not only on the MASH but also on the practice of medicine.

As it turned out, the Norwegian MASH arrived in Tokyo and deployed there to serve as an adjunct to an American general hospital. After a short service there, the MASH redeployed north of the thirty-eighth parallel and served in the vicinity of MASH 8055. During the heavy fighting in the fall of 1951, the Norwegians helped out tremendously, even though some critics claimed the MASH capacity was too small to make a significant difference.

As we stabilized just north of the 38th parallel, we began to see more of the international troops in their garrison mode rather than as wounded soldiers in our operating tent. Our MASH served all the United Nations troops as well as the North Koreans, the Chinese, and Korean civilians. As the lines stabilized, the rear areas moved forward and were safer for noncombat troops. Rear echelon U.S. troops came to the MASH to deliver supplies and mail as if the MASH were a part of the garrison command. We began to see more senior officers who wanted to look in on a real MASH. During times when the intelligence reports forecast little activity, politicians would inspect the MASH and have their pictures taken with the wounded soldiers. With the hectic pace of the war diminished, rear echelon troops had more time on their hands. These were sure signs that the lines were stabilizing—and that the MASH was becoming a part of the stabilized army.

In this configuration, more foreign troops came to the MASH for one reason or another. None were more delightful than the French troops who came as patients and who came to visit us when the French battalion bivouacked near us. We had a good working relationship with the French. They had a battalion surgeon who stopped by occasionally and spent time in the operating tent with us. They had several officers and NCOs who liked to visit and chat with the nurses and pass the time. They particularly liked Agnes, our Korean friend.

The French also had several female officers assigned to their battalion in the combat zone; they came to the MASH occasionally for business. The French were elegant and, to many Americans, cosmopolitan. The French female officers were reticently pleasant but appeared very plain in their dull green French uniforms. Without makeup and with hair pulled sternly up under their caps, they had a cold, distant countenance. A particular female captain, a special services officer, came to the MASH on business and lingered to visit. She was pleasant and could speak passable English. This captain had a French aura about her, and we enjoyed her company even though she was somewhat remote.

When the French came to visit, they always wanted us to reciprocate. They repeatedly invited us to come to their battalion and visit in their tents and drink their wine and coffee. We were pleased to be invited but always, as graciously as we could, we declined the invitations. Nearly everyone who stopped by invited us to visit their units. We simply did not have the time to go from unit to unit on a social basis. Some we did not want to visit. No one was excited about visiting regimental headquarters in the infantry or armor divisions. But other outfits, corps headquarters and higher, made enticing invitations. We knew, at least most of the doctors knew, that the invitations were often extended to us in hopes that the nurses would come along also.

The French were very insistent that we come to their unit and eventually insinuated that it would somehow offend their social honor if we did not grace them with our presence. So Ed Ziegler, the aviation officer, and I and several others caved in and agreed to go to the French battalion for a cup of coffee. One afternoon when the casualty flow was slow, we jumped in the jeeps and headed out on an adventure to find the French. It was very cold, and the snow was deep and frozen. We slid over the icy roadway to a cantonment area of brown tents much like our own. There was not a soul in sight. If it had not been for the French vehicles in the motor pool, the place could have passed for a ghost town. Eventually, we were greeted by a French sergeant who pointed us to a drab brown tent that looked like all the rest. The flaps were closed tight. He opened the flaps and led us into the tent.

On the inside were several officers seated around small café tables. They greeted us warmly and invited us to join them. The air smelled of warm bread. Bottles of red wine perched on the tables. We sat in wrought iron chairs that matched the tables. The tent was decorated like a Parisian café. Lights were strung across the tent poles, and the ceiling was decorated with red and white material that looked much like a deployed parachute. The tables sported red and white checked table cloths like those used in French cafés. A garçon, white napkin over his forearm, brought a bottle of wine and opened it with great ceremony, and we toasted the French battalion.

Shortly after we arrived, the special services captain greeted us. As the senior French officer present, she was an elegant hostess. Dressed in a short black skirt, black net stockings, black heels, and a white silk blouse, she looked the part of the French hostess. An engaging conversationalist, she sat at the table and drank wine and brightened our afternoon. Later, the chef brought warm bread and cheese, which we ate with great gusto as we drank a superb French wine. It was an excellent afternoon of companionship and esprit, and it never touched on the topic of the war. We felt as if we had spent the afternoon in a Paris café.

When we left the tent and passed out into the Korean winter, we walked like formless phantoms through the brick walls separating our international cultures. Inside was the glowing, movable feast of Paris, outside the harsh topography of Korea, and finally, back at the MASH, the gray tedium of an American combat hospital. The French provided a distinctly international view of this war that we had not seen and could not see in the operating tent. For a brief afternoon, the Parisian hospitality rescued us from the oppression of the war and liberated our spirits.

I am not sure when Agnes came to us or how she got there. She was about five feet five inches tall and very well built. It was a strange situation. Her beauty was such that her reputation flashed throughout the theater of operations, and soon soldiers stopped by for the sole purpose of catching a glimpse of her. She was dark and Korean and seemed to radiate with a cosmopolitan splendor. In her smile lurked the enigma that westerners attribute to the Orient. At first we laughed about the situation and were very tolerant about times and places that people could interrupt the operation of the MASH to visit with Agnes. It was good for morale. Then we joked that we needed MPs to direct traffic near our MASH because of the soldiers stopping to see her. It was all in good fun.

Agnes had not been with us long, but already the men who came to see her were a bit unruly. Perhaps it is an American trait to be possessive about women; I don't know. But the soldiers who came gawked at her. Even the internationals who were more debonair than some of our men could not contain themselves. The British would smile at her and avert their eyes. The French cooed and clucked. The Turks gazed with an eye of inspection. The ROKs beamed with pride and stood near her with an attitude of ownership. The Canadians were like the Americans. They wanted to push close as if proximity meant importance.

We began to have a problem with the men touching her. That may be understandable in a combat zone. Everyone wanted to get close to her and put his hands on her. They were not rough. She had a very inviting pose. Like children in a candy store, the men would gaze and reach out tentatively as if reaching for a glass-enclosed store case of candy. They just wanted to rub her smooth texture. We had to handle the matter somewhat delicately, of course. Too many soldiers rubbing her might cause an incident.

Near Christmas, a loud ruckus erupted on the road outside the MASH. Shouting and cursing drew us from our tents. The night was cold and clear, and the menacing voices of angry men carried in the frigid air and echoed off the mountains. Several deuce-and-a-halfs and a few jeeps were jammed together in the small muddy road, and soldiers were jumping out of the vehicles and spilling into the field between us and the road.

We were not at all surprised that it had come to this. The notoriety about Agnes was surely leading to a confrontation of this nature. Someone in the MASH had the good sense to call the MPs. In a moment, the men in the field began pushing and shoving and shouting, and a general melee broke out. The MPs arrived in their jeeps, riot batons in hand, and waded into the fray. After several wild swings of stick and fist, the action subsided and the MPs took control. The troops were loaded back into the trucks and driven away.

An MP sergeant came over to us and asked for the commander.

"I'm the executive officer," I said.

"You have someone here by the name of Agnes?" he asked. I said that we did.

"That was an armor company and a transportation company. They both came up here to see her. Neither wanted the other to see her while they were here."

"So they fought about it?"

He shrugged. "Who is this Agnes anyway?"

"Just a Korean," I answered.

He looked at me closely. "Mind if I talk to her?"

"Not at all," I said. He whistled to the other MPs congregated near the jeeps on the roadway, and they joined him. We took the MPs into the tent where Agnes stayed, and we had a very nice visit. When they left, the MP sergeant said, "Now, I see what they were fighting about."

Everywhere we went, Agnes went with us. We all felt obliged to take very good care of her; she rode in the convoys in the most comfortable place we could find. Everyone liked her—even the nurses. In every move we made sure that she was the first one on the vehicles and the first one off. As time went by, nothing was too good for Agnes.

Somewhere near Chunchon we picked up a pup that was blond in color and was probably part setter, part retriever, and mostly Korean mutt. He was on the road looking at us with a longing expression that would not allow us to pass him by. We put him in the back of a deuce-and-a-half and adopted him as the MASH mascot. We called him Iddi Hwa, which in Korean means "Come here." Iddi Hwa fit into the MASH very well. He was always welcome in the mess hall and the sleeping tents. We hastily

Iddi Hwa, the
MASH mascot.

checked his gender to see whether he slept with the men or the women.
A male, he often lounged in the men's tents and chewed nearly everything
he could fit between his teeth.

He patrolled the trash cans outside the mess hall and delighted in
getting into the trash before it was dumped. More than one KP shouted
curses at him and ran him out of the trash. When we had time to throw
a football or a softball, he would chase it with unceasing energy. We often wondered what language Iddi Hwa spoke. He was at ease with both
the American troops and the Koreans around the MASH. Choi often fed
him scraps and talked to him in Korean. But there were times when he,
like most pups, acted as if he did not understand any language.

On one occasion we had loaded the trucks and were ready to move
out. Iddi Hwa was still playing in the field, and we called and called, but
he would not come. When we went to get him, he thought it was a game
and ran away and barked playfully. It was time to go, and the truck began to pull out. Still, Iddi Hwa wanted to play in the field. None of us
wanted to leave him behind. Finally, one of the men shouted in exasperation, "Iddi goddam Hwa!" With that, Iddi Hwa ran from the field and
bounded up into the back of the truck and was ready to go.

As I deliberated over staying the extra four months in Korea, I had the opportunity to think about this enigmatic country. I had seen doctors and nurses come and go and, after eight months in the MASH, considered myself one of the old-timers. Strangely, I had a sense of loss, a sense of nostalgia about Korea and the MASH. I wanted very badly to go home, but eight months was not long enough. In the back of my mind was the thought that I had something else to do here. It struck me one night as I left the operating tent and went to my sleeping tent. Choi was there, and he had cleaned the quarters and done the laundry.

"Choi, what are you going to do when all this is over?" I asked. He turned to me with his dark eyes and his dark features. He shrugged and said something in Korean that is the equivalent of "Life goes on."

"Sit down," I said. He sat on the field table, and I sat on the edge of the bed. We had talked a lot together but always on the surface, always as officer to servant, as American to Korean. There was always that gulf between us. In spite of all the United Nations troops and all the ROK troops that had come through the MASH and all the Koreans that helped us on a daily basis in the operation and maintenance of our facilities, in cooking and cleaning and caring for equipment, this war in Korea, in the final analysis, was American owned and operated. The Americans were financing, fighting, and directing the show. This was an American war. We, like many other Americans, were isolated in our own cultures and purposes. The Koreans, in many respects, were merely there, merely shadows behind us as we fought the war and lived the best we could. Choi had been a servant, a houseboy, a help, occasionally a distraction from the tedium of the war, but more often a little brother whom we cared for but would not let on that he meant anything to us.

These things began to weigh on my mind as I thought about an extra four months. Four months was an eternity in that environment, yet I had that lingering feeling that I could do something else. I did not have an altruistic sense of completing unfinished business. This was much larger than me personally or the MASH or the medical profession. This was much larger than the U.S. government. But it was something I had committed to for the time that I was to be there.

For the more fortunate young men of Korea who were not drafted into the army or conscripted as Choggi boys, the American troops provided an excellent asylum from the ravages of war. The younger boys like Choi could serve as houseboys to the Americans and have a supply of food and a roof over their heads. Sometimes they were drafted into the army, and sometimes they slipped away to go to another unit. Choi arrived at the MASH before I got there and had been faithful through this time.

Choi was one of the many Koreans who attached themselves to American units. He became very special to us for his sense of humor, for his loyalty, and for his sincere desire to help others. The Koreans helped each other in that way. Choi, after he was established as a member of the 8076th, began taking other Koreans in and providing them with food and shelter. The first was a teenage orphan, younger than Choi, whom we called Georgie. Georgie followed Choi like a shadow everywhere he went. It came to be two for the price of one. He helped where Choi helped, he provided Choi with company, and he became one of our group. He lived with us just as we lived there with one another.

A very young Korean we called Boy came to our MASH, and Choi took him in. We called him Boy because that is all he was—a small boy about seven years old. No one ever knew where he came from. He just appeared one day, and from that time on Choi made sure he had something to eat and a place to sleep and clothes to wear. Choi mothered him all the time, making sure that he stayed out of trouble and out of the Americans' way. One of the fondest images I have of Korea is Choi pushing Boy on an ice sled on the frozen Hwachon Reservoir like a father pushing his infant in a wagon. Boy was still there when I left.

Choi took care of all the Korean orphans who came to live with us at the 8076th. He would make sure they behaved as properly as they could, that they were clothed, and that they worked. He would bring them to us for physical examinations and for treatment of illness. He acted as the mother, the father, and the scout leader all rolled into one. And he was sixteen at the time. Choi himself had been orphaned early in the war and had been forced to find shelter wherever he could. He knew the meaning of being orphaned and knew that he wanted to do something about it. We considered it our privilege that he would choose the 8076th as his new home.

Many of the Koreans were simply laborers; "Choggi boys" they were called. They were young men reminiscent of the day laborers in the industries of the United States at the turn of the century. They worked when the work was available, and they were paid by the job. Often they were

Choi pushing Boy on an ice sled at the Hwachon Reservoir.

paid in currency or meals or clothing. They were given what we had left over or what we had discarded. Choggi boys did the heavy labor. Korea was rugged, mountainous country, and the roads were often impassable because of the weather or the terrain. Choggi boys carried the heavy equipment on their backs over the mountains. I will have the image always in my mind of the Choggi boys winding up a mountainside, one after another, each with a heavy pack, twisting up the dirt path like a line of ants, each stooped under the weight, staring at the ground beneath them. It was manual labor reminiscent of the slave labor of sixteenth- and seventeenth-century Latin America, human machinery at the disposal of the conquering army.

"How would you like to go to the United States," I asked Choi. I did not have a plan when I asked.

"I would like that, Cop'n" he said. There was no outpouring of great enthusiasm. It was a matter-of-fact statement.

"You could go to American schools, get a good education, go to college. It would not cost very much. I'll be a doctor in the United States soon. I can help with all that."

Choggi boys, carrying loads, standing atop a mountain.

He nodded slowly as the thought of America sank in. "I would like that very much," he said.

"We can work on it. We can talk about it some more."

He hopped up and with his characteristic smile said, "Thanks, Cop'n."

When he left, the decision to stay the four months extra was sealed. As I reflect upon it, it was because of Choi; but to a greater extent, it was a decision personal to me and for me. We had seen much in Korea, and I was concerned about the purposes and the answers. I did not know what I would do with Choi, but I began to plan for him to come to America. I could find a place for him to stay and a school to educate him. As a doctor, I planned on financing that myself. It would be the one little thing that I could do to advance the Korean culture and help the Korean people.

During the time I was there, the ROKs established their own MASH. They sent administrative personnel, doctors, and nurses to the 8076th as well as to other MASH units, to observe the operations of the MASH so they could make their own copy and take some of the load from us. We gladly showed them the things we had learned in both the medical and the administrative sides of the operation and shared with them all our manuals, standard operating procedures, and shortcuts. They were an attentive group, smiling at our comments, but they did not completely understand English and did not have a clue as to our idioms and our inside jokes. They absorbed everything we had to offer and took it, no doubt, with the idea that they would improve on it.

In the spring of 1952, the ROK MASH was taking its share of the workload. Waldo Schwing and I visited the ROK MASH one day to check on their procedures and offer any assistance we could. The day was cold and snowy, and we found the ROK MASH nestled in a valley not too far from us. It looked like an American MASH, olive drab tents everywhere. The wards and operating tent were configured like ours. They were proud to show us a MASH that looked just like the original.

As we chatted with the ROK doctors, we enjoyed their enthusiasm. They were bright and polite, and when we could not communicate in English, a translator stepped in and helped. We drank a cup of thick Korean coffee with them, and they asked if we would eat with them. Having seen the local delicacies such as kimchee (a foul-smelling cabbage-like food loved by Koreans), we decided that we probably should return to our own MASH for meals.

While we talked with the ROK doctors, they asked about arterial repair. Waldo and I made an appointment to return and discuss it with them at greater length. Some time later, Waldo and I spent time with the Korean doctors and showed them what we had done with arterial repair. They picked it up quickly and began to use it as the occasions arose. We checked on them later, and they shared with us their successes and their failures. They were very eager to provide their countrymen with the best medical care possible.

Some years later, a Korean surgeon joined the staff of our hospital in Ohio. A very competent and well-liked man, he was quiet about his experiences and background. I had the opportunity to sit with him in the doctors' lounge one afternoon, and I asked him where he was from in Korea. He told me, and I asked him where he was during the war. He told me he had begun his medical career as an orderly in a Korean hos-

Santa and his reindeer. Note the guitar in his hands. He sang Christmas carols to the MASH.

pital in Chunchon. When I asked him the time frame, he said that he had been there in the summer of 1951. I had to laugh inside because that was the time I was there. He said that he assisted Korean doctors in their work and had met several American doctors. I do not know whether I ever actually ran into him in Korea. But it was fun to speculate that our paths may have crossed nearly a half-century before.

Christmas 1951 was a time when we stopped, took a brief respite from the fighting, and enjoyed the spirit of the season. The mess hall fixed a Christmas meal with all the trimmings, and the nurses decorated the mess hall with a Christmas tree and Christmas lights. The tree was a Korean evergreen that some adventurous group had braved the snow and sub-zero weather to go up on the mountain and chop down and drag into the MASH. The enlisted personnel of a truck battalion down the road decorated a jeep like a float in a Christmas parade by attaching a plywood sleigh to its sides and a white reindeer to its front. The passengers dressed as Santa and the elves and sat in the jeep seats. They played guitars and sang "Jingle Bells" as the jeep circled the MASH. Santa's sleigh visited the surrounding units and made a trip through the local Korean villages serenading and caroling in the spirit of the season.

Christian missionaries had been very active in Korea for many years, so the Koreans were familiar with Christmas and its meaning. Although much of the Korean population professed Buddhism, Christianity spread rapidly through the cities and the countryside. Since the end of the war, Christianity has exploded throughout the peninsula, and Korea now has one of the highest per capita Christian populations in the world. Nowhere was the promise of Christmas more appealing than in the devastation of Korea in 1951.

The Koreans who worked at the MASH joined us for the Christmas meal that year. It was an enjoyable time. We sang Christmas carols and ate turkey, cranberry sauce, dressing, mashed potatoes, and gravy at the mess tables, which had been decorated with evergreen twigs and red bows made from string we had in supply. Christmas, then as now, provided a time to reflect upon the war and life in general. It was my first time away from home on Christmas, and I, along with everyone else, longed to be back in the United States. Armed Forces Radio played the best of Christmas music, both hymns and popular tunes. "I'll Be Home for Christmas" seemed to come on every five minutes.

Santa Claus brought in the gifts that we had bought or made for each other. Some were gags and some were useful. Santa then brought a box for Choi. Surprised, he did not know what to do with it. We gathered around him and cheered as he gawked at it. Each time I wrote to my wife I had described what was going on in the MASH, and I had mentioned several individuals. One of those, of course, was Choi. My wife passed along my letters to the members of the churches in my home town, and they had recognized Choi as a special young man. The churches gathered gifts for the MASH for Christmas, including a special box that was made and addressed directly to Choi. He was flabbergasted. The doctors and nurses gathered around him, and we cheered and clapped as he sat and gazed, mystified, at the big box. We urged him to open the box, and finally he began to understand that this gift was actually for him. He tore off the wrapping and tentatively, like a small child on his first Christmas, took the contents out of the box and held them up. The churches had sent several sweaters and a pair of warm pants and a hat and gloves. But

Choi in his gift shirt from the United States.

the special gift was a red and black plaid wool shirt, which Choi put on
right there and wore until it became his trademark. Christmas 1951 was
a very special time for each person in the 8076th.

Perhaps it was the visits to the orphanages that made me think about
staying four extra months. The fabric of Korea was ripped by war. This
was nowhere more evident than in the many orphanages in Korea. War
always leaves orphans and refugees as homes and families are caught in-
nocently between the warring factions and obliterated. The U.S. government as well as the ROK government tried to help the orphans and
refugees in every way possible.

When we had stabilized near Hwachon, we returned to Chunchon
and visited an improvised orphanage in the city to provide clothing and
Christmas gifts to the children there. Our MASH had become a drop-
ping-off point for the units in our area. We set out boxes for clothing and
gifts and tools and anything else we could part with. The project started
off as a local effort, but before long we were receiving clothing from the

French and the Turks and the British and the Australians and nearly every other outfit in central Korea. As the word got around, several churches in the United States heard about the effort and sent gifts for the project. We wrapped as many of the presents as we could and stuck the others in sacks or wrapped them in old newspapers.

We took Iddi Hwa with us and went by jeep down to the low tan building on a narrow street in the urban sprawl of Chunchon that served as an orphanage. It was a bright day that made you squint at the reflection of the sun off the snow. The sun warmed the air and belied the brutal cold of the Korean winter. The operator, a slender, middle-aged Korean man, met us as we pulled up in front. He was happy to see us and ushered us into the low, open building that housed the administrative part of the orphanage.

I am not sure we were ready for what we saw there. I am not sure you can ever be ready. We considered ourselves hardened by what we had seen in the operating tents and on the roadways in Korea. Something like this was not likely to affect us any more than the operating room. As I reflect on it, we entered the orphanage with that American confidence that borders on arrogance. There were few signs of children there, no pictures of stick figures on the walls, no finger painting of green trees and yellow suns, no toys abandoned on the floor in a moment of delight.

The children were ushered into a courtyard by two Korean women. The children were dressed in heavy, ill-fitting, tan winter jackets, which accented their smallness and made them look like Pillsbury dough boys. They were full of energy and shouted and played as they waited in line. They chattered in Korean to one another, but their playing was an international language of children. They were no different from American kids you might see in an orphanage or a foster home or in an elementary school. When they got inside and saw us, they suddenly became apprehensive and crept forward with the prodding of their Korean caretakers.

That morning we saw a variety of children who had children's ailments common to American kids at Christmas: sore throats, mild ear infections, colds, and toothaches. Most of these children had lost their parents in the one-and-a-half-year-old war and had been shipped hastily to this orphanage. The orphanage was supported by missionaries, by the ROK government, by the U.S. government, and by private contributions. Much of the support came in kind: clothing, blankets, food, shoes, and volunteer help around the grounds.

Dr. Apel and Archie Breedlove visiting the orphanage at Chunchon.

Archie Breedlove talking with a child at the orphanage at Chunchon.

These children were small and frail. They stood rigidly still and flinched a bit at the presence of an American soldier. Some stared out of wide, scared eyes, and some fixed their eyes on the Korean women as if to say, "Don't let them do anything to me." Some of the small bodies carried the stains of war: missing limbs, lost eyesight, and massive scars from wounds or burns—the marks of great treachery in the midst of innocence. We went into the courtyard and mingled with the children and talked with them. At first, it was a bit awkward because of the language barrier. But the Korean women interpreted as best they could, and we spoke the international language. We gave them chocolates and picked them up and hugged them. They giggled that excited giggle of small children, and that made us laugh as we looked at them; we could only shake our heads and wonder what would become of them.

We posed for photographs with the children, and that too was somewhat awkward. We had come to the orphanage to do our part of doing good. But the human side of the orphanage did not strike us until we came into contact with these children. Their faces lit up like the faces of American kids, their smiles spread from ear to ear when they saw candy, their eyes squeezed shut and they gasped when they cried about parents and homes and families. They were little children not any different from those in New York City or Miami or Houston or in the backroads of Mississippi or Appalachia. Their faces betrayed their questions as they looked to an uncertain future. When we left, we ached with the grief that had accosted them in the form of war.

For many years I did not know what became of Agnes. By the time I left Korea, she was a legend. We had to guard her constantly. I have asked about Agnes, but no one has seemed to know where she went. In the presentations on the MASH that I have given to medical meetings over the years, I have often referred to her as the friend I left behind. Recently, I learned that we did not really leave her behind. I am told that she has not lost one bit of her beauty.

She came to the United States after the war. It is not quite clear how she got into the country. Someone may have smuggled her in. I suspect there will be several who claim credit for it. She now lives in San Antonio, Texas, at the Armed Forces Medical Museum. I hope they are taking very good care of her.

Agnes, about five feet five inches tall and very well built, was made

Agnes posing with
Archie Breedlove.

of golden brown teakwood, and each of her anatomical features was carved to perfection. She posed au naturel. Because teakwood tends to dry out very easily, she had a small hole at the top of her head that ran the length of her body. Oil was poured into the hole weekly to keep her fresh. Someone had to rub her smooth skin with oil to keep her from wrinkling and cracking in the harsh Korean climate. The oil, of course, made her skin shine and look soft and inviting. Perhaps it was the American in me. I confess that I looked many times at Agnes and smiled. She was the secret of the 8076th, and we all smile when we think about her.

I ended up staying the extra four months in the 8076th. On the front end, it seemed an eternity. Now, from the perspective of five decades, it was only a tick of the clock of history. I hope that extending for the four months was advantageous to the Medical Corps, but I know that the ex-

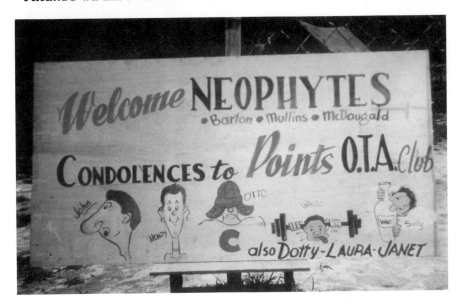

A sign at the 8076th welcoming new personnel, including those who had extended for four months.

tra time continued to broaden my view of the war, the Koreans, and the world.

In that extra four months, I recognized the swan song of the MASH. The war continued on hot and heavy as the peacemakers convened for peace talks in mid-1951, U.S. Adm. C. Turner Joy appearing for the United Nations. The talks broke down for the first of many times. In October 1951 the talks moved to Panmunjom, where they progressed at glacier speed until the final armistice in July 1953. In the meantime, battle lines stabilized at or near the 38th parallel.

In my last four months, I had the opportunity to see some of Korea beyond the narrow paths of the 8076th. We flew down to Seoul and toured the city. Seoul was devastated. Back and forth, back and forth, the trail of two armies had cut the city to shreds. The national capitol, once a proud and marvelous monument to the Korean people, now stood a mere empty shell. Government buildings, factories, homes, roads, and everything that housed humanity were reduced to rubble.

Symbolically, the bridge over the Han River from Yongdungpo to Seoul was still a mass of twisted, tormented steel sticking up out of the brown river like a huge skeleton's hand pleading for forgiveness from the

Bridge over the Han River.

heavens and grasping for anything it could hang on to. The bridge was the major civilian thoroughfare between the two cities. Early in the war, on one of the passages through the capital, the South Koreans, in retreat, had packed the bridge with explosives to destroy it before the pursuing North Koreans could cross it. In the midst of the fighting, as always, the refugees streamed across the bridge. At the militarily correct time, the detonated explosives cast the bridge and countless refugees into the air and scattered the bodies over the river like a priest spreading ashes over the sea. The remains of the bridge collapsed, exhausted, into the water below.

The streets of the cities were strewn with rubble. I now knew where we got all the brick to put on the floors of our tents. Brick was all over the streets of the cities. Several of us, doctors and nurses, walked the streets of Seoul in the twilight. We fell into a reverent silence when we came upon a wall covered with Chinese propaganda slogans, graffiti scrawled on a crumbling wall, offering Americans leniency if they would throw down their weapons. Beneath the whitewashed slogans were the initials CPVF, which, I think, stood for Chinese People's Volunteer Forces. In that moment I wondered whether those who painted that propaganda on the wall believed any of it. Ten percent? Fifty percent? All of it? In a glimmer of thought in the twilight, I recognized that both sides of the conflict were worn out with war, but on both sides, true believers car-

Chinese propaganda graffiti on walls in Seoul.

Bombed-out Capitol Building, Seoul.

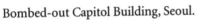

Bombed-out hotel in downtown Seoul.

ried on in the hope that the righteousness of their respective causes would prevail. In the spoiled beauty of Seoul, you could easily see that this was much more than capitalism versus communism. This was much more than freedom versus slavery. This war was incapable of reduction to convenient words. The Chinese People's Volunteer Forces could not do it with promises painted on a war-torn wall. Nor could the negotiators in Panmunjom or the journalists in the United States or the politicians in Congress capture the complexity of Korea in simple slogans. As we walked that day in Seoul, the enormity of Korea and Asia and the war grew in me slowly like the tide rolling into the Han River Estuary, unnoticed, until it was over your head. We went back to the MASH that night in silence. Only a few years before, Seoul had been a city of great charm and beauty. Now Seoul was a city of soiled rubble and graffiti. A sense of profound sadness swept over us all.

9 ROTATING OUT

Twelve months in Korea—and my rotation date—rolled around; this time there were no letters asking me to stay, no offers of a regular army commission. This time only a sheet of paper ordering me to return to the United States for duty at the U.S. Army Hospital, Fort Monroe, Virginia. When the final day drew near, I began to pack my bags and make arrangements to ship my goods back to the United States. At the MASH the custom was to paint a large sign in honor of the departing comrades. I was rotating out with three other doctors and four nurses. We had the obligatory going-away party, and we said our good-byes to people who had become very close friends over that short period.

I had talked to Choi several times about the possibilities of coming to America, and he had expressed interest each time. But he was always reserved about the prospect. I made up my mind that it was the least I could do. The morning I left MASH 8076, a jeep came to my tent to carry my duffel bags the short distance to the helicopter landing zone. Choi and I loaded my duffel bags into the back of the jeep, and before I got in, I turned to Choi and said, "When I get back to the States, I'll send for you."

He smiled and squinted. I shook his hand. We had taught him to shake with a firm grip like a westerner. Our hands clasped firmly. Then we hugged, and I hugged him like a little brother for a long time.

"I'm serious," I said. "When I get home, I'll send for you to come to the United States."

He paused and he smiled no longer. He looked into my eyes and said, "It'll never hopp'n, Cop'n."

Little did I realize that Choi knew more about Americans than I did. He—and the Korean people—had heard our promises before. When I returned to the United States, I began to ask about bringing a Korean national to the state of Ohio. I ran into the brick wall of the federal bureaucracy. All my efforts were to no avail. I remember Choi's words as if

Choi (in white shirt) at
the 8076th.

he had said them yesterday. He knew better than I did that it would never
happen.

Ed Ziegler gave me a lift by helicopter down to Chunchon to catch an L-
19 into Pusan. It was a bittersweet trip. From the air, Korea is a beautiful
country. I said good-bye to Ed and hoped that I would see him again. We
had become very close in the past months. Ed had several more months
to serve before he returned to the States. From Pusan I went to Sasebo
and then boarded the SS William Weigel, a transport ship bound for San
Francisco. There were many soldiers on board. Some were being medically evacuated to the United States, others rotating out and going home.
There was not an air of great excitement on the ship as you might expect among soldiers bound for home. It was a rather somber atmosphere.
We had a long way to go, and we knew that we were leaving many behind. It was a long trip but a trip that begged contemplation. Standing
on the deck and watching the sun set on the endless sea, I was ready to
go home and wanted to go home. But Korea had left its mark on me, a

Debarkation point at Pusan on the way home.

sense of great sadness and grief, and I was not quite able to comprehend the depth of that.

The stopover in Hawaii was brief and uneventful. There were no hula girls, no leis, no tours to see exquisite waterfalls. There were only wounded soldiers standing and hobbling around the deck of the ship. The rest of us ventured on shore, browsed in the souvenir shops, and returned early to the ship in hopes that we might hasten its departure.

The announcement of our approach to San Francisco sent us scrambling to the decks to view the Golden Gate Bridge. As we looked to the east, we saw only a misty gray shroud over the city. We stood silently on the deck for a long time and watched from the distance as the coastline came into view. The sun was coming up and the fog going away, and the city appeared on the coast. At that time, the sense that we were really coming home swept over me. It had been only sixteen months since I left the United States, but it seemed an eternity.

We left the decks and went below to change into our best clothing

Troops lined up at Sasebo, Japan, to board the SS *William Weigel* for the trip back to the States.

for arrival in the United States. Before I left for Korea, a good friend of mine, Dr. Lou Chaboudy, had given me an Eisenhower jacket as a going-away present. I had packed it in my duffel, and there it remained for sixteen months. I had never worn it. Down in my sleeping quarters, I dug it out, put it on, and inspected myself in the mirror. I felt pretty sharp.

At the port of San Francisco, I reported to the military office where we could draw an advance on our pay to help with our travel expenses. Two young civilian women sat behind a counter and displayed a most diffident attitude that a soldier was asking for an advance on pay. Without even a glance, one of them lazily extended her hand, palm up, and said, "Identification. Orders." She demanded each without inflection. Disguising my considerable irritation, I dutifully produced them, and she read over them disinterestedly.

I was just about to give her a piece of my military mind when her face lit up. She said, "Are you returning from Korea?"

I answered that I was.

She turned to her cohort and thrust the papers to her. "Look where this guy's from," she said. The coworker read the orders and looked up at me.

"Is there some problem?" I asked.

"Are you really a doctor?" she said. I nodded.

"We've heard so much about the MASH," she gushed. "You're the first one we've ever seen."

With that revelation, they quickly and enthusiastically gave me an advance on pay and I went on with my journey. I have laughed about that over the years. I am not sure of the meaning of "We have heard so much about the MASH." I had the same hesitation as when someone you are meeting for the first time says, "I have heard a lot about you." I assumed that whatever it was that they had heard about the MASH was positive.

That incident seemed to mark a change of attitude toward the MASH and military doctors. The debate about our involvement in the Korean War was abroad in the country. The debates over preparedness in the military and in the medical community had been hashed and rehashed. Now the soldiers were coming home, a few at a time, and the country was beginning to see them. On an individual and social basis, service in the MASH attached an importance to the Korean experience.

At Fort Monroe, Virginia, I was assigned as chief of surgery in the Army Hospital even though there were career officers senior in rank to me. I attributed the appointment to my service and experience in the MASH. The hospital commander, a full colonel, was enthralled by the MASH and its operations. Neither he nor any of his staff were Korean veterans, but they displayed an attitude much different from the one we had encountered on the trip over to Korea. They expressly wanted to learn from the returning doctors.

I spent four months at Fort Monroe. I rejoined my wife and two sons and daughter, and we lived in military housing on the base. Once again I came home from the hospital in the late afternoon and enjoyed the family. I played on the hospital softball team. The work was not heavy, and we only occasionally performed surgery. When Colonel Welsh went to Europe for several weeks, I was appointed acting commander and commanded the facility until he returned. It was a small thing, but I was honored by it. I had command over senior medical officers, and again I attributed that appointment to my experience in Korea.

The turning point of our stay occurred one afternoon when my older son was reported missing. We searched and searched for him but to no avail. He had just turned seven years old and was at the age when children wander. We fretted and paced and questioned. Finally, an MP vehicle arrived at our quarters and told us they had found him. They took us in the car several blocks away, and there sat our son on the lap of a young soldier. The MPs told us that the two had been talking sports and that they were having a good time. The young man, not knowing where our son came from, had stayed with him until someone came looking for him. It turned out that the fellow was one of the boxers on the installation boxing team. He wanted very much to win the All-Army championship. As we talked with him, we learned that he worked out every day at the gym and did his roadwork on the streets of the installation. While he was doing that, he saw my son wandering down the street. We thanked him for watching out for our son, and later we watched for the fight results in the local newspaper. That series of events made me understand that the world had kept on turning while we were gone in Korea, that people had lives to live and interests to pursue, and that the war had not slowed them down to any appreciable degree. At home, America continued to work and play baseball and box and live and laugh and love. Those in Korea were far away.

Twelve months in Korea had impressed upon me, a mere raindrop in the sea of humanity, one great truism: our human capabilities are very limited. That is not an attitude of defeatism. We tackled the problems of the MASH with a great confidence and optimism. We overcame many of the obstacles that confronted us. And yet, although we advanced emergency medical care by great leaps and bounds, a deep sense of humility hung over the MASH. The problems often overwhelmed us. Many times all we could do was try our best and, when we failed, sit down and critique our procedures and learn from our mistakes. The next day, having been thrown from our high horse, we would soothe our bruises, dust ourselves off, and climb back on. We owed that to the young men out in front of us.

As time went by, different problems arose to take the place of those solved, and different people were called upon to confront them. I recognized that I was just one of many, many thousands who had answered the call to address the immediate needs in Korea, who had gone home full of questions, and who, unsatisfied by easy answers, sought the purpose of that year spent in Korea.

The answers were not forthcoming. If we thought that we would receive any satisfaction from our role in the military and any lasting public reward for our service, we were mistaken. The initial interest in military medicine soon cooled under the urgency of continuing demands. In the military, the Korean War was an unpleasant experience. Within a decade after the United States had fielded the greatest army in all history, its combined military forces, reinforced by troops from a dozen other countries and scrutinized by a worldwide audience, fought to a stalemate against a third-rate army backed by an army second to many in equipment and tactics but second to none in heart and purpose. As an army we learned that the human spirit could neutralize superior technology. As a nation we found that our seemingly limitless resources, unleashed in Europe and Asia in the 1940s, were indeed limited. But that was not all due to the military, and therein lay much of the unpleasantness within military circles.

The United States was much less effective at the bargaining table than it had been on the battlefield. The peace talks lingered month after month amidst bickering over the smallest of diplomatic or military points. The term negotiations dwindled to triviality as the armies continued to fight and kill on the fields around Panmujon, the site of the summit between the warring factions. After nearly twenty-five months of incessant haggling, the negotiators reached a compromise and an armistice silenced the sounds of war.

The propaganda war erupted immediately. The official Chinese pronouncements declared a great victory for the People's Republic. On the other side, UN commander Gen. Mark Clark declared that the United Nations military presence would continue in South Korea as a reminder to the Chinese that the world community would stand firm behind its promises to defend the Koreans against communist aggression. Yet everyone knew that little change had taken place in Korea—no change of boundaries or governments or understandings, nothing except the wholesale destruction of the two countries. Hollow declarations of victory and empty pledges of military support did little to dispel the haunting realization among the veterans that the courage and sacrifices of hundreds of thousands of people in waging that war were in vain. The cessation of hostilities prompted a stunned silence rather than a joyous celebration.

As a result of the often disagreeable experiences associated with Korea, the military moved on to other things. The Cold War was in full swing, and the air force saw its modern proficiency as unlimited. In the second half of the fifties, the air force paraded its hardware before all who would watch. In the eyes of the air force generals, aviation made ground warfare obsolete. Yet, in one short decade, the experiences of Korea were placed on a shelf to gather dust, and we found ourselves tiptoeing around our traditional military principles and floundering in places with strange names like the Ia Drang Valley, Khe Sanh, and the Mekong Delta.

The MASH itself changed after I left. In a time of immobility, what do you do with a unit that was developed for mobility? The army thought it had some ideas. In the eyes of the career officers, it was another step in the evolution of the MASH as a part of immediate surgical care for the wounded. Eighth Army Surgeon Brig. Gen. Holmes Ginn was determined that surgery was to be done closer to the front. Groups of surgeons would be attached to units closer to the front, and the immediate surgery would be done in the clearing stations. Surgeons moved in with the tactical units, but the tactical units were stabilized also, and there was little movement. The MASH units stayed in a central location, one behind each corps. The MASH itself settled into the work of an evacuation hospital. It no longer had a unique purpose. It had evolved into just another field hospital.

By New Year's Day 1953, after I was gone, the name of the MASH changed. No longer called Mobile Army Surgical Hospitals, the medical units became Surgical Hospitals (Mobile Army). On February 1, 1953, the army deactivated MASH 8076 and renamed and reorganized it as the 45th Surgical Hospital (Mobile Army). The change apparently reflected more than mere nomenclature. In January 1953 the MASH admitted only 155 people, less than 10 percent of the monthly average for 1951. Of those 155, 42 were battle casualties. Of 74 surgical procedures done in January 1953, only 42 were battle wounds. In contrast to the number of battle casualties, 208 patients were treated on sick call, down from 366 in December 1952. The wounded patients were being routed to the clearing stations closer to the front.

The stabilization apparently caused a decrease in medical service and professionalism. I do not know this to be true because I was not there. Several allegations concerning the medical care provided and the military conduct of the Medical Corps in Korea have surfaced over the years. Charges of apathy, slipshod medical procedures, failure to maintain equipment, drunkenness, and general dereliction of duty have stained the performance of the Medical Corps in Korea. If those allegations have any substance, they are characteristic of the attitudes within the military at large and in the civilian sector toward the conduct of the war in Korea. The nation often wondered aloud what we were doing there. Although this collective murmuring fell far short of that heard a decade and a half later concerning Vietnam, the fact remains that it was abroad in the country.

In the MASH itself, the officers' club was symbolic of the change. MASH 8076 had no recognizable officers' club when I was there. I learned that an officers' club started in a tent the same size, shape, color, and smell as every other tent in the MASH. Joe Jacko, a good friend and an excellent Medical Service Corps officer, organized a band for the Officers' Club to play for dances on Saturday nights. Joe played the accordion, another doctor played the guitar, and a nurse played the piano. The nurses were responsible for the "furniture" in the officers' club. They procured army cots and padded them with blankets, one to sit on and another turned upright to served as a backrest. A dance floor was rigged from four squares of plywood laid on the floor of the tent. A bar was shaped from plywood that was scorched and varnished and shined nicely and placed in the back of the tent at a strategic location. A dance band in the MASH? Many of us smiled and shook our heads. Times had changed.

The fact was that things had cooled down considerably in the last year of the war, and as in every other war, when the urgency diminished, gone also was the discipline. Vietnam is another example of that phenomenon, but it is not the only example, and the phenomenon is not exclusively American. It is a fact of life.

In early 1953 I was discharged from the army and returned to a surgical residency at Saint Luke's Hospital in Cleveland, Ohio. I picked up right where I had left off two years earlier. The things of the MASH suddenly became academic. After the first flurry of discussions about arterial repair and medical evacuation and shock, my attention turned once again to the civilian ailments. Surgery in the 1950s concerned gall bladders and ulcers and organ repairs, and most of it was performed on elderly patients. In those days, only very rarely did we see a gunshot wound or an acute cranial injury or severed arteries. Combat medicine was not needed in America. Our experiences had made us better doctors, but they were not in great demand in middle America of the 1950s.

In the civilian sector, the medical advances in Korea were studied and improved upon and sent to hospitals around the world. By the Vietnam era, medevac was commonplace. Arterial repair had advanced beyond anything recognized two decades before. The use of antibiotics was light years ahead of the Korean era. Treatment of shock and psychiatric disorder had advanced way beyond our knowledge in the early 1950s. Medicine had left the Korean era behind.

In 1954 I returned to my hometown of Portsmouth, Ohio, and began the private practice of medicine. The medical problems and challenges were completely different from those of the MASH in Korea. After several years, we were once again submerged in our daily lives, and Korea was far away. It was not until the early 1970s that Korea came back to the public eye. Vietnam was over, and in the antiwar, antiestablishment attitudes of the day, *M*A*S*H* became a household word.

The new Korean War Memorial, opened in Washington on July 27, 1996, bears the inscription "Our nation honors her sons and daughters who answered the call to defend a country they never knew and a people they never met."

I like that inscription very much. But it is not altogether true. Perhaps the correct thing to say is that it is not complete. Very few of us knew Korea or the Koreans before we went. Many went for varying periods of time and came home and still did not know Korea or the Koreans. But many who answered the call came home and knew something more of Korea and the Koreans. We did meet them and see their faces and their families and their orphans and their cities and their lives and their culture. We came to know something of them. And in knowing Korea and the Koreans, we came to know something more of ourselves. I was inspired by an article by journalist and syndicated columnist Charles Krauthammer, who contrasted the purposes of the Vietnam War and the Korean War. Writing at the time of the dedication of the Korean War Memorial, Krauthammer highlighted the similarities and the dissimilarities between that memorial and the Vietnam Memorial. The Vietnam

Memorial, he noted, is a wall with three soldiers in the background. "At the Korean Memorial, the figures [soldiers] are central; the wall, complement. The Vietnam Memorial envelops you in war's aftermath, its legacy of loss; the Korean Memorial thrusts you into war's actuality, its crucible of fear and courage. The one memorializes death, numberlessly multiplied; the other: struggle, faithfully rendered."

For many years the Korean War has been overshadowed by our collective frustration in Vietnam and our struggle for identity at home. Some question whether we are indeed a people, diverse as we are. Part of our question about who we are has to do with purpose. Korea was a time when purpose was present and the struggle for that purpose was faithfully rendered.

Charles Krauthammer concludes his column with this comment: "The Vietnam Memorial was a vessel for saying: This is war. Never again. The Korean Memorial, dedicated thirteen years later, reflects a different sensibility. In the interim, the horrors of Rwanda and Bosnia have made even those once most adamantly anti-war rethink and indeed reverse themselves. Thirteen years later, we are not so sure that 'learning war no more' is a good idea. Thirteen years later, we agree: There are battles worth fighting, they should be chosen with great care and fought with great purpose, but there are purposes worth fighting for. Korea was one."

Those ideas focus us on the purpose of the Korean War and what it meant in our lives. "The purpose worth fighting for" taught us lessons on courage and preparedness and humanity. As I reflect on Korea, I marvel at the courage of those in the fight. I feel a great kinship with the men and women who served there. The memories of the 8076th are still very present in my thoughts. Some years ago, I learned through a mutual friend that one of the doctors who went to Korea at the same time I did lived and practiced only 150 miles from me. We had been good friends back then. We have exchanged very sincere letters and promised to visit each other in the near future. But life goes on, and we have yet to travel that 150 miles. Our present conditions captivate us.

The courage of Korea was one moment when the purpose worth fighting for drew out the best of those who answered the call to serve. In our lives, however, it was only one moment, and it has passed. Courage, like friendship, is not permanent in its present state but dynamic, always alive yet always changing. Courage, like friendship, never dies, but it often lies dormant in the human spirit so that it is not present in power or politics or economics. The courage we saw in Korea will not return in the same form. But it will instruct us in the future and, like old friendships, when resurrected, will draw us together in common purpose.

Korea is a lesson in national preparedness. Certainly, after the Persian Gulf War, our military has declined greatly, and many military people conclude that our nation is not as prepared for international conflict. Much of that has to do with the cyclical nature of preparedness. Historically, in times of peace we have not prepared for war. In some ways that has been a wise course. In other ways we have paid dearly for it. Preparedness is the job of the executive branch of our federal government and of the military. The yearning for preparedness is the job of the American people. It is the prerogative of the people to demand an appropriate level of preparedness for it is the people who will pay, as they did in Korea, for our failure to prepare. Our lesson is that the extraordinary courage and sacrifices of our young men and women are not appropriate substitutes for preparedness.

Finally, Korea is a lesson in the meaning of the human experience. We have exercised our military might several times since then. And we have let our military decline several times in that same period. As time goes by, different problems face us. The rhetoric of the Cold War is mercifully behind us. But as we look back over the fifty years, we must ask where the purpose of humanity has prevailed. Certainly not in the rubble that we left in the Korean peninsula in 1953. Today the 38th parallel still separates North and South, and the two constantly rattle sabers at one another. Certainly not in the superpowers who have faced off in the years since. One has folded and cracked into a number of smaller countries according to the dictates of nationalism. The optimistic and exceptional future of the other is in great doubt. Perhaps we can see the purpose of humanity in the field of medicine. But medicine, like every other endeavor of humanity, can be used by individuals or groups for greed and power and corruption.

Medicine supports physical life but does not replace the purpose worth fighting for or build the human spirit. Korea was indeed an essential step in our nation's search for a human purpose worth fighting for. To find that sense of purpose, we must first define that purpose. And today, in the bantering of our politicians and the truculence of our business community and the rootlessness of our laws and courts, the definition of what is worth fighting for eludes us. As an essential step in that search for purpose, Korea has caused us to question our confidence in the course of our nation. We see many parallels between the pre-Korea years and our course today. But that is the purpose of history—to draw parallels between the past and the present and to learn about today from the actions of yesterday.

In our lives the search for purpose takes us to many destinations. But our journeys begin in our hearts: they are individual journeys, and they compel us to travel a path toward what is right and good about humanity. We often lose our way and become embroiled in private and public distractions. Regardless of national goals and strategies, Korea was on that path toward what is right and good about humanity. Our purpose is found in that eternal quest for the universal in right and good, that which transcends cultures and nationalities, that which is found in helping another to live a better life. Often elusive and overshadowed by our own pursuits, that duty to help others defines the meaning of our human purpose. In our own way, we tried to do that in Korea.

Some think our nation has taken a dangerous turn in the past half-century. I do not think so. I am a great believer in the American experience. The development of the United States over the past three centuries has been unique in history and has produced a unique nation. The United States, as a Western nation, has viewed itself as endowed with an exceptional mission to evangelize the world with its economic and political and military principles. We went to Korea with the firm expectation that the Koreans would be eager to learn from us and to adapt their own ways to ours. Perhaps that attitude has not served us well internationally, but it prevailed among Americans in the 1950s. After a year in Korea, I learned that the Koreans had been on that peninsula many centuries longer than we had. They had their own culture and their own traditions and their own purpose. They often looked upon ours as inferior to theirs. Unprepared though we may have been, we went to Korea with the self-perception that we were cultural superiors seeking to help a cultural inferior. We saw there a culture that, in many respects, dwarfs the American culture. We came back as equals in the human experience.

Collectively and individually we will always continue on that trail toward our human purpose. We will stumble into the future, confident that the answers are within our grasp. We will make wrong turns, convinced that our course has been conclusively and righteously charted. We will set false goals, certain that our destinations are worthy. We will continue to search right up until the end. May the Korea that has dwelled within many of us for the past fifty years enlighten us and guide us on the paths of our journey.

BIBLIOGRAPHY

BOOKS

A number of books have been very helpful in researching the various facets of the Korean War. I found that Clay Blair's *The Forgotten War* (New York: Anchor Press, Doubleday, 1987) provided an interesting insight into the tactical aspects of the war. Concentrating on the first year, Blair takes a close look at the Army's officer corps and at its readiness in 1950. Another helpful work is Joseph C. Goulden, *Korea: The Untold Story of the War* (New York: McGraw-Hill, 1982). This book is written with a journalist's flair for covering the war and speaks of aspects of the war not covered by Blair. A variety of books have been written about the war, but not nearly so large a volume as one would expect given the nature and length of the war. S.L.A. Marshall's books are interesting commercial accounts of specific aspects of the war. Robert E. Appleman gives an excellent account of the first year of the war in *South to the Naktong, North to the Yalu*, the official history published by the Office of the Chief of Military History, Department of the Army, in 1961. D. Clayton James's *Refighting the Last War: Command and Crisis in Korea 1950-1953* (New York: Free Press, 1993) is also an interesting view of command in Korea. Bruce Cumings's two-volume work, *The Origins of the Korean War* (Princeton, N.J.: Princeton University Press, 1981, 1990) lays an excellent foundation for any discussion of the war and of U.S. foreign policy in Asia.

On the medical aspects of the Korean War, much less is written. The most helpful is the excellent official history by Albert E. Cowdrey entitled *The Medics' War* (Washington, D.C.: Center of Military History, 1987). William L. White's *Back Down the Ridge* (New York: Harcourt, 1953) is a journalist's popular account told in the vernacular of the soldier of the day. Though not altogether accurate on technical points, it has some interesting insights into the medical care given to soldiers in Korea. Other helpful titles include Graham A. Cosmas and Albert E. Cowdrey, *The Medical Department: Medical Service in the European Theater of Operations* (Washington, D.C.: Center of Military History, 1990); Albert E. Cowdrey, *Fighting for Life: American Military Medicine in World War II* (New York: Free Press, 1994); Frank A. Reister, *Battle Casualties and Medical Statistics: U.S. Army Experience in the Korean War* (Washington, D.C.: Government Printing Office, 1973); and U.S. Army, Walter Reed Institute of Research,

Recent Advances in Medicine and Surgery Based on Professional Medical Experiences in Japan and Korea, 1950-1953 (Washington, D.C.: Government Printing Office, 1955). In addition, all students of medical history or social history should read Paul Starr's *The Social Transformation of American Medicine* (New York: Basic Books, 1982).

ARTICLES

The following articles were of great interest in the research for this work:

Albert, Janice. "Air Evacuation from Korea—A Typical Flight." *Military Surgeon* 112 (April 1953): 256-59.

Castle, Donald E. "Medical Experiences in Korea." *U.S. Armed Forces Medical Journal* 2, no. 11 (Nov. 1951): 1623-30.

DeBakey, Michael E., and Fiorindo A. Simeone. "Battle Injuries of the Arteries in World War II." *Annals of Surgery* 123, no. 4 (April 1946): 534-79.

Duke, Raymond E. "Training Activities of the Army Medical Department." *Military Surgeon* 102 (May 1948): 339-42.

Fielding, Fred J. "About the Army Medical Service: Operation NavMed." *U.S. Armed Forces Medical Journal* 2, no. 2 (Feb. 1951): 335-40.

Fielding, Fred J., and C.R. Moon. "Naval Reserve Physicians Serve with the Army." *Military Surgeon* 110, no. 5 (July 1951): 35-36.

Fox, Ted. "Division Combat Medical Services." *Military Surgeon* 108, no. 5 (May 1951): 427-29.

Ginn, L. Holmes, and H. Haskel Ziperman. "Surgery in Division Clearing Stations." *Military Surgeon* 113, no. 6 (June 1953): 443-47.

Hughes, Carl W. "Acute Vascular Trauma in Korean War Casualties." *Journal of Surgery, Gynecology, and Obstetrics* 99 (July 1954): 91-100.

———. "Arterial Surgery during the Korean War." *Annals of Surgery* 147 (April 1958): 555-61.

Jahnke, Edward J. "Late Structural and Functional Results of Arterial Injuries Primarily Repaired." *Surgery* 43 (Feb. 1958): 175-83.

Jahnke, Edward J., and Sam F. Seeley. "Acute Vascular Injuries in the Korean War." *Annals of Surgery* 1138, no. 2 (Aug. 1958): 158-77.

Link, Mae M. "Development of the Armed Services Blood, Blood Derivatives, and Plasma Expanders Program." *U.S. Armed Forces Medical Journal* 4, no. 8 (Aug. 1953): 1221-25.

Maluf, Noble S.R. "Use of Veins in Surgery: A History." *Sudhoffs Archiv. Zeitschrift fuer Wissenschaftsgeschichte* 67 (1983): 50-73.

Mason, James B. "The Army Medical Services Reserve Program." *Military Surgeon* 111, no. 4 (April 1952): 246-52.

Mothershead, John L., and Samuel L. Crook. "Operation of the 8076th MASH."

In *Combat Support in Korea,* 116-19. Washington, D.C.: Center of Military History, 1987.

Neel, Spurgeon H. "Medical Considerations of Helicopter Evacuation." *U.S. Armed Forces Medical Journal* 5, no. 2 (Feb. 1954): 220-27.

Robinson, Paul I. "About the Army Medical Service: Draft of Doctors of Medicine, Dentistry, and Veterinary Medicine." *U.S. Armed Forces Medical Journal* 1, no. 11 (Nov. 1950): 1359-65.

————. "About the Army Medical Service: The Physician in the Present Emergency." *U.S. Armed Forces Medical Journal* 2, no. 4 (1951): 691-95.

————. "About the Army Medical Service: Procurement of Medical Officers." *U.S. Armed Forces Medical Journal* 2, no. 3 (May 1951): 843-45.

Salyer, John M. "Training of Medical Officers." In *Recent Advances in Medicine and Surgery Based on Professional Medical Experiences in Japan and Korea, 1950-1953,* vol. 2, 83-93. Washington, D.C.: Army Medical Service Graduate School, 1954.

Scoles, Peter S. "Anecdotes of a Combat Medic." *Military Surgeon* 110, no. 5 (May 1952): 356-57.

Seeley, Sam F., Carl W. Hughes, Francis N. Cook, and Daniel C. Elkin. "Traumatic Arteriovenous Fistulas and Aneurysms in War Wounded." *American Journal of Surgery* (March 1952): 471.

Smith, Allen D. "Medical Air Evacuation in Korea and Its Influence on the Future." *Military Surgeon* 110, no. 5 (May 1952: 323-32.

Smith, Sidney. "Studies in Experimental Vascular Surgery." *Surgery* 18 (1945): 627-29.

Spencer, Frank C., and Roy V. Grewe. "The Management of Arterial Injuries in Battle Casualties." *Annals of Surgery* 141 (March 1955): 304-13.

Thornton, W.H. "The 24th Division Medical Battalion in Korea." *Military Surgeon* 109, no. 1 (July 1951): 11-20.

"United States War Losses in Korea." *U.S. Armed Forces Medical Journal* 4, no. 9 (Sept. 1953): 1288-90.

Van Buskirk, Kryder. "The Mobile Army Surgical Hospital." *Military Surgeon* 113, no. 1 (July 1953): 27-32.

INDEX

Adjusted Service Rating, 7
Agnes, 107, 182, 184-85, 197-98
antibiotics, 143-44
ANZACS, 87, 164
Armstrong, Don, 71
Army Specialized Training Program
  (ASTP), 10, 11, 14, 15
army units:
  Far East Command, ix, 11, 37, 38, 48,
    139, 161
  Eighth United States Army Korea, 69,
    76, 91
  I Corps, 76
  IX Corps, 76, 178
  X Corps, 41
  1st Cavalry Division, 11, 18, 49
  2nd Infantry Division, 18, 34, 41, 81,
    82, 112
  7th Infantry Division, 18, 81
  24th Infantry Division, 11, 18, 41, 49,
    87
  25th Infantry Division, 11, 18, 41, 60-
    61, 71, 81, 87
  17th Infantry, 7th Division, 2
  5th Cavalry Regiment, 60
  5th Regimental Combat Team, 87-90
  23d Infantry Regiment, 81
  24th Infantry Regiment, 87
  187th Regimental Combat Team, 74
  1st Battalion, 5th Infantry, 87
  2nd Battalion, 5th Infantry, 87
  3rd Battalion, 5th Infantry, 87
  555th Field Artillery Battalion, 86-90
  695th Field Artillery Battalion, 28
  584th Ambulance Company, 100
  2d Helicopter Detachment, 69
  8193d Helicopter Detachment, 69-70, 73
arterial repair, 152; procedure, 153-54,
155-56; suture, 156, 158, 167; instruments, 156; clamp, 162
auxiliary surgical group, 46

Bedcheck Charley, 113-16
Bethea, James A., 11
blood: distribution, 139-40; Type O, 140;
  infusion, 141
Bloody Ridge, x, 41, 61
Boatwright, Bob, 82-83
Bowler, Joe, 69
Boy, 188
Boysen, Alexander, 33
Breedlove, Archie, 71, 84, 90, 111
British Brigade, 87
Brown, Marilyn, 105

Canadians, 87, 164
Casberg, Melvin A., 146
casualties, x
Chaboudy, Lou, 206
Childers, James E., 71
Chinese Fifth Offensive, 87-88
Chinese New Year's Offensive, 69
Choggi boys, 187-89
Choi, 22, 39, 43, 53, 66, 187-90, 193, 203-4
Chorwon, 180
Chosin Reservoir, x
Chunchon, 20-21, 56, 91, 97, 151, 191
Churchill, Edward D., 26
Coleman, John, 22, 33, 127, 142, 147, 151,
  162
Columbia College of Physicians and
  Surgeons, 5
Commonwealth Brigade, 87
Connolly, Maurice, 70, 105, 121, 163, 164,
  166
convalescence, 145

Dai Ichi Building, 161
Daniels, George, 81-82
Davis, John, 163
Deane, Philip, 131
Doctors Draft Act, 9, 13, 14-15, 39
Dovell, Chauncey, 60, 69
Duckworth, Dorothy, 105

early ambulation, 144-45
Esensten, Sidney, 34
Ethiopians: colonel, 40-42; soldiers, 61
evacuation, 44-46; air, 67-68, 76-78;
    priority, 79

Far East Command. *See* army units
Farmer, James A., 60
Fast Flying Virginian (train), 4, 5
Folb, Jay, 92
Fort Monroe, Virginia, 207-8
French, 182-84

George Washington (train), 4
Georgie, 188
German Trail, 4
Ginn, Holmes, 27, 210
Glover, Donald M., 151, 167

Hamner, Louis, 71
Han River, 199-200
Heartbreak Ridge, x, 42, 61, 73, 81, 122
helicopters, xiii, 67, H-13s, 69, 74; H-13D
    74-75; H-13E, 74, 80; H-19, 74; H-25, 75
hemorrhagic fever, 81
Henderson, Elmer, 70
Howard, John, 163
Hughes, Carl, 150, 153, 168
Hwachon, 97, 130-31, 180, 194
Hwachon Reservoir, 40, 55, 80, 107

Idi Hwa, 185-86
Indians, 87
Iron Triangle, 41, 179-80

Jacko, Joe, 59, 101-02, 211
Jahnke, Edward, 150, 153, 168
Jones, Jimmy, 91-93
Jordan, Rusty, 105
Joy, C. Turner, 199

Kaye, Danny, 178-79
Kirk, Norman T., 9
Knighton, Jim, 71, 90
Korean War Memorial, 212
Krauthammer, Charles, 212-13

L-19, 81
Lamar, Henry, 71
Laucks, Phyllis, 112, 146
laundry, 112-13
Little, Lou, 5, 6
Lovelace, Richard, 61, 160

Main Supply Route (MSR), 19, 54
M*A*S*H (film and television series),
    x-xi, 48, 71, 92-95, 118, 122
MASH: T/O&E, 48-49; organization,
    51, 100-101; diagram, 52; helicopters,
    67
MASH, 1st, 49
MASH 8055, 49, 60, 69, 80, 95, 131-32,
    155, 181
MASH 8063, 49, 62-63, 69, 80, 91, 132
MASH 8076, 20-22, 35, 41, 49, 87-90,
    132, 155; patient load, 56-57, 128-31;
    living conditions, 95; strength, 98;
    turnover, 98; operating tent, 133; use
    of water, 135-36; international troops,
    181; deactivation, 210
MASH 8209 (8225), 81
MASH, Norwegian, 181
MASH, ROK, 164, 190, 191
Mayo, Charles, 34, 61, 102, 160
McConnell, Amy, 105
Medical Corps: strength, 8, 35; training,
    xii, 25, 35, 38
medical units:
    279th General Hospital, 29
    8054 Evacuation Hospital, 69
    45th Surgical Hospital (Mobile Army),
    210
    Army Medical Service Graduate School,
    36
    auxiliary surgical groups, 46
    field surgical hospitals, 45
    medical groups, 46
Meyers, Bob, 127, 147

Miryang, 61, 136
mobility, xii, 50, 56
Mothershead, John L., 59, 159, 162
Munsan, 74

Naktong River, 59
Newport, Eswick, 71

Old Baldy, x, 180
Operation NavMed, 15, 27
Operation Touchdown, 41
orphans, 194-97
Osaka, 18, 28-32

Pagano, Major, 104
penicillin, 5, 143
Pork Chop Hill, x, 180
Public Law, 779. See Doctors Draft Act
Punch Bowl, x, 41, 139, 160
Pusan, port of, 18-19, 49, 69, 204
Pusan Perimeter, Battle of, x, 49, 60, 68,
    139

regiments. See army units
Robison, Jacob, 149-50
Roosevelt Administration, 12

Saint Luke's Hospital, 12, 91
Salyer, John M., 38
Sams, Crawford, 34
Samson Naval Base, 5
Schwing, Donald "Waldo," 127, 142, 147,
    158, 162
Seeley, Sam, 33, 37
Seoul, 199, 202
Shambora, William E., 165
Sheets, Jerry, 99-100

shock, blood-loss, 137-38
shower tent, 72, 118-20
silversmith, 161-62
Spaulding, Jim, 71
Spellman, Francis Joseph, 102-3
Starr, Albert, 127, 147, 148
Stone, Sergeant Major, 117
Strawn, Willie, 69
Surgical Research Team, 151

Townsend, Harry, 71
training. See Medical Corps
Truman Administration, 12
Turkish soldiers, 60-61, 120-21, 130

units. See army units
USO, 120, 178

V-12 (Navy), 5, 10, 12, 14-15, 26, 27
vascular surgery. See arterial repair
Valentino (enlisted man), 120-21
Van Buskirk, Kryder, 49-51, 62-63, 73
V-E Day, 7-8

Warren, Dayton, 71, 88-90, 161
Warren, Richard, 155
Whispering Manor, 103
Wiltse, Bill, 71
women in combat, 54, 107
worms, 63-64

Yale, 6-7
Yokohama, 48, 62
Yongdungpo, 199

Ziegler, Ed, 64, 71, 81-82, 84, 90, 120,
    204